Lecture Notes in Economics and Mathematical Systems

Managing Editors: M. Beckmann and W. Krelle

Subseries: Institute for Mathematics and its Applications, Minneapolis
Advisers: H. Weinberger and G.R. Sell

264

Models of Economic Dynamics

Proceedings of a Workshop held at the IMA,
University of Minnesota, Minneapolis, USA
October 24–28, 1983

Edited by Hugo F. Sonnenschein

Springer-Verlag
Berlin Heidelberg New York Tokyo

Managing Editors

Prof. Dr. M. Beckmann
Brown University
Providence, RI 02912, USA

Prof. Dr. W. Krelle
Institut für Gesellschafts- und Wirtschaftswissenschaften
der Universität Bonn
Adenauerallee 24–42, D-5300 Bonn, FRG

Editor

Prof. Hugo F. Sonnenschein
Department of Economics, Princeton University
Princeton, NJ 08544, USA

ISBN 3-540-16098-1 Springer-Verlag Berlin Heidelberg New York Tokyo
ISBN 0-387-16098-1 Springer-Verlag New York Heidelberg Berlin Tokyo

Printing and binding: Beltz Offsetdruck, Hemsbach/Bergstr.
2142/3140-543210

INSTITUTE FOR MATHEMATICS AND ITS APPLICATIONS

PUBLICATIONS

CURRENT VOLUMES:

The Mathematics and Physics of Disordered Media
Editors: Barry Hughes and Barry Ninham
(Springer-Verlag, Lecture Notes in Mathematics, Volume 1035)

Orienting Polymers
Editor: J.L. Ericksen
(Springer-Verlag, Lecture Notes in Mathematics, Volume 1063)

New Perspectives in Thermodynamics
Editor: James Serrin
(Springer-Verlag, in press)

Models of Economic Dynamics
Editor: Hugo Sonnenschein
(Springer-Verlag, Lecture Notes in Economics, this volume)

FORTHCOMING VOLUMES:

Homogenization and Effective Moduli of Materials and Media
Liquid Crystals and Liquid Crystal Polymers
Amorphous Polymers and Non-Newtonian Fluids
Oscillation Theory, Computation, and Methods of Compensated Compactness
Metastability and Incompletely Posed Problems
Dynamical Problems in Continuum Physics

* * * * * * * * * * *

The INSTITUTE FOR MATHEMATICS AND ITS APPLICATIONS was established by a grant from the National Science Foundation to the University of Minnesota in 1982. The IMA seeks to encourage the development and study of fresh mathematical concepts and questions of concern to the other sciences by bringing together mathematicians and scientists from diverse fields in an atmosphere that will stimulate discussion and collaboration.

Hans Weinberger, Director
George R. Sell, Associate Director

* * * * * * * * * * *

YEARLY PROGRAMS

1982-1983 STATISTICAL AND CONTINUUM APPROACHES TO PHASE TRANSITION

1983-1984 MATHEMATICAL MODELS FOR THE ECONOMICS OF DECENTRALIZED RESOURCE ALLOCATION

1984-1985 CONTINUUM PHYSICS AND PARTIAL DIFFERENTIAL EQUATIONS

1985-1986 STOCHASTIC DIFFERENTIAL EQUATIONS AND THEIR APPLICATIONS

1986-1987 SCIENTIFIC COMPUTATION

1987-1988 APPLIED COMBINATORICS

PREFACE

During the week of October 24-28, 1983, a group of mathematicians and economists met at the Institute for Mathematics and it Applications at the University of Minnesota. The workshop dealt with economic models in which time plays an essential role, and both the description of adjustment to a static equilibrium and the description of equilibrium paths were considered. From a mathematical point of view, discrete dynamical systems and the dynamics of ordinary and partial differential equations played a major role.

The conference consisted of lectures by economists and by mathematicians which treated some of the principal ideas of economic dynamics. Donald Saari provided some discrete dynamical systems background for a paper by Jean-Michel Grandmont on business cycles; the Grandmont paper was a major focus of the Workshop. Daniel Goroff, Jose Scheinkman, Christopher Sims, Neil Wallace, and Michael Woodford discussed the Grandmont paper after its presentation. The ideas of tatonnement were introduced by Leonid Hurwicz and extended by Andreu MasColell and H. Jerome Keisler. Four papers on economic dynamics follow (W.A. Brock, Truman Bewley, W.A. Brock and M. Rothschild and Yieh-Hei Wan). The remaining papers are devoted to issues of quantity and/or price adjustment (William Novshek and Hugo Sonnenschein, Phillipe Artzner, Carl Simon and Hugo Sonnenschein), equilibrium with a continuum of commodities (Larry Jones), and the adjustment of expectations (Lawrence Blume and James Jordan).

A distinctive feature of the Workshop was the substantial interaction between mathematicians and economists, many of whom had not been previously exposed to the ideas that were presented. This volume is intended to introduce a wider audience to the contents of these lectures and to stimulate further dialogue between economists and mathematicians.

ACKNOWLEDGEMENTS

The organizers of the Workshop thank Debbie Bradley and Kaye Smith for their careful typing of this volume.

TABLE OF CONTENTS

DYNAMICAL SYSTEMS AND MATHEMATICAL ECONOMICS

Donald G. Saari

Department of Mathematics
Northwestern University
Evanston, Illinois 60201

1. INTRODUCTION

The modern mathematical economics literature is permeated with dynamics. This starts with a simple tatonnement story of how prices adjust according to supply and demand, and it continues with the more sophisticated price adjustment models which involve speculation, etc. Dynamics arise from the Euler, or the Bellman equations, to define the optimal paths in growth models, as well as in other optimization problems. Arguments based upon dynamics are advanced to justify various forms of equilibria; here we find issues such as the accessibility of pareto points or the comparison of different bargaining solution concepts. In recent years, as manifested by several of the papers presented at this conference, dynamics has been used to explain non-stationary behavior such as business cycles.

It became clear in the 1970's that mathematical economics is blessed with almost an overly rich supply of dynamical systems. This is the period when the work initiated by H. Sonnenschein and advanced by Mantel, Debreu, and Mas Colell culminated in the conclusion that just about any differential equation, or vector field on the price simplex, can be viewed as being the aggregate excess demand function for some economy. (A good reference would be the expository paper by Shafer and Sonnenschein [1].) Other topics from mathematical economics also admit a wealth of dynamical systems with the accompanying varying behavior of the solutions. For example, in optimal growth models or overlapping generations models, a large class of systems can be generated by altering the production sets, the utility functions, and the discount rates. In what follow, I will indicate how these simple changes can lead to all sorts of unexpected orbit behavior.

Because the modelling admits an abundance of dynamical systems, mathematical economics can benefit from most advances in Dynamical Systems. Consequently, it is fortunate for economics that during this same period of the late 60's and the

70's, mathematicians made significant advances in the geometric study of these systems. Part of the earlier intuition concerning solutions resulted from the behavior of dynamical systems in the plane. Here, under some general conditions (known as the Poincare - Bendixson Theorem), it is known that all bounded solutions asymptotically approach either a fixed point or a periodic orbit. But it has been known for some time that the solution behavior isn't as nicely described in a higher dimensional space. Important progress has been made on the difficult problem of describing the "general" or "generic" behavior of solutions; an earlier exposition of this is in [2] while a more recent one is [3].

We now know that the flexibility acquired by increasing the dimension of the phase space from two to three admits orbits which only a decade ago would have been viewed as being pathological. For example, it is natural to think of a periodic orbit as being a distortion of a simple loop. However, in a three dimensional space, there are periodic orbits for differential equations which define almost any conceivable knot one can tie. That is, tie a piece of string into a complicated knot. Once this is done, attach the loose ends of the string together. It turns out that there are differential equations where a periodic orbit ties this knot! (An excellent, recent paper by Franks and Williams [4] shows that an infinite number of different knots occur in a system which satisfy a certain "topological entropy" condition.) Furthermore, we are learning that the limiting sets of orbits can assume complicated and strange structures; such sets are described by the now standard term "strange attractors".

Although this orbit behavior may seem to be bizarre, it can occur in models from economics! For example, as soon as four commodities are admitted into an economy, the tatonnement story is modelled by a dynamic in a three dimensional price simplex. The Sonnenschein result asserts that the defining system can be quite arbitrary, so all of the above orbit behavior is admitted. Thus, the story of the auctioneer admits some knotty consequences.

It is natural to question whether this unusual orbit behavior can be dismissed on the grounds that it only occurs either in isolated, or in complicated examples. This is not the case. For example, in the 60's Lorenz introduced the following differential equation as a model for turbulence.

$$\begin{pmatrix} x' \\ y' \\ z' \end{pmatrix} = \begin{pmatrix} -a & a & 0 \\ b & -1 & 0 \\ 0 & 0 & -c \end{pmatrix} \begin{pmatrix} x \\ y \\ z \end{pmatrix} + \begin{pmatrix} 0 \\ -zx \\ xy \end{pmatrix}.$$

Here, a, b, and c are positive constants where the original values are $a=10$, $b=28$, and $c=8/3$. The linear part of this equation can be studied with a standard eigenvalue analysis. Because the equation is only a quadratic system, it might appear that the full system shouldn't be unduly difficult to analyze. The fact is, in spite of the efforts of several very good mathematicians, this equation is yet to be completely understood. It is known that this quadratic equation, admits solutions such as the knotty periodic orbits described above, and that there are other, more complicated trajectories. (A recent book by Guckenheimer and Holmes [5] discusses this system in great detail.) The important point, which is why this example is introduced here, is that <u>although a nonlinear system is elementary in form, it can admit a very complicated orbit structure</u>! (For an example of a simple, nonlinear, second order scalar equation with a periodic forcing function which has complicated solutions, I refer you to Mark Levi's seminal work on the van der Pol equation [6].)

When the modelling of an economic setting involves discrete units of time, the analysis yields an iterative, discrete dynamic. (Indeed, often the intended model is a discrete one, but a continuous model is used to approximate and to simplify the analysis; e.g., a differential equation is the limiting case of the desired iterative system.) Since discrete, iterative dynamics play a vital role in economics, it is important to determine whether their orbit structures can be as complicated as above. They can, and these complexities already appear in one dimensional systems!

In this paper, I will provide an elementary introduction to selective aspects of this area. The explanation of the causes for "chaos" in discrete dynamics are easier if only because they occur for one-dimensional systems. This permits the ideas to be described in terms of graphs of functions. For this reason, this is the topic I'll emphasize. But, because Dynamical Systems is such an exciting and rapidly growing field of mathematics, any introduction cannot be complete. So, my approach is to present those ideas which I suspect are of immediate interest and applications to mathematical economics. My emphasis will be to indicate why certain types of orbit behavior occur, and to describe the identifying features of the defining system. These properties will be illustrated by suggesting how this relates to models in economics such as cycles in growth problems and price dynamics. (The details for some of these models will be given elsewhere.) A selection of the appropriate references for the mathematics will be cited for the reader interested in more detailed information.

2. DISCRETE DYNAMICS AND THE TATONNEMENT PROCEDURE

In this section, I will discuss a simple dynamical system represented by a mapping G from an interval I back into itself. To be specific, suppose the graph of G is given in Figure 1 where the iterative dynamic is given by

$$x_{N+1} = G(x_N). \tag{2.1}$$

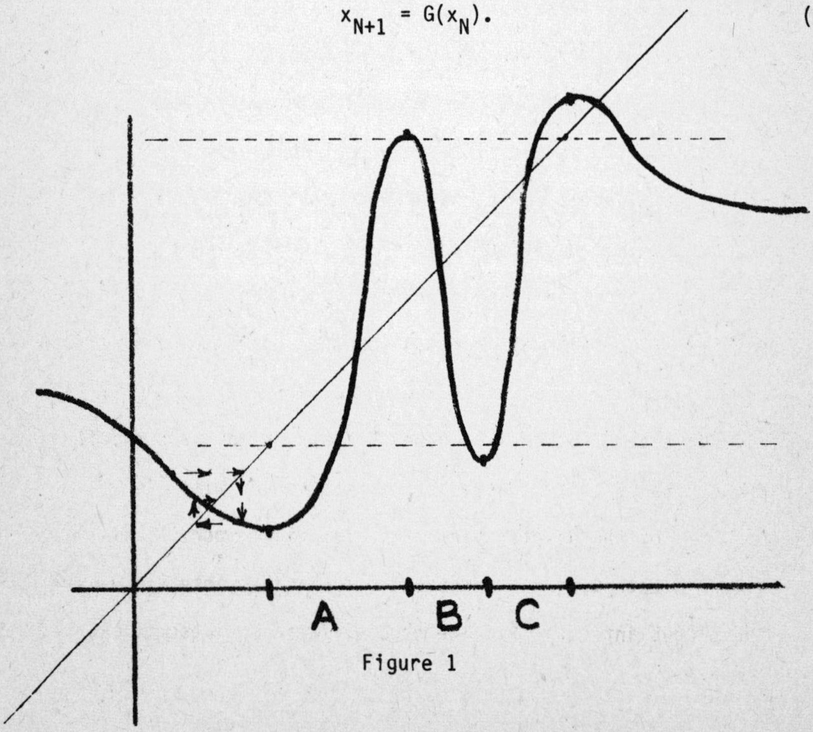

Figure 1

Geometrically, this can be described in the following way. The value of $x_{N+1} = G(x_N)$, which is found from the graph of G over x_N, provides the next value for x. To determine the location of x_{N+1} on the x-axis, move horizontally from the graph of G until you reach the diagonal $y=x$, then move vertically to the x-axis. The next iterate, x_{N+2} , is given by the value on the graph of G over this point. An equivalent description of this iteration, which omits the vertical projection, is to move horizontally from the graph of G to the line $y=x$ and then move vertically to the graph of G . The process is continued, and it is depicted by the directed lines in the figure.

It is obvious from the above that the intersection of the graph of G with the diagonal $y=x$ determines a fixed point p of the map; $G(p)=p$. By use of the mean value theorem, it is an elementary exercise to show that a fixed point is stable at $x=p$ if $|G'(p)| < 1$ and unstable if $|G'(p)| > 1$. This is because $|x_{N+1}-p| = |G(x_N) - G(p)| = |G'(c)||x_N-p|$ for some c between x_N and p. Thus if $|G'(p)| < 1$, then once an iterate x_N is sufficiently close to p, all future iterates are closer. If $|G'(p)| > 1$, then the future iterates are pushed away from p. These conditions are the basis for the usual analysis of fixed points in mathematical economics.

This system admits much more interesting activity than that captured by an equilibrium analysis; for instance, it admits a highly random, orbit behavior in the three regions labelled A, B, and C. More specifically, select a region in which you wish the initial point to be, say region C. Next, specify the interval in which you wish the first iterate to land, say A. Continuing in this fashion, a sequence of intervals is specified, say (C,A,A,B,...), where the $(N+1)^{th}$ term in the sequence identifies the interval in which you wish the Nth iterate to be. What I will show is that for any specified sequence, there exist points for which their trajectories have this future! In other words, for any random defined future, there are orbits of this deterministic system which will obey it.

To show this, all of the points which satisfy a finite portion of this future will be found. Let $C(C,\overline{A})$ be the set of points in interval C which are mapped to the closed interval $\overline{A}$. The crucial factor in describing this set is to notice that on each of the intervals, the graph of G intersects both of the dotted lines. This means that when G is restricted to any of these labelled intervals, the range of G covers the union of all three intervals. Therefore, $C(C,\overline{A})=G_C^{-1}(\overline{A})$, where G_K denotes the restriction of G to the interval K, K=A,B,C. The continuity of G ensures that $C(C,\overline{A})$ is a closed subset of C, and the surjectivity of G_K ensures that this inverse image is non-empty. Similarly, $C(A,\overline{A})=G_A^{-1}(\overline{A})$ is a non-empty, closed subset of A which represents those points of A which are mapped to $\overline{A}$. The set $C(C,A,\overline{A})$, which designates all points which are mapped from C to $\overline{A}$ and then to $\overline{A}$, is a non-empty, closed subset of $C(C,\overline{A})$ which is given by $G_C^{-1}(C(A,A))$. (For the discussion in Section 3, it is important to emphasize that $C(A,\overline{A})$ is contained in the image set of G_C.)

Let S represent the sequence describing the desired future of some point, and let S_N correspond to the first N terms. Let $C(S_N)=\{x|$the ith iterate of x under G lies in the interval denoted by the $(i+1)^{th}$ symbol of S_N, $i=0,.., N-2$, and the $(N-1)^{th}$ iterate of x is in the closure of the interval denoted by the Nth symbol of $S_N\}$. The obvious extension of the above argument shows that

$$C(S_2) \supset C(S_3) \supset C(S_4) \supset \ldots\ldots \supset C(S_N) \supset \ldots \tag{2.2}$$

and that $C(S_2)$ is a closed, non-empty subset of the interval represented by the first symbol of S. Any point which is contained in all of these sets has the orbit described by S; denote the set of all such points by C(S). So,

$$C(S) = \bigcap C(S_N). \tag{2.3}$$

C(S) is non-empty because it is the intersection of a nested sequence of non-empty, compact sets. (This fact can be found in any introductory analysis text.)

The above example suggests a link with mathematical economics. Quite often in economics, equilibrium conditions are described as the intersection of the graph of a given function with the y=x diagonal, where explicitly or implicity it is understood that the equilibrium is achieved through the iterative dynamics defined by the function. (This is a tacit assumption whenever there is an accompanying stability analysis.) But, by relying solely on an equilibrium analysis, are we missing some of the relevant economics? Away from the equilibria, the system may admit interesting, and unexpected, dynamics which can be found by a version of the above nested set argument. This orbit structure results from the economics model, so perhaps it corresponds to various forms of cycles, etc.

This happens in price dynamics. With standard boundary assumptions, price equilibria exist. Also, it is well known that for any initial condition, the usual tatonnement story for two commodities, as modelled by a differential equation, must always converge to some price equilibria. But, this global convergence need not happen when the price dynamic is modelled as an iterative one! To see this, first use standard methods to map the price simplex to the unit interval. According to the Sonnenschein result, any smooth function, $D(x)$, for which $D(0) > 0$ and $D(1) < 0$ can be viewed as being an aggregate excess demand function. The price dynamic is given by 2.1 where $G(x) = x+hD(x)$ and where h is some constant used to determine the "step size". Since there is freedom in the choice of D, it can be selected so that the graph of G is given in Figure 1. For any S where the terms are not eventually constant, $C(S)$ corresponds to a set of points which can never converge because they will never remain in any one interval. Thus the auctioneer story already collapses for two commodities unless the story is adjusted to include the additional knowledge how to avoid a set like $C(S)$. This requires global information, and it isn't clear how it should be incorporated into the standard story. Indeed, a related argument shows that if such global convergence is required for any iterative tatonnement process, then this process depends upon an immense amount of information, and it is still unresolved as to what form it should take for the general problem. (See Saari [7].)

3. OTHER MAPS, INFORMATION THEORY, AND GROWTH MODELS

Although the above choice of G was made to simplify the exposition, the essential ideas extend to a large class of mappings. In this section, I'll show why this is so while emphasizing the properties of a mapping which create these "random" orbits. In particular, it will turn out that correspondences or mappings from a multi-dimensional domain back to itself can admit orbits of this type. To illustrate these mappings, I will outline how they provide new results about growth models and about the evolving theory of information for economics.

The main property of G which we used in the nested set argument is that when G is restricted to any interval, its range includes the union of all three intervals. That is, these orbits depend only upon the continuity of G and its image set over the subintervals; it doesn't involve anything about the slope or any other property of G. Thus it is easy to extend the class of functions which admit these orbit structures. For example, the choice of three subintervals isn't of importance; the argument will work as long as there is more than one such subinterval. Of course, with more subintervals, more interesting dynamics can be admitted. At the other extreme, such behavior already will occur for two intervals, say with $G(x) = |2x-1|$ or a quadratic map, should the range condition be satisfied. Here the two regions are to the left and to the right of the sole extreme point. (Indeed, recently these maps have received considerable attention. An important survey and discussion of this literature is given in the book by Collet and Eckman [8]. Also, I recommend the monograph by Preston [9] and the preprint by Coppel [10].) Because all of this orbit structure can occur with a quadratic map, this underscores the fact that <u>it isn't the complexity of the form of the defining system which causes the complexity of the orbit structures, but merely the properties of the image sets of a non-invertible G over certain subintervals!</u>

The range of G_K need not include all of the subintervals. For instance, suppose for a different choice of G that the range of G_A covers only C, the range of G_B covers A and B, while the range of G_C covers B. This imposes a restriction on the sequences S which describe the orbits of G. In particular, any sequence which requires that a point in A is mapped either to A or B cannot be realized; e.g., the sequence (C,A,A,...) is not allowed for this choice of G. To describe an orbit, a sequence must obey certain rules which are extracted from the properties of the image sets of G when restricted to the subintervals; e.g., an A must be followed by a C; a B must be followed by either an A or a B, and a C must be followed by a B.

To cause a "random dynamic", the range of G_K need not cover a full subinterval, but rather only part of it. (This can occur for a parameterized family of maps where the parameter affects the size of the image sets.) However, here the description of the dynamics will require even a more subtle modification of the rules which define an admissible sequence. For instance, suppose for some G, G_C maps C into, but not onto A. Even if the range of G_A covers A, it may be that the set G_C misses the set $C(A,\overline{A})$, so the sequence (C,A,A,...) is not admissible. The range set of G_K is more complex because it may meet some inverse sets of G_K, but not others. The rules defining admissible sequences must manifest this, so the rules will involve not only what letters can follow other letters, but also which sets of letters can follow certain other letters or sets of letters. One way to determine these rules could be to adopt a refined redefinition of the subintervals; they could be defined not in terms of the extreme values of G, but in terms of inverse iterates of extreme points, etc. The complete analysis of the orbits of such maps is very difficult, and it is not completely understood. We will briefly return to this topic in Section 5 (the Sarkovskii sequence), but for our present purposes it suffices to note that

a) random dynamics still may exist,

b) the larger the range of G over the subinterals, the more varied the orbit structures which are admitted, so

c) the orbit structures will be intermediate between what is permitted by a similar mapping with a smaller range and one with a larger range.

For example, suppose for some G that G_A covers all of A, B and part of C. The set of orbits, as represented by sequences S, are more complicated than if G_A had covered only A and B, but less than if it had covered A, B, and C. (Here I'm assuming that the rest of G remains the same.)

In the nested set argument, the continuity of G was used only to force the inverse image of certain closed sets to be closed sets. Anything which will ensure this condition can be substituted; in particular, appropriate piece-wise continuity conditions will suffice. (Consider the orbit structure of the mapping which has the value 2x over the interval [0,1/2] and 2x-1 over (1/2,1].) This fact is of interest to economics because occasionally discontinuities are admitted to handle such problems as boundary conditons; e.g., a multicommodity growth problem may admit discontinuities to avoid the possibility of a capital good becoming negative.

Perhaps the most important extension of the above is that the argument remains valid for a mapping from a higher dimensional space back into itself. This is because the proof relies only upon properties of compact, nested sets and the continuity of the map; it does not use any properties peculiar to the real line. Here the subintervals are replaced by subsets. What needs to be checked are the properties of the image sets of G when restricted to various subsets; do they meet the subsets? If they cover other subsets, then the above analysis holds immediately. If they only meet, but do not cover some subsets, then a more delicate analysis is required to completely describe the orbit structure, but a rough analysis may show whether the system admits chaos. (An immediate application of such maps to economics would be to extend the observations made in Section 2 concerning the iterative, tatonnement processes from the two good setting to n goods. The existence of an excess demand function which maps each of several specified subsets from the price simplex onto the union of the subsets is assured by the Sonnenschein result.)

The economics literature is replete with models where "correspondences" are used in place of mappings. Again, with the appropriate conditions which ensure that the inverse image of closed sets are closed sets and that the image set conditions are satisfied, iterates of correspondences also admit a chaotic dynamic. The mathematical arguments are similar, and applications to economics are plentiful.

To conclude this section, multidimensional mappings will be used to illustrate some issues from information theory and from growth theory which arise in economics. We start with information theory, which can be viewed as being an extension of the tatonnement process discussed above. A more complete description of the tatonnement process has each agent sending to the auctioneer information which is based upon his state of the economy; namely, he describes his excess demand function at the quoted price. Then, at an equilibrium point (i.e., whenever the markets clear), this information is used to determine the designated economic solution (the net trades which yield a competitive equilibrium).

This general framework has been extended to more general situations by L. Hurwicz [11]. In a simple setting, the designated allocation (or reallocation) of goods is described by a performance standard $P(\underline{x},\underline{y})$ where $\underline{x}$ and $\underline{y}$ are vectors representing, respectively, the economic characteristics of the first and the second agent. The design problem is to determine the analogue of the excess demand function for the solution represented by P. That is, the designer must determine the appropriate form of messages m_1 and m_2, as well as the communication rules (given in an iterative form where the superscript T designates the time)

$$m_1^{T+1} = g_1(\underline{x}, m_1^T, m_2^T), \qquad m_2^{T+1} = g_2(\underline{y}, m_1^T, m_2^T). \tag{3.1}$$

An equilibrium point for this dynamic is one where

$$(m_1,m_2) = (g_1(\underline{x},m_1,m_2),g_2(\underline{y},m_1,m_2)).$$

As part of the design problem, a function h must be determined which will assign an equilibrium message to the allocation $P(\underline{x},\underline{y})$. (To see how the design problem can be solved, see Saari [12], or Hurwicz, Reiter, and Saari [13,14].)

While this theory admits global dynamics, its formulation relies upon reaching an equilibrium point of the message dynamics. A stability analysis of the equilibria has been made (e.g. see Mount and Reiter [15], and Williams [16]), but I'm unaware of any study of the global aspects of the (message) iteration process. By what we have seen above, if the communication rules, g_i, are not linear in the m's, then there are excellent reasons to suspect that the iterations will admit chaos. That they can is demonstrated by the following simple example where the performance standard is $P(x,y) = [-2 + y + ((2-y)^2 + 8x(1-y)^2)^{1/2}]/2x(1-y)$. This performance function admits the communication rules $g_1 = 2 - xm_1^2 - m_2$, $g_2 = ym_2 + m_1$, and $h = m_1$. Let $G=(g_1, g_2)$. If x and y (the states of the economy) are greater than 3 in value, then when G is restricted either to

$L = \{-1 < m_1 < 0,\ -1 < m_2 < 1\}$, or $R = \{0 < m_1 < 1$, or $-1 < m_2 < 1\}$, the image set includes both sets. This means that for any sequence S consisting of L's and R's, the set C(S) is non-empty; there are orbits of G which have this behavior. For those S's which are not eventually constant, the corresponding orbits never approach an equilibrium. This violates the central, tacit assumption in the formulation of the dynamical theory! (However, the so-called "one-shot" formulation is not affected.)

A second application from economics, which utilitzes a mapping from a multi-dimensional space back into itself, comes from growth models with several goods. Traditionally in this area, attention is focused upon equilibria, but in recent years there have been some papers which explore the existence of cycles admitted by the Euler equations. An example of a period 2 cycle (i.e., $x_{N+2} = x_N$, but $x_{N+1} \neq x_N$ for all N) for a two commodity economy where the utility function is quadradic was described by David Gale at this conference. (A more ambitious program was described by Grandmont [17].) There is an earlier paper by Benhabib and Nishimura [18] where they demonstrate the existence of period two orbits for appropriate technologies, discount rates, and utility functions. In both of these papers, the cycles were established by use of standard analytic techniques, and the proof involved considerable detailed analysis. By use of the method used here, it can be shown that these results hold for any number of goods (greater than unity) and there exist orbits which are far more complex than a simple period two cycle. Moreover, as we see from the previous examples, the method is simplier to verify because only the range of G needs to be checked.

Recall that in a stationary model for growth, the function being maximized is

$$\sum_{T=1}^{\infty} p^T\, U(\underline{k}_{T-1}, \underline{k}_T) \tag{3.2}$$

where p is the discount rate, $\underline{k}_T$ is an m dimensional vector corresponding to the amount of capital stock of m goods at time T, and U is the utility function. (Because the utility function depends upon the capital stock at two different periods of time, the technology is incorporated in U. See McKenzie [19].) The Euler equations are

$$U_2(\underline{k}_{T-1}, \underline{k}_T) + pU_1(\underline{k}_T, \underline{k}_{T+1}) = \underline{0} \tag{3.3}$$

where U_i is the gradient of U with respect to the ith set of m variables. Eq. 3.3 can be viewed as being

$$(\underline{k}_T, \underline{k}_{T+1}) = G(\underline{k}_{T-1}, \underline{k}_T) = F\{p^{-1}U_2(\underline{k}_{T-1}, \underline{k}_T)\} \tag{3.4}$$

where F is the term resulting from the inverse function theorem. (Actually, to force G to have the correct properties, often it turns out that U_i is not globally invertible.) Now, if $\underline{V}_{T+1} = (\underline{k}_T, \underline{k}_{T+1})$, this can be expressed as

$$\underline{V}_{T+1} = G(\underline{V}_T) \tag{3.5}$$

This equation is in a form where we can suggest why, under certain circumstances, it will admit cycles of any desired period and chaos. The main item to check is whether the image set of G satisfies the appropriate conditions. This will occur with the non-linear form of G should it be sufficiently enhanced. But an increased range for G is easily achieved by letting the discount factor $p \to 0$. (This increases the range of the term $p^{-1}U_2$.) An appropriate choice of the utility function (and the accompanying implicit choice of technology) can be made so that G, with a small p, will map certain sets into others. In this way, as p gets smaller, an increasing variety of orbit behavior is admitted into this stationary model. (This is the case for the Gale model. The way he obtained period two points shows that the image set of G maps certain regions into others. For a smaller value for p, the image set of the new G will extend over even more of these regions, and eventually all sorts of motion will occur. Notice that this is a parameterized family of maps and that as p varies, we can expect situations where certain sets are mapped into, but not onto certain other sets.)

4. PROPERTIES OF THE DYANAMICS

The fact that our approach is based upon a nested set argument was used in Section 3 to extend the conclusions to large variety of mappings. This similarity in the argument provides an additional benefit-- even for widely differing settings, the orbits will possess certain similar characteristics. In this section, I will outline some of the more important ones.

1. These chaotic orbit structures run against a natural prejudice that the equilibrium points should dominate the dynamics in economic models. So, I will start by showing that there can be an uncountable number of these C(S) sets. For each admissible sequence S, the set C(S) is non-empty. If S' doesn't equal S", then it is clear from the argument that C(S') and C(S") are disjoint sets. Thus, whenever there are an uncountable number of such sequences, there are an uncountable number of sets, C(S), of points with a "random" future behavior. This happens whenever the defining rules for admissible sequences permit more than one choice to follow each letter; i.e., for each restriction, the image set of G meets at least two subintervals in an appropriate fashion. In particular, this uncountability statement hold for all of the mappings described above.

2. The above statement asserting the abundance of such sets also implies that most of them must be very small. This follows from the impossibility of having more than a countable number of open sets, or sets with positive Lebesgue measure in any Euclidean space. Consequently, most (all but perhaps a countable number) of these (closed) sets must be meager in that they have an empty interior and are of measure zero.

3. Since most of the sets C(S) are meager in size, one might hope that the "small" sets include all C(S)'s where S corresponds to non-convergent dynamics. Of course, this isn't always so, as counter-examples are easy to construct. (See Section 5.) Even in those situations where it is true, it only assures us that any particular non-convergent orbit is unlikely -- the set of all non-convergent points may have positive measure. In any case, it turns out that the set of non-convergent points defines a complicated set structure. To simplify the discussion we will assume that the dynamic, G, is a smooth function with bounded derivatives defined on a compact region of Euclidean space.

A given G admits an infinite number of different orbit structures when the defining rules permit an infinite number of entries to be changed in an admissible

S, and any such resulting sequence is again admissible. Whenever this is the case for an S which isn't eventually constant, there is some point q in C(S) which is an accumulation point for the set of non-convergent points. In other words, certain non-convergent points tend to be close to, and accumulate on other non-convergent points. To see this, notice that if q is an interior or a boundary point of C(S), then the conclusion follows immediately. The basic idea of the proof for the general case is that if S and S' differ only after the Nth entry in the sequence, then $C(S_N)$ contains both C(S) and C(S'). But both sets must be close to each other because as N grows, $C(S_N)$ is decreasing in size to meet the points C(S). The formal proof follows.

Assume that C(S) consists of isolated points $\{q_i\}$. The assumption that the dynamic is restricted to a compact region means that there are only a finite number of these points. Since these points are isolated, this means that the diameter of each of the components of $C(S_N)$ tends to zero as N grows. So, let e be a number greater than zero, and let $B(q_i)$ be a ball of radius e about q_i. Since there are only a finite number of balls, and since the diameter of each component of $C(S_N) \to 0$, there is some N so that $C(S_N)$ is in the union of these balls. Now, let S' be an admissible sequence obtained by altering S only after the Nth entry. Since C(S') is contained in $C(S_N)$, there is some point of C(S) which is within distance e of a point of C(S'). Because there are only a finite number of points in C(S), a point in this set can be found with this property for any choice of e. This completes the proof. (Actually, Cantor sets can occur. For example, see Saari and Urenko [20].)

4. While the above conclusion may seem to be a bit abstract, the basic ideas illustrate that when these strange orbits occur, the system becomes highly sensitive to the choice of initial conditions. This is true even for a subset of points which define convergent orbits. To see the first part of this assertion, notice from the construction that there is a set $C(S_N)$ which is arbitrarily close to that of C(S). However, if S' differs from S only after the N^{TH} entry, then C(S') is in $C(S_N)$. This means that although the dynamics of S' can differ radically from that of S, initial conditions for each orbit can be found

arbitrarily close to each other.

Because the system is highly sensitive to initial conditions, the slightest error can sharply alter the future behavior of the system. (Choose S' to differ significantly from S.) This statement seems to run counter to the usual concept of "continuity with respect to initial conditions", where the assertion is that a small change in the initial conditions results in only minor changes in the resulting dynamics. But, recall that this result requires a <u>compact</u> time interval. In the above example, the dynamic is similar for the first N-1 iterates; it differs only after the Nth iterate.

This sensitivity issue can also affect our concept of "convergent orbits". The sets $C(S_N)$ can contain orbits which are eventually convergent. This happens whenever all the sets C(S) which correspond to non-convergent orbits consist of isolated points, while the sets $C(S_N)$ have non-empty interiors. (For example, this is true whenever for each K in the sequence, G_K covers the interior of the subset represented by the next entry of the sequence.) Indeed, in this setting, the eventually convergent points in $C(S_N)$ contain an non-empty open set. But if the last two entries of S_N are not the same, then the convergence of these points cannot be manifested until at least after the Nth iterate. If N is sufficiently large, like 10^{52}, then it will exceed the capacity of any computer. For all practical purposes, such a set of convergent points is "non-convergent". This phenomena occurs in all of the examples previously cited; e.g., the growth models, the models for information theory when the communication rules are non-linear in m, the price dynamic models, etc. Thus, even should the sets of non-convergent points be of no real consequence, the above demonstrates that <u>for models coming from economics, there can be open sets of convergent points which are, for any practical purpose, non-convergent!</u>

These sensitivity statements can be disconcerting; after all, one of the purposes for using dynamics in economics is to discover rules of predictability. These sensitivity statements appear to run counter to this goal. Fortunately, there are methods to rescue some of this predictability. However they assume a probabilistic form. The basic idea is much in the spirit of statistics; if a careful, microscopic examination of the data demonstrates sensitivity and chaos, perhaps an aggregation will supply some order. The same thing occurs in dynamics; here the statements assume a probabilistic flavor coming from the ergodic theorem and they are of the form "the probability that an orbit is in a specified region is ...". This goal of finding order through aggregation is still in its early stages, and some of the existing theorems involve hypotheses which are difficult to verify for specific problems. However, for a partial description of some of this work for one dimensional, iterative systems, see Chap. 9 of [9].

5. PERIODIC ORBITS, STABILITY, AND THE SARKOVSKII SEQUENCE

Although the nested set argument demonstates the existence of a wide range of orbit structures, it is, as it stands, too gross to admit other types of conclusions. For instance, for the mapping G described in Section 2, an admissible sequence is S"=(A,C,A,C,A,C,...) where the entries alternate between C and A. This is a periodic sequence, but the nested set argument doesn't offer any clue whether there is a period two orbit in C(S"). Furthermore, supposing there is a period two orbit in this set, is it stable? (That is, does any point sufficiently close to the orbit defines a trajectory which approaches the orbit?) In this concluding section, a refinement of the above argument will be provided which demonstrates the existence of periodic orbits, and which leads to the appropriate stability conditions. In addition, a surprising assertion concerning the ordering of the periods of periodic orbits for mappings from the line to the line will be introduced. (This is the important Sarkovskii sequence.)

The basic idea for this section comes from the description in Section 2 of a fixed point. If a point is of period two, then every second iterate must have the same value. That is, $G(G(p)) = p$. So, if we define G^2 as the composition $G(G)$, then a period two point becomes any fixed point for G^2 which is not a fixed point for G. In the same way, a period N point is any fixed point for G^N which is not a fixed point for G^K when $K<N$. (Of course, G^N is the mapping obtained by composing G with itself N times.) This means that one way to demonstrate the existence of periodic orbits is to graph G^N and check the points of intersection

with the line $y=x$.

This task is much easier than it may appear. This is because an accurate graph for G^N isn't required. We need only to show whether it intersects the line $y=x$. To illustrate this, parts of G^2 will be graphed for the choice of G given in Figure 1. First the graph of G^2 will be found over the interval A. Over this interval, G is increasing, and G(A) covers the union of all three intervals. The graph of G over G(A) is given in Figure 1 when the appropriate restriction is made on the domain. Thus, the graph of G^2 over A is <u>a translation to the interval A and a contraction in the x direction of the graph of G over G(A).</u> This contraction is non-linear and it depends upon G, so the actual graph of G^2 can be difficult to determine. But because the graph of G over G(A) intersects the dotted lines over three subintervals, we know that the graph of G^2 also will intersect both dotted lines over each of three subintervals of A! These subintervals are C(A,A), C(A,B), and C(A,C).

The continuity of G and the location of the dotted lines ensures that over each of these subintervals, G^2 must intersect the line $y=x$. This means that <u>there are at least three candidates for period two points</u>. All that remains is to determine whether these points are fixed points. Since a fixed point must remain in the same interval for each iterate, such a point must be in C(A,A). Therefore, the intersections of G^2 with $y=x$ over the intervals C(A,B) and C(A,C) must correspond to period two oints, and, respectively, they correspond to points in C(S') and C(S") where S' = (A,B,A,B,...) and S" = (A,C,A,C....). This argument now is extended to find the period two points which start in interval B and in interval C. However, because G_B is decreasing, the graph of G^2 over B will be a reversed version of G over G(B). I wish to emphasize that while this description is too crude to obtain the exact properties of G^2, it is refined enough to establish the existence of period two points.

The obvious induction argument holds to demonstrate that there are periodic orbits of any desired period and orbit structure as captured by a sequence S. That is, if the entries of S can be described in terms of a repeating block of N entries, but not in terms of a repeating block of K entries when $K<N$, then there

is a period N orbit in C(S). To show this, we need to find the graph of $G^N = G(G^{N-1})$.

Consider the interval $C(S_{N-1})$. According to the nested set argument, G^{N-1} maps this interval onto the interval represented by the last entry of S_{N-1}. Consequently, the graph of G^N will resemble the graph of G over this interval, except it will be over the interval $C(S_{N-1})$ and it will be a translated, contracted (in the x-direction), and possibly reversed version. The actual graph may be very difficult to determine, but because the y values are not affected (some may be repeated if some points in S_{N-1} have more than one pre-image), it is clear that over the interval $C(S_{N-1})$, the graph of G^N must intersect the diagonal y=x at least once. That these points are not periodic points of a smaller period follows from the assumption that S cannot be described in terms of blocks of symbols of length less than N. (Obviously, a periodic point of period K will define a sequence S' where S' has repeating blocks of length K.)

The important point to note is that the above argument is nothing more than a refinement of the nested set argument found in Section 2. The main difference is that the properties of the image set of G are included in the last step. Again, because this argument uses nothing peculiar to the real line, it extends to a wider class of mappings and as well as to correspondences. The development follows in much the same manner as described in Section 3 where the existence of these periodic points depend only on the boundaries of the image set of G and whether the sets will intersect the diagonal $y=x$. Applications of all of this to problems of mathematical economics are immediately obtained by modifying the above examples. In particular, with the appropriate choices of modelling ingredients, periodic orbits of any desired period exist in growth models, in the message iterates of information theory, for optimal solutions in overlapping generation models, and in the price dynamics.

The stability of a periodic orbit can be analyzed in much the same way as that of a fixed point. After all, if p is a periodic orbit with period N, then p is a fixed point for G^N. The same argument appies to show that if $|\{G^N(p)\}'|$ is less than unity, then the orbit is stable in that the orbit of near-by points tend to that of p. If this value is greater than unity, then the periodic orbit is unstable. (Of course, if G is a mapping from a multidimensional domain back into itself, then G' is the usual Jacobian matrix, and the relevant values to check are the eigenvalues. If all the eigenvalues are less than unity in magnitude, then the periodic orbit is stable; otherwise it is unstable.)

By use of the chain rule, the stability condition becomes

$$\left| \prod_{K=1}^{N} G'(G^{K}(p)) \right| < 1 \tag{5.1}$$

That is, the stability is determined by the N-fold product where the terms are G' evaluated at each iterate of p. For this product to have magnitude less than unity, it isn't necessary that $|G'|$ is less than unity at each of the iterates; at some of the iterates it can be greater than unity if it is sufficiently less than unity at other iterates. In particular, notice that if one of the iterates happens to be at a critical point ($G'=0$), then the orbit is automatically stable independent of what happens at any other iterate. (This is called a "superstable" periodic orbit.)

The above argument shows that there exist G's with open sets of non-convergent points. For example, at a period N point, the slope of G could be altered so that it becomes an inflection point. This means that the period N point is now stable, so an open interval of points will converge to it. In turn, this means that if S is the sequence corresponding to the periodic orbit, C(S) will have a non-empty interior.

These stability arguments can be applied to problems from economics. For instance, consider the example discussed in Section 3 concerning the iterates of the communication rules. Here the conclusion may be attacked by questioning the size or measure of the non-convergent points. However, it isn't difficult to use the same example to illustrate that for certain parameter values, the mapping admits stable periodic orbits. The same assertion applies to the tatonnement process, as well as for growth models, etc.

The existence of periodic orbits is easy to prove when G is a one-dimensional smooth mapping (with bounded derivatives) which maps each subinterval onto the union of the subsets. In this case a periodic orbit of any order is possible. But if the image set of G is only into, but not onto these intervals, then the argument becomes far more delicate. For continuous mappings of the line back into itself, there is a surprising statement by Sarkovskii [21] which asserts that there is a natural ordering for the periods of the periodic orbits. The statement claims that if the system admits a periodic orbit of period k, then it must also admit a periodic orbit of period m if m follows k in the following sequence:

$$3,5,7,9,11,\ldots;2(3),2(5),\ldots;2^2 3\ ,\ldots;\ \ldots,2^3\ ,\ 2^2,\ 2,\ 1. \qquad (5.2)$$

This sequence, which contains all of the positive integers, first lists all of the odd integers in increasing order, then it lists in increasing order all of the integers which have a factor of 2 but not 2^2, then those which have a factor of 2^2 but not 2^3, etc. Finally, the multiples of 2 are listed in decreasing order. At the extreme, this means that if a mapping has a periodic point of period 3, then it also admits a periodic point of any desired period. (See the paper by Li and Yorke [22].)

The proof of this result is difficult. (The interested reader can find a nice proof in [23].) However, it can be thought of in terms of the nested set argument. Namely, if G^k intersects the line y=x, then we have some knowledge about the location of the extreme points of this graph over some subintervals. It turns out that they are such that the graph of G^m, where m follows k in the Sarkovskii sequence, must also intersect the diagonal. This proof, then, uses the properties of the real line, so we cannot expect the result to extend to higher dimensional mappings. Indeed, it doesn't. The problem is that in higher dimensions the diagonal $\underline{y=x}$ doesn't divide the $\underline{x\text{-}y}$ space into two parts as it does for a mapping from the real line. (So, an intermediate value theorem doesn't apply.) Thus, just knowledge of the extreme points of the image set isn't sufficient to ensure that the graph of other iterates will intersect the diagonal.

This concludes my introduction to this field and its applications to economics. Most of what I have presented is based only on the image sets. Other than the stability conditions, I haven't used other properties of the slope or the curvature of G. One would expect that once these conditions are used, more delicate conclusions follow. This is the case, and in these final paragraphs I'll suggest what they are. Some excellent references for these results are [8,9,10]. (Also, see the references cited in these books.)

To start, the Sarkovskii sequence suggests potential properties for parameterized maps from the real line back into itself. For example, suppose that for certain parameter values, the mappings admit only fixed points. If the mappings will eventually admit periodic orbits, then it is reasonable to expect that they would follow the Sarkovskii ordering. Namely, as the image sets becomes larger, first we would expect a period two orbit to occur, then a period four orbit, etc. Under the appropriate conditions, this happens. This, then, describes for one-dimensional maps what occurs as the image sets cover more and more of the various subintervals.

Under the appropriate conditions, we would expect the values of G' to change smoothly with parameter values. From this and 5.1, we might expect that when certain periodic orbits arise, they may be stable. Again, we do find stability regions for certain maps and periodic orbits when the parameters enter certain windows. Of particular interest to mathematical economics, it would be nice to know when certain periodic orbits tend to define the total behavior of the system. For example, we would like to know whether a stable periodic orbit (e.g., a business cycle) is the only one and whether most of the orbits tend toward it. That is, under what conditions does a business cycle dominate the behavior of the system? Conditions have been found which ensure this, and the best known one concerns what is known as the Schwartzian derivative. Indeed, Grandmont [17] exploited these conditions for a special class of mappings in his study of business cycles.

Acknowledgements

This work was supported, in part, by a grant from the NSF IST-8111122. This paper is a written version of a talk entitled "Periodic and aperiodic discrete dynamical systems" which I gave on October 25, 1983, at a conference on price dynamics hosted by the Institute for Mathematics and its Applications (IMA) at the University of Minnesota and organized by Hugo Sonnenschein and Hans Weinberger. Most of this paper was prepared while I was a member of the IMA, and I would like to thank Hans Weinberger and George Sell for their kind hospitality during my stay at the Institute.

References

1. Shafer, W. and H. Sonnenschein, Market demand and excess demand functions, Chap. 14 in Handbook of Mathematical Economics, vol II, edited by K.J. Arrow and M.D. Intriligator, North Holland Publishing Company, 1982.

2. Nitecki, Z., Differentiable Dynamics, MIT Press, 1971.

3. Palis Jr., J. and W. de Melo, Geometric Theory of Dynamical Systems Springer-Verlag, 1982.

4. Franks, and R. Williams, Entropy and Knots, Northwestern University preprint, 1983.

5. Guckenheimer, J. and P. Holmes, Nonlinear Ocillations, Dynamical Systems, and Bifurcations of Vector Fields, Springer-Verlag, 1982.

6. Levi, M., Qualitative analysis of the periodically forced relaxations, Memoirs of the American Mathematical Society no. 244, Providence, Rhode Island, 1981.

7. Saari, D.G., Iterative price dynamics, Northwestern University preprint. November, 1983; to appear in Econometrica, 1985.

8. Collet, P. and J.-P. Eckmann, Iterated maps on the interval as dynamical systems, Progress in physics, Vol. 1, Birkhauser, Boston 1980.

9. Preston, C., Iterates of maps on an interval, Lecture Notes in Mathematics, Vol. 999, Springer-Verlag, 1983.

10. Coppel, W.A., Maps of an interval, Discussion Paper No. 26, (June 1983), Institute for Mathematics and its Applications, 514 Vincent Hall, University of Minnesota.

11. Hurwicz, L., Optimality and informational efficiency in resource allocation processes, in Mathematical Methods in the Social Sciences, ed. by K. Arrow, S. Karlin, and P. Suppes, Stanford University Press, 1960.

12. Saari, D.G., A method for constructing message systems for smooth performance functions, to appear in Jour. Econ. Theory.

13. Hurwicz, L., S. Reiter, and D.G. Saari, On constructing mechanisms with message spaces of minimal dimensions for smooth performance functions, April 1978, Conference Seminar on Decentralization, University of Minnesota.

14. ———————, On construction of an informationally decentralized process implementing a given performance function, Preprint July, 1980, Notes for lectures at Boulder, Colo.

15. Mount, K., and S. Reiter, On the existence of a locally stable dynamic process with a statically minimal message space, Northwestern University Discussion Paper no. 550.

16. Williams, S., Manipulating a message process to achieve stability, IMA and SMU preprint, August, 1983.

17. Grandmont, J.-M., On endogeneous competitive business cycles, CEPREMAP Discussion paper no. 8316, September 1983.

18. Benhabib, J. and K. Nishimura, Competitive equilibrium cycles, NYU preprint, 1983.

19. McKenzie, L.W., Optimal economic growth, turnpike theorems and comparative dynamics, Dept. of Econ, Univ. of Rochester preprint (Sept 1983), to appear in _The Handbook of Mathematical Economics_, Vol. III, edited by Arrow and Intriligator.

20. Saari, D.G., and J. Urenko, Newton's method, circle maps, and chaos, in American Math Monthly, 91(1984), 3-17.

21. Sarkovskii, A.N., Coexistence of cycles of a continuous map of a line into itself, Ukranian Math J., 16 (1964), 61-71.

22. Li, T.Y. and J.A. Yorke, Period three implies chaos, American Math Monthly 82 (1975), 985-992.

23. Block, L., J. Guckenheimer, M. Misiurewicz, and L.S. Young, Periodic points and topological entropy of one dimensional maps, in _Global Theory of Dynamical Systems_, edited by Z. Nitecki and C. Robinson, _Lecture Notes in Mathematics_, Vol. 819, Springer-Verlag, 1980.

ON ENDOGENOUS COMPETITIVE BUSINESS CYCLES

Jean-Michel Grandmont*
CEPREMAP, France

The belief that the long run equilibrium of a competitive monetary economy that does not experience any exogeneous shocks - whether originating from the external environment or from policy - should be modelled as a state that is stationary or perhaps growing at a constant rate, seems to be deeply rooted in the mind of some economists.

The most outspoken believers in the market's invisible hand go indeed as far as claiming that any departure from a long run Walrasian equilibrium should be regarded as purely transitory and that accordingly the basic tendencies of a competitive economy may be represented adequately by such a "Classical" stationary equilibrium. The most recent reformulation of the Classical approach has been to model economic fluctuations by adding random shocks to the deterministic stationary state and to underscore the role of incomplete (and asymmetric) information in the influence of economic policy on real equilibrium variables. The outcome of this reformulation is a model that very cleverly preserves stationarity while incorporating in the analysis something that looks like business cycles (Barro (1981), Kydland and Prescott (1982), Lucas (1972, 1975, 1977, 1980, 1981), Sargent and Wallace (1975)).[1] An important implication of many, but not all, of these models is that the systematic (deterministic) component of economic policy can have no real effect whenever it is anticipated by the private sector.

---

* CEPREMAP, 140 rue du chevaleret, 75013 Paris, France. This is a short summary of a longer paper with the same title that is forthcoming in Econometrica, and that was presented at the Workshop on Price Adjustment, Quantity Adjustment and Business Cycles, in October 1983, at the Institute for Mathematics and its Applications of the University of Minnesota. I wish to thank warmly Hugo Sonnenschein who organized the meeting, our hosts, Leo Hurwicz, George Sell, Hans Weinberger, as well as Neil Wallace, who made my participation possible. Special thanks are due to the discussants of the paper, Daniel Goroff, Jose Scheinkman, Christopher Sims, Neil Wallace and Mike Woodford for their valuable comments and constructive criticisms. Financial support from the France Commissariat General du Plan, the University of Lausanne and the U.S. Office of Naval Research under contract ONR-R00014-79-C-0685 at the Institute for Mathematical Studies in the Social Sciences at Stanford University is also gratefully acknowledged.

1 See also Grandmont and Hildenbrand (1974).

The arguments put forward by the opposing (Keynesian) school often appear, by contrast, almost exclusively defensive. Proponents of this school seem to accept in effect the **theoretical** validity of the claim according to which the long run equilbrium positions of a competitive economy may be described by (deterministic or stochastic) stationary states. They tend to question primarily the **practical** relevance, for the description of short run and medium run phenomena, of the mere notion of a long run stationary equilibrium and of its underlying assumptions. The list is long: prices cannot move fast enough to clear markets, anticipations adjust slowly, New Classical macroeconomic models rely upon extremely specific assumptions concerning the distribution of information, the Classical stationary state may be unstable or convergence to it may be slow that it becomes practically irrelevant in calendar time, and so on.[2]

The purpose of this work is to demonstrate that, by contrast to currently accepted views, a competitive monetary economy of which the environment is stationary may undergo persistent and large deterministic fluctuations under **laissez faire**. That these cyclical fluctuations may display, moreover, the sort of correlations that recent Classical macroeconomic models have sought to incorporate, even under complete information. And finally, that the Government, in the face of such autonomous deterministic fluctuations, has indeed in principle the power to stabilize the economy by implementing simple deterministic - and publicly known - countercyclical policies.

Although one of the goals of the present work is to develop concepts and methods that can be applied, it is hoped, to a larger class of situations, the analysis proceeds by studying a particular example, namely an overlapping generations model very much like the model developed by R.J. Lucas in his seminal paper (1972), with the noticeable difference that we assume that the economy is **not** subjected to any shock of any sort. Business deterministic cycles are shown to appear in a purely endogenous fashion under **laissez faire**. Markets are assumed to clear in the Walrasian sense at every date, and traders have perfect foresight

---

[2] For an excellent account of the long feud between Keynesian and (Old, Neo or New) Classical economists, see e.g. Tobin (1980).

along the cycles.

The origin of these endogenous deterministics cycles is the potential conflict between the wealth effect and the intertemporal substitution effect that are associated with real interest rate movements. Business cycles emerge, in particular, when the degree of concavity of a trader's utility function - which we measure, although there is no uncertainty in the model, by the so-called Arrow-Pratt "relative degree of risk aversion" - is sufficiently higher for old agents than for younger ones.[3] An important outcome of the analysis is that cycles of different periods typically coexist - in some case, there may be a countable number of these. The techniques employed to study the occurrence and the stability of such business cycles are partly borrowed from recent mathematical theories that have been constructed by using the notion of the "bifurcation" of a dynamical system in order to explain the emergence of cycles and the transition of turbulent ("chaotic") behavior in physical, biological or ecological systems.[4] The equilibrium level of output is shown to be negatively related to the equilibrium level of the real interest rate. A similar relation exists (but in the opposite direction) between equilibrium real money balances and real interest rates. These relations hold both in the long run, i.e. along business cycles, and in the short run, i.e. on the transition path, and whether movements of the real

---

[3] The idea that endogenous deterministic cycles may emerge in an overlapping generations model is already present in the literature. For instance David Gale (1973) presents a numerical example of a cycle of period 2, while David Cass (1980) discussed graphically the possibility of their occurrence. Moreover, the deterministic business cycles that are the subject of this paper may be assimilated to what has recently been called "sun spots" equilibria. The analysis of sunspot equiilbria has been started by Karl Shell (1977) and later developed by C. Azariadis (1981) and D. Cass and K. Shell (1981, 1983). Independently of the present work, a forthcoming paper by C. Azariadis and R. Guesnerie (1983), which I have not yet seen, establishes that there are sunspots equilibria if and only if deterministic cycles exist.

Finally, a recent paper by P. Diamond and D. Fudenberg (1983) provides an example of an endogenous rational expectations business cycle in a search equilibrium model, in an otherwise stationary environment.

[4] One important mathematical reference in this field is Collet and Eckmann (1980). For a stimulating review of variuos applications of the theory, see May (1976). Part of this theory has been already applied in economics or game theory, in particular by Benhabib and Day (1981, 1982), Dana and Malgrange (1981), Day (1982, 1982), Jensen and Urban (1982), Rand (1978). The results of this theory that seemed (to me) relevant and useable by economic theorists are reviewed in Grandmont (1983).

interest rate are anticipated or not. The basic ingredient there is the condition that older agents have a higher marginal propensity to consume leisure.

Finally, monetary policy by means of nominal interest payments is shown to be extremely effective. A permanent change of the rate of growth of the money supply by these means is seen to be superneutral. Yet, it is shown that there exists a very simple deterministic countercyclical policy that enables monetary authorities to stabilize completely business cycles and to force the economy back to the unique (Golden rule) stationary state. Due to the nonlinearity of the model, such a policy affects not only the variances of real equilibrium magnitudes but also their means. The central point here is that there are typically many long run periodic equilibria that coexist under **laissez faire**, and that policies may be designed which force the economy to settle at only one of these - here the stationary state.[5]

The particular model used to get these results is a very simple version of the overlapping generations model of the Lucas type (1972). It is shown in the original paper that this sort of model with variable production can be reduced to a simple exchange model (without production). One can thus focus attention in this brief presentation directly on the latter case. Traders live two periods, and agents are identical (equivalently there is a single agent) in each generation. There is only one (non durable) good, and "money" is the only asset. For most of the paper, its stock is constant over time and equal to $M > 0$.

Each agent has a nonrandom endowment of the good in each period of his life, $\ell_1^* > 0$, $\ell_2^* > 0$. Intertemporal tastes among lifetime consumption streams (a_1, a_2) are represented by the utility function $V_1(a_1) + V_2(a_2)$, with $a_1 \geq 0$, $a_2 \geq 0$, in which each V_τ has the usual properties of strict concavity and continuous differentiability up to the second order.

The behavior of a young agent observing the current price $p > 0$ of the good

---

[5] The idea that there may be large number of "rational expectations" or perfect foresight equilibria in a monetary economy and that accordingly, one possible role of policy is to select one of these, is also already present in the literature. In particular, this fact has been well known by theorists who worked with the overlapping generations model. The point has been most forcefully reiterated recently by F. Hahn (1982).

and expecting the price $p^e > 0$ to prevail in the future is to maximize his intertemporal utility function under the current and the expected budget constraints

$$pa_1 + m = p\ell_1^*$$

$$p^e a_2 = p^e \ell_2^* + m$$

in which $m > 0$ stands for his demand for money. Optimum excess demands for the good at each age $a_\tau - \ell_\tau^*$ are then functions of $z_\tau(\theta)$ $(\tau = 1,2)$ $\theta = p/p^e$, i.e. The associated demand for money is then given by

$$m^d(p,p^e) \equiv - pz_1(\theta) \equiv p^e z_2(\theta) \tag{1}$$

It is assumed throughout the paper that agents have an incentive to save when the price of the good is constant over time, i.e. $\tilde{\theta} = V_1'(\ell_1^*)/V_2'(\ell_2^*) < 1$.

A competitive equilibrium at a given date t is then described by the following relations that represents the equality of supply and demand on the good and the money markets

$$z_1(p_t/p_{t+1}^e) + M/p_t = 0 \tag{2}$$

$$m^d(p_t,p_{t+1}^e) = M \tag{3}$$

in which p_t is the current price and p_{t+1}^e is the price that is expected to prevail at $t + 1$. Of course (1) implies that the two equations are equivalent (Walras's Law).

Periodic competitive equilibria with perfect foresight are defined as periodic sequences of prices $\{p_t\}$ that are solutions of (2) (or (3)) satisfying $p_{t+1}^e = p_{t+1}$, for all t. A straightforward manipulation shows that such a periodic equilibrium satisfies the following system

$$z_1(\theta_t) + z_2(\theta_{t-1}) = 0 \tag{4}$$

$$M/p_t = z_2(\theta_{t-1}) \tag{5}$$

in which $\theta_t = p_t/p_{t+1}$, all t. Indeed (5) says that the excess demand of an old trader at date t, which is equal to M/p_t, must be equal, under perfect foresight, to what he planned to do for the current date one period earlier, i.e. $z_2(p_{t-1}/p_t)$. Using that fact with (2) yields (4).

Equation (4) induces a well defined backward <u>perfect foresight dynamics</u> on real interest rates, i.e. on the variables $\theta_t = p_t/p_{t+1}$. Indeed, under the assumptions of the paper, z_2 is a differentiably increasing function and thus (4) can be rewritten

$$\theta_{t-1} = z_2^{-1}\,[-z_1(\theta_t)] \equiv \phi(\theta_t) \tag{6}$$

The function ϕ so defined maps $[\overline{\theta},+\infty)$ into $[\overline{\theta},z_2^{-1}(\ell_1^*))$, and is continuously differentiable. It has two fixed points, $\theta = \overline{\theta}$ which corresponds to the non-monetary stationary state of the economy, and $\theta = 1$ which is the unique monetary stationary state.

Periodic competitive equilibria with perfect foresight are in a one-to-one correspondence with periodic orbits of the map ϕ by using (5). Once this remark is made, it is relatively easy to get some information about the occurrence of cycles in the present model, by applying a few mathematical results on the existence and the bifurcation of periodic orbits of one-dimensional difference equations. Among the results obtained in the paper, one may select the following ones.

1. If the concavity of an old trader's utility function V_2 is not too large, i.e. if $R_2(a_2) = -a_2V_2''(a_2)/V_2'(a_2) < 1$ for all $a_2 > 0$, then the map ϕ has no critical point (it is increasing everywhere) and thus it can have no non-degenerate cycle.

2. If $R_2(a_2)$ is nondecreasing, and if $\alpha_2 = \text{Sup}\, R_2(a_2) > 1$, then the map ϕ is unimodal with a unique critical point $\overline{\theta} < \theta^*$, i.e. ϕ is increasing for $\theta < \theta^*$ and decreasing afterward. It is then straightforward to see that a cycle of period 3 exists when the iterates of the critical point θ^* satisfy

$$\phi^2(\theta^*) < \phi^3(\theta^*) < \theta^* < 1 < \phi(\theta^*)$$

It is shown in the paper that this condition obtains in the present economic model whenever the concavity of an old trader's utility function, as measured by $R_2(a_2)$, is large enough, provided that other mild conditions on the endowments ℓ_1^* and ℓ_2^* are satisfied. Then it follows from Sarkovskii's Theorem, that cycles of all periods also exist.

3. Let us index in a continuous way all characteristics of the model (i.e. ℓ_1^*, ℓ_2^*, V_1 and V_2) by some parameter λ, so that for $\lambda = 0$ case 1 above obtains (no cycle) while case 2 obtains for $\lambda = 1$ (a cycle of period 3). Then when λ moves from 0 to 1, one observes the usual cascade of period-doubling "flip" bifurcations of ϕ-stable cycles, for λ in some interval $[0,\lambda_\infty^*)$, and then beyond λ_∞^* one enters the "chaotic" region. A computer experiment along these lines is carried out by increasing the concavity of an old trader's utility function.

The above bifurcation results concern ϕ-stable cycles, i.e. cycles that are stable in the backward perfect foresight (b.p.f) dynamics on θ_t described by (4) or (6) (or equivalently the b.p.f. dynamics on equilibrium prices p_t given by (2) with $p_{t+1}^e = p_{t+1}$). They may accordingly appear difficult to interpret since time should go forward after all in any meaningful dynamics. One possible interpretation is the following one. Suppose that ϕ has several cycles, but that at most one of them is weakly ϕ-stable, as in the case in which ϕ has a negative Schwartzian derivative (sufficient conditions on the utility functions V_1 and V_2 that yield this property are given in the paper). Then the forward perfect foresight dynamics is locally well defined around all other cycles that are ϕ-unstable (by an appropriate linearization of the associated iterate of ϕ), and these ϕ-unstable cycles are locally stable under this forward dynamics. The interpretation of the bifurcation results reported in 3. above is then that the map ϕ becomes more and more "humpy" as the parameter λ moves from 0 to 1, and more and more cycles appear that are locally stable under the forward local perfect foresight dynamics.

It is further argued in the paper that ϕ-stable cycles may not be "unstable" after all. In this economy, if there are several cycles with perfect foresight, traders will have a hard time figuring out on which one (if any) they are going to end up. In other words, one should model traders as <u>learning</u> the dynamics of prices on the transition path toward long run equilbria. The way that is chosen in the paper to portray this learning process is to postulate that the expected price p^e_{t+1} in (2) is a fixed function of current and past prices

$$p^e_{t+1} = \psi(p_t, p_{t-1}, \ldots, p_{t-\tau}) \tag{7}$$

in which τ is a fixed "large" number. It is shown in the paper that under some reasonable conditions on the expectation function ψ, (2) and (7) determine uniquely the short run equilibrium price p_t at date t as a (continuously differentiable) function of past prices $(p_{t-1}, \ldots, p_{t-\tau})$. It is further proved under some not implausible assumptions on the learning scheme ψ, that a cycle of period k of the map ϕ that is ϕ-stable (in which k is relatively small by comparison to the memory lag T) is also stable in the <u>forward</u> dynamics induced by (2) and (7).

The outcome of the study is that this economy may behave very badly as soon as there is a multiplicity of long run periodic equilibria. As mentioned before, traders are then bound to have great difficulties in guessing where they are going to end up and thus about the dynamics of prices. On the transition path, they are bound to make mistakes that entail efficiency losses, and this is likely to last for a significant amount of time. There is thus a need of a stabilization scheme. It is shown in the paper that there is indeed such a countercyclical policy, using proportional money transfers or equivalently nominal interest payments on money balances. This scheme obeys the following rule. If r_t is the nominal rate paid at t, then one should have for all t

$$(1 + r_t) = \frac{p_t}{p_{t-1}} \, g\left(\frac{p_{t-1}}{p^*_{t-1}} \right)$$

in which $\{p^*_t\}$ describes a target sequence of prices given by $p^*_0 = \frac{M}{z_2(1)}$ and $p^*_t = (1 + r^*)^t \, p^*_0$, r^* being the inflation rate. This policy therefore links the <u>real</u> rate of interest $(1 + r_t)p_{t-1}/p_t$ between dates $t - 1$ and t (through the countercyclical part of the policy described by the function g) to the deviation of the actual price p_{t-1} from the target price p^*_{t-1} at $t - 1$. It is shown that under some mild conditions on g, this policy succeeds in stabilizing completely economic fluctuations by locking the economy into the unique (Golden rule) monetary stationary state $\theta = 1$ immediately.

References

1. Azariadis, C. (1981), "Self-Fulfilling Prophecies", Journal of Economic Theory 25, 380-396.

2. Azariadis, C. and R. Guesnerie (1983), "Sunspots and Cycles", Caress Working Paper 8322, University of Pennsylvania, Philadelphia.

3. Barro, R.J. (1981), "The Equilibrium Approach to Business Cycles", Ch. 2 in Money Expectations, and Business Cycles, Academic Press, New York.

4. Benhabib, J. and R.H. Day (1981), "Rational Choice and Erratic Behavior", Review of Economic Studies 48, 459-472.

5. Benhabib, J. and R.H. Day (1982), "A Characterization of Erratic Dynamics in the Overlapping Generations Model", Journal of Economic Dynamics and Control 4, 37-55.

6. Cass, D (1980), "Money in Consumption-Loan Type Models: An Addendum", in J.H. Kareken and N. Wallace (eds.), Models of Monetary Economies, Federal Reserve Bank of Minneapolis.

7. Cass, D. and K. Shell (1981), "Do Sunspots Matter?" Caress Working Paper 80-09R, University of Pennsylvania, 1981. Also appearing in French as "Les taches solaires ont-elles de l'importance?" Cahiers du Seminaire d'Econometrie 24 (1982), 93-127.

8. Collet, P. and J.-P. Eckmann (1980), Iterated Maps on the Interval as Dynamical Systems, Birhauser, Boston.

9. Dana, R.A. and P. Malgrange (1981), "The Dynamics of a Discrete Version of a Growth Cycle Model", Cepremap Working Paper, forthcoming in Analysing the Structure of Econometric Models, J.P. Ancot (ed.), M. Nijhoff, Amsterdam.

10. Day, R.H. (1982), "Irregular Growth Cycles", American Economic Review 72, 406-414.

11. Day, R.H. (1983), "The Emergence of Chaos from Classical Economic Growth", Quarterly Journal of Economics 98, 201-213.

12. Diamond, P. and D. Fudenberg (1983), "An Example of Rational Expectations Business Cycles in Search Equilibirium", M.I.T., Mimeo.

13. Gale, D. (1973), "Pure Exchange Equillibrium of Dynamic Economic Models", Journal of Economic Theory 6, 12-36.

14. Grandmont, J.M. (1983), "Periodic and Aperiodic Behavior in Discrete Onedimensional Dynamical Systems", Cepremap D.P. N^{O} 8317. Also available as a Technical Report of IMSSS, Economics, Stanford University and a Technical Report of EHEC, University of Lausanne.

15. Grandmont, J.M. and W. Hildenbrand (1974), "Stochastic Processes of Temporary Equilibria", Journal of Mathematical Economics 1, 247-277.

16. Hahn, F.H. (1982), Money and Inflation, Basil Blackwell, Oxford.

17. Jensen, R.U. and R. Urban (1982), "Chaotic Price Behavior in a Nonlinear Cobweb Model", Yale University, mimeo.

18. Kydland, F.E. and E.C. Prescott (1982), "Time to Build and Aggregate Fluctuations", Econometrica 50, 1345-1370.

19. Lucas, R.E. Jr. (1972), "Expectations and the Neutrality of Money", Journal of Economic Theory 4, 103-1224.

20. Lucas, R.E. Jr. (1975, "An Equilibrium Model of the Business Cycle", Journal of Political Economy 83, 1113-44.

21. Lucas, R.E. Jr. (1977), "Understanding Business Cycles", Journal of Monetary Economics 3, (Supplement), 7-30.

22. Lucas, R.E. Jr. (1980), "Methods and Problems in Business Cycle Theory", Journal of Money, Credit and Bankings 12, 696-715.

23. Lucas, R.E. Jr. (1981), "Tobin and Monetarism: A Review Article", Journal of Economic Literature 19, 558-567.

24. May, R.B. (1976), "Simple Mathematical Models with Very Complicated Dynamics", Nature 261, 459-467.

25. Rand, D. (1978), "Exotic Phenomena in Games and Duopoly Models", Journal of Mathematical Economics 5, 173-184.

26. Sargent, T.J. and N. Wallace (1975), "Rational Expectations, the Optimal Monetary Instrument, and the Optimal Money Supply Rule", Journal of Political Economy 83, 241-254.

27. Shell, K. (1977), "Monnaie et allocation intertemporelle", CNRS Seminaire d'Econometrie Roy-Malinvaud, Paris, mimeo.

28. Tobin, J. (1980), Asset Accumulation and Economic Activity, Yrjo Jahnsson Lectures, Basil Blackwell, Osford.

COMMENTARIES ON THE GRANDMONT PAPER "ENDOGENOUS COMPETITIVE BUSINESS CYCLES

Daniel Goroff, Harvard University

Professor Grandmont studies business cycles by identifying them with periodic points of certain functions. As parameters of his model vary, cycles appear, disappear, and become stable or unstable. The mathematics which governs qualitative changes of this kind is called bifurcation theory.

A more formal description of bifurcation theory begins by specifying when to consider two functions qualitatively the same. For mathematical purposes, the usual criterion is topological conjugacy, or, in other words, equivalence up to a continuous change of coordinates. We say a one parameter family of functions undergoes a (codimension one) bifurcation as it passes through the boundary of the conjugacy classes determined by this relation.

What bifurcations befall or beget business cycles? On a neighborhood of a periodic point, only three qualitative changes of behavior are possible as a parameter varies. At a saddle-node bifurcation, for example, an unstable and a stable periodic point collide and both disappear. A stable periodic point becomes unstable at a flip bifurcation, giving birth to a pair of stable periodic points of twice the original period. The last possibility, called the Hopf bifurcation, occurs only in two or more dimensions. Here a stable periodic point changes to an unstable one which is encircled by an attracting invariant closed curve.

Professor Grandmont's results on the existence and stability of business cycles with various periods rely on the regularity and order with which flip bifurcations occur in maps of the interval. His sixth figure, for example, illustrates the period doubling cascade whose universal properties were explored by Feigenbaum. Despite progress on this one dimensional case, there are few rigorous descriptions of how successive birfucations organize themselves in general. Even in the plane, counterexamples rule out natural analogues to the Sarkovskii ranking cited by Professor Grandmont. Moreover, the attracting invariant circles which appear at Hopf bifurcations in two or more dimensions also need analysis since these could model business cycles as well.

Finally, there is the problem of global dynamics. On the interval, the assumption of a negative Schwarzian derivative insures that at most one stable business cycle exists, and that the economy converges to such a cycle from almost every initial condition. In contrast, periodic points and their local bifurcations do not exert such a decisive influence on the global behavior of typical multidimensional systems. A rich variety of other qualitiative features, such as homoclinic orbits and strange attracters, also come into play.

Indeed, examples show that there are no simple characterizations of the equivalence classes determined by requiring large scale topological conjugacy. The mathematical tendency to define "qualitatively the same" as meaning "gives the same answer to all coordinate-free questions" does not produce a useful theory of global birfurcations.

Fortunately, economic analysis turns on far fewer and far more special questions. As in Professor Grandmont's last chapter, understanding the effects of certain policies is often the ultimate goal. Therefore, models which differ in the mathematical sense above may nevertheless be considered qualitatively the same for all economic purposes. The fundamental challenge in studying multidimensional economies as dynamical systems is to specify these purposes.

Jose A. Scheinkman, University of Chicago

Grandmont's paper provides, among other things, an example of a fully articulated model in which "endogenous" (i.e. independent of the existence of random shocks) cycles appear. Another example may be provided by optimization problems of the type

$$(p) \max \int_0^\infty e^{-\beta t} u(x\ \mu)dt \quad \text{s.t. } (x,\dot{x},\mu) \in A, \quad x(0) = \zeta .$$

Such control problems just as Robinson Crusoe's famous example, may be "decentralized" i.e. its solution may be seen as the outcome of a competitive system where consumers and firms face prices parametrically, provided enough convexity is present.

Control problems such as (p) may well posess periodic solutions. Though this cannot happen when β is close to zero (cf. Scheinkman [1976]), periodic solutions appear for large β's. Benhabib and Nishimura [1975], using the Hopf bifurcation, produce an example with two capital goods (i.e., $x \epsilon R^2$) and a simple consumption good ($\mu \epsilon R$), in which a periodic (stable) solution exists.

Though an inattentive reader of Grandmont's paper may think that there is something inherently bad about cycles, which would require government intervention to smooth them out, in decentralized models of the type discussed above the cycles represent <u>the optimum solution</u> and then any attempt to smooth them out would cause a lowering of every agent's utility. The situation is entirely different in models where cycles are caused by market failures. Scheinkman and Weiss [1983] present a model where all cycles are caused by the lack of certain insurance markets. Though one should be careful in specifying which instruments are available to the government, it may well be that in this type of economy, government action to correct for market failure will by itself eliminate cycles.

References

1. Benhabib, J. and Nishimura, K. [1979] The Hopf Bifurcation and the Existence and Stability of Closed Orbits in Multisector Models of Optimal Economic Growth -<u>Journal of Economic Theory</u> 21 - pp. 421-444.

2. Scheinkman J.A. [1976] - On Optimal Steady States of n-Sector Growth Models When Utility Is Discounted. <u>Journal of Economic Theory</u> 12-pp. 11-30.

3. Scheinkman, J.A. and Weiss, L. [1983] - Borrowing Constraints and Agregate Economic Activity U. of Chicago, Unpublished.

Christopher Sims, University of Minnesota

Economics is a peculiar science, like the "hard" sciences in that both its theory and its empirical work use sophisticated mathematics, but still a social science in that its theories are suggestive aids to intuition rather than serious attempts at precise description of the real world. As someone whose professional work is mainly statistical, using vague or simple theories to understand a much finer-grained description of the "business cycle" than that underlying this paper, my first role as discussant must be to point out the obvious--that this paper explains a very much simplified picture of the real business cycle. The business cycle is not exactly periodic. It is not even approximately periodic in any useful sense. Aggregate economic variables behave to a first approximation as realizations of multivariate linear stochastic processes with smooth spectral densities. The model in this paper cannot generate this sort of time series.

The paper counts it as an advantage that it avoids the need for "the ad hoc assumption that cycles are due to exogenous shocks". But what is critical to the stochastic models the paper implicity criticizes is not that shocks come from "outside" the model, but rather that they may not be predictable from the history of the economy; that is, that at any given date the future of the economy is uncertain to those active in it. This is a central fact about the world; a model which avoids assuming agents are uncertain about the future is not avoiding ad hockery, it is making a counterfactual simplification which requires justification.

The behavioral mechanism generating cycles in this model could of course be introduced into a more realistic model. I doubt that the mechanism at work here is important in actual business cycles, however. In an economy with a time-stationary, smoothly convex technology and long-lived individuals with concave utility functions, perfect foresight will tend to keep cycles negligibly small. If a cyclical path of consumption is feasible in such an economy, so will also be something close to the same path shifted in time by half a cycle. Convexity guarantees that the sum of the two paths, which should be nearly smooth, is also feasible; and concavity of utility guarantees that the smoother path is preferred. Because individuals discount future consumption, and because a long cycle may deliver high consumption immediately, long cycles may arise despite the foregoing heuristic argument. But it is unlikely that a realistic model would show individuals with perfect foresight choosing to let production fluctuate much at business cycle frequencies.

This paper generates fluctuations of "short" period, but only, in my view, because the period is "one generation". The welfare of generations fluctuates in this paper, not the consumption levels of individuals living many periods. In a cyclical equilibrium market forces do not damp the cycle, because the less fortunate generations have been known since the beginning of time to be unfortunate and have nothing of value to trade to the more fortunate generations with whom they overlap. I doubt that this sort of mechanism could generate a cycle of realistic magnitude in an economy in which each generation was modeled as living 40 periods or more.

The paper points out that the model generates a positive relation between inflation and output level and a negative relation between real interest rate and output level. The former of these relations, the "Phillips Curve", is only very roughly realistic. In recent U.S. history (the '70's), it has been closer to false than true. The negative association between real interest rates and output levels is at least equally dubious as an empirical generalization.

The paper begins by placing its model in opposition to those of the New Classical school. The paper does display cycles which policy of a certain kind can eliminate, in contrast to the simplest New Classical models. But, because the cyclical equilibria are Pareto-efficient, the gains from countercyclical policy are small relative to its redistributional effects. New Classical models can easily be constructed which imply that countercyclical fiscal policies are desirable and produce efficiency gains, probably larger than those implied by a realistic version of this paper's model. (One assumes the efficiency losses from taxation depend on the fraction of income taxed--then one should time the largest efficiency losses to coincide with the periods of greatest wealth). New Classical theorists see these sorts of gains as inherently smaller than those implicitly claimed for policies of Keynesian interventionism, and they are right. Keynesianism rests on an analysis of the large aggregate effects which might flow from small market failures of certain types in dynamic economies. If these play an important role in the business cycle, countercyclical policy may have large effects on welfare. From such a truly Keynesian perspective, the model in this paper carries much the same message as that of other New Classical models.

Neil Wallace, University of Minnesota

Grandmont studies a nonstochastic version of Lucas' "Expectations and the Neutrality of Money" (Journal of Economic Theory, 1972) and shows that there are parameter values for which there are perfect foresight cyclic equilibria in which there is a positive association between total output and inflation. The Lucas model, in contrast, produces such a positive correlation only through the presence of aggregate demand randomness and other randomness, the realizations of which have to be inferred from prices.

The two models have some common implications and some different implications. One common implication is that an observed positive association between total output and inflation cannot be exploited in any simple way to, for example, maintain permanently some peak level of total output. Among the differences are the following: using the standard welfare criterion for overlapping-generations models, a cyclic equilibrium in Grandmont's model is known to be Pareto optimal. A plausible conjecture is that an equilibrium in the Lucas model with aggregate demand randomness and, hence, with a positive association between total output and inflation is not Pareto-optimal.

Grandmont studies a broader class of policy than that considered by Lucas. He studies a rule which promises to pay real interest on money held from t to $t+1$ at a rate that depends on the time t price level, with interest financed, as in Lucas, by creation (or destruction) of money.

This rule, as he claims, selects one out of many perfect foresight equilibria that exist under laissez faire. The properties of such rules deserve further study if only because so much is achieved so easily. One interpretation of the Grandmont rule is that the government announces a target path of the price level (which, by the way, had better be precisely one of the laissez faire equilibria) and, in effect, says: behave in a way consistent with this target or we will create (or destroy) money so that there is no equilibrium.

M. Woodford, Princeton University

One of the most striking ideas proposed in Professor Grandmont's paper is that important properties of the temporary general equilibrium dynamics (what he calls the "actual dynamics") may be ascertained from a consideration of the backward perfect foresight dynamics. His prop. 2.3 establishes that the set of periodic temporary general equilibria (periodic orbits of W) coincides with the set of periodic orbits of ϕ, while his prop. 3.1 establishes that ϕ - stability of such a periodic orbit implies stability of the same orbit in the t.g.e dynamics. These results are important for two reasons. First, they allow the theory of iterated maps of an interval to be applied to his model, so that one may draw conclusions about conditions for the existence and stability of periodic orbits of arbitrarily large period, the coexistence of a multiplicity of periodic orbits, and the appearance of more complex cycles through bifurcations as certain parameters are varied. Since the mathematical results involved in section 4 apply only to univariate maps, they could not be applied to the t.g.e. dynamics directly. Second, the conclusions that are drawn (e.g., the conditions for global stability of the monetary steady state given in Lemmas 4.2) involve only the preferences and endowments of agents, not the properties of their expectation functions.

In order to establish props. 2.3 and 3.1, certain assumptions are made regarding the expectation function ψ ; in particular, that

(2.f) ψ is continuously differentiable,

(2.g) if $(p_t,\ldots, p_{t-T})$ displays period k, $\psi(p_t,\ldots,p_{t-T}) = p_{t-k+1}$, and

(2.h) at any k-cycle, $\psi'_j > 0$ for all j.

(it is not stated for what values of k these conditions are to hold; one may suppose that some bound related to the size of T is intended, such as $k < \frac{T}{2}$.) These conditions might seem to be reasonable properties for a forecasting rule that is to perform well in whatever environment one happens to find oneself. However, the conditions are not as weak as they seem. For example, one can show that if $T = \infty$, and the conditions are to hold for all k, no function exists that satisfies all three. If the conditions need hold only for all k up to some finite upper bound, functions satisfying all three conditions can be found for T large enough but unless the upper bound on k is very small, T must be very large. For example, if the conditions are to hold for all $k < 20$, one must have $T > 957,695,759$. And even if one grants this, the properties of the functions satisfying the three conditions are not attractive. For example, if one demands that the conditions hold for all $k < 20$, and lets $T = 1,000,000,000$, then in the neighborhood of a constant price sequence $(p,p,p,\ldots)$, the ψ function must be approximately

$$\psi(p_t, p_{t-1}, \ldots, p_{t-1,000,000,000}) = p_{t-957,695,759} + O((p_\tau - p)^2)$$

That is, to first order, the expectation function is sensitive only to deviations from the trend level in one of the past billion periods, and that one period is located far, far in the past. Such an expectation function is plainly not desirable if one is interested in sensitivity to things other than possible cycles; for example, it will not be sensitive to drift in the parameters of the economy.

Various responses to this problem are possible. (1) the paper still stands as a demonstration that one could construct examples of stable competitive t.g.e. cycles of any desired periodicity. One finds an example for which there is a stable orbit of the desired periodicity in the b.p.f. dynamics (which are well understood), then constructs an expectation function satisfying the above conditions only for the particular periodic orbit of interest, then uses Props. 2.3 and 3.1 to show that one has a stable obit of the desired periodicity in the t.g.e dynamics.

(2) One might suppose that the expectation function ψ is not "a characteristic of the traders on the same level as preferences and endowments," but instead that it evolves so as to eventually adapt itself to the dynamics of the particular economy that exists. Then one might assume that the outcome of this evolution is a function satisfying (2.f,g,h) in the case only of a particular periodic orbit that occurs in that particular economy. But these conditions are not as plausible as the outcome of learning in a particular economy, as they are

for a forecast function intended to be reasonable in all environments. While one may suppose that expectations eventually converge to a function satisfying $\psi(p_t^*,\ldots,p_{t-T}^*) = p_{t-k+1}^*$, whose $(p_t^*, \ldots, p_{t-T}^*)$ represents a particular period k orbit of the b.p.f. dynamics, there would be no reason for that function to satisfy $\psi(p_t, \ldots, p_{t-T}) = p_{t-k+1}$ for all $(p_t,\ldots, p_{t-T})$ close to $(p_t^*,\ldots, p_{t-T}^*)$. Yet the latter property is needed for the proof of Prop. 3.1. Nor is there any reason to expect the updating process to converge to a function satisfying (2.h). Furthermore, resort to an evolutionary story of this sort requires that one investigate the stability of the process by which ψ is updated, in the case of the particular periodic orbit and associated ψ function of interest.

(3) Perhaps differentiability everywhere is not a requirement for a reasonable expectation function; one might instead demand differentiability almost everywhere, but allow it to fail at exactly the points (such as constant price histories) considered in proving the mutual inconsistency of the various assumptions. For example, OLS autoregression as a forecasting method yields a ψ function that is continuous, and that is differentiable except on a set of Lebesgue measure zero in R^{T+1}, which set happens to include all histories which are k-periodic for low k. It is an open question whether functions exist satisfying the modified conditions

(f') ψ is continuous, and differentiable almost everywhere,

(g') as above, and

(h') in the neighborhood of any k-cycle, ψ is non-decreasing in all arguments,

(OLS autoregression fails to satisfy (h').) Furthermore, in the case of such a generalization, the methods used to analyze stability of periodic orbits of w in the present paper become inapplicable. It is an open question whether similar results could nonetheless be obtained using more sophisticated methods.

(4) One might simply argue that perfect foresight equilibrium, rather than temporary general equilibrium, is the approximate equilibrium concept, and that b.p.f. stability ("ϕ - stability") is the appropriate stability concept, and omit consideration of t.g.e. dynamics altogether. In this case all the results

of sections 4 and 6 based on analysis of the b.p.f. dynamics remain of interest. But one needs in this case a convincing story as to how perfect foresight equilibria are realized outside of a periodic orbit, and in particular as to why backwards p.f. stability is to be demanded.

On the Stability of the Tatonnement Approach to Competitive Equilibrium

Leonid Hurwicz
Economics Department
University of Minnesota

The notion of tatonnement goes back to Walras who studied its stability properties in the case of two goods ([14], Lesson 7). It is patterned after an auction where goods do not change hands hands until the final price has been agreed upon.

Formally, in a pure exchange economy with n agents and ℓ goods, a Walrasian tatonnement process with a discrete time parameter can be written as

$$(1) \quad p_{j,t+1} - p_{j,t} = H_j(f_j;\omega_o, R)), \; j = 1_1,,,\ell, \; t = 0,1,2,\ldots \quad .$$

Here $\omega_o = (\omega_o^1,\ldots, \omega_o^n)$; $\omega_o^i = (\omega_{1,o}^i ,,,\omega_{\ell,o}^i)$, $i = 1, \ldots, n$;

$p_t = (p_{1,t},\ldots, p_{\ell,t})$; $R = (R^1 \ldots, R^n)$; $\omega_{j,o}^i$ is the i-th agent's initial endowment in good j ; $p_{j,t}$ is the price of good j at time t ; R^i is the preference relation of the i-th agent. $f_j(\cdot;\omega_o,R)$ is the aggregate excess demand function for good j ; i.e., $f_j = \sum_{j-1}^{n} f_j^i$ where f_j^i is the excess demand function of the i-th agent for the j-th good. H_j is sign preserving (often also monotone).

By contrast, a non-tatonnement process involves varying the commodity holdings of the participants. Thus (1) may be replaced by

$$(2) \quad p_{j,t+1} - p_{j,t} = g_j \,(p_t, \omega_t, R), \; j=1,\ldots, \ell, \; t = 0,1,2,\ldots,$$

where $\omega_t = (\omega_t^1,\ldots,\omega_t^n)$; $\omega_t^i = (\omega_{1,t}^i,\ldots, \omega_{\ell,t}^i)$, $i = 1,\ldots, n$, $t = 0,1,2,\ldots$. To make the specification complete for such a non-tatonnement process one would also have to prescribe the law governing the variations over time of ω_t, but we shall not formalize this here.

It is worth noting that special problems arise when dealing with economies in which irreversible physical phenomena (production, consumption) take place. Thus if production were to take place while the adjustment process is "seeking the right prices," irreversible "errors" would typically occur, and the final outcome would, in general, not be Pareto-optimal with respect to the initially given resources, technology, and preferences. On the other hand, in a tatonnement process no physically irreversible actions take place, and Pareto-optimization is achievable.†

Given the initial dispersion of information in a non-tatonnment process for economies with irreversible physical changes, it would be appropriate to justify the notion of optimality, taking into account the unavoidable costs in the 'learning' stages.

Turning back to tatonnement processes, much of the work has been devoted to the problem of stability of solutions of systems such as (1) above, or, more precisely, their differential equations counterparts, such as

$$(1') \qquad \frac{dp_j}{dt} = H_j(f_j(p)) \quad , j = 1,\ldots, \ell.$$

(Here we suppress ω_0 and R , since ω_0 will not vary, and R may be regarded as incorporated in the excess demand functions f_j, $j=1,\ldots,\ell$.)

From static analysis (going back to Walras and Marshall), it is known that, even under very plausible circumstances, systems such as (1') have multiple equilibria, i.e., solutions $\overline{p}$ of

$$(3) \qquad 0 = H_j(f_j(\overline{p})), \quad j = 1,\ldots,\ell \quad .$$

Thus even for $\ell=2$, $n = 2$, with one of the prices normalized (say $p_2(t) = 1$ for all $\underline{t}$), the excess demand function $f_1(p_1,1)$ may have three zeros, and assume positive values when p_1 is close to zero and negative values when p_1 is sufficiently large.

Taking H_1 to be the identity function, the dynamics in this case reduces to

---

†Walras did consider tatonnement process in economies with production, using 'tickets' (in French 'bons') to stand for input-output proposals. ([14], p. 242).

$$(4)\quad \frac{dp_1}{dt} = f_1(p).$$

It is easily seen that of the three equilibrium points $\bar{p}_1 < \bar{p}_2 < \bar{p}_3$, the outside ones are locally stable but $\bar{p}_2$ is locally unstable.

Hence it is not to be expected that, in a reasonably broad class of economic environments (i.e., here: aggregate excess demand functions) every equilibrium point of a Walrasian tatonnement process will be stable. This leads to the following milder definition called global stability of the system (1): that, for every initial value p(0), there exist an equilibrium point (i.e., a solution of (3)) $\bar{p}$ such that the trajectory p(t)

$$(5)\quad p(t) = \psi\,(t;p(0))$$

converges to $\bar{p}$. I.e.:

$$(6)\quad \lim_{y\to\infty} \psi\,(t;p(0)) = \bar{p}.$$

It turns out (see, e.g., Arrow, Block, and Hurwicz [2] and Arrow and Hahn [1]), that certain classes of economies are globally stable in this sense. This, in particular, is true when all goods are "gross substitutes" ($\frac{\partial f_j}{\partial p_\ell} > 0$, all $j \neq k$) and in some less interesting cases such as $n=1$ or $\ell=2$. (In some cases, additional restrictions are imposed on the functions H_j.)

On the other hand, as shown by Scarf [10] and Gale [4], it is possible to construct economies satisfying the usual postulates of the static ("Arrow-Debreu") theory with $\ell>2$ and $n>1$ (in Scarf's case $n=\ell=3$) which lack global systems stability. It should be added that the results due to Sonnenschein and others provide a blueprint for constructing many more such examples.

From a normative or computational point of view it is natural to conclude that the possible absence of global stability calls for replacing the Walrasian tatonnement by another dynamic process such as, e.g.,

$$(7)\quad \frac{dp}{dt} = (Df(p))^{-1}\, f(p)$$

(Saari and Simon [9] Smale, [11]).

Clearly, the informational burden of this system is greater than that of (1'). But as shown, from different viewpoints, by Saari and Simon [9] and Reiter [7], one must, in general, be prepared to require a bigger message space when stability is demanded.

From a descriptive point of view, it is not obvious that instability as such indicates lack of realism. However it is my impression that the types of instabilities exhibited by the Walrasian tatonnement processes may not mirror the instabilities many economists believe to be present in real economies.

NOTES ON PRICE AND QUANTITY TÂTONNEMENT DYNAMICS*

Andreu Mas-Colell

Department of Economics
Harvard University
Cambridge, MA 02138

1. Introduction

1.1 In these notes we present an exposition of some modern versions of L. Walras' tâtonnement theory (see (1926)) with special emphasis on simultaneous price and quantity dynamics.

1.2 Walras proposed his theory as an approach to the determination of equilibrium prices and productions which rested on dynamic laws intended to mimic the actual functioning of competitive markets. His main laws were two: (I) prices move according to the difference of demand and supply ("loi de l'offre et la demande"), and (II) production moves according to the difference of price and cost ("loi de prix de revient").

1.3 By modern versions we mean the formalization via differential equations first suggested by Samuelson (1947) and pursued by Arrow-Hurwicz (1958). Although a convenient and powerful approach, there is no intrinsic reason why Walras' laws should be embodied into differential equations. Difference equations have a long tradition in economics (e.g. the cobweb). A stochastic treatment would also be quite natural.

1.4 The literature on the tâtonnement is very extensive. See the above reference and also the recent survey by Hahn (1982). Much of the research, however, has concentrated on the limit pure price dynamics (with production, if at all there, automatically adjusted to equilibrium) or, to a lesser extent, on the limit pure quantity dynamics (see the contribution of Novshek and Sonnenschein to this volume). The general case treated here, where prices and quantities stand on the

* This paper has been written for the Workshop on Price-Quantity Dynamics organized by H. Sonnenschein and H. Weinberger at the Institute for Mathematics and its Applications, University of Minnesota, October 23-26, 1983. I am indebted to the audience of my talk for useful comments and references.

same footing, is much less familiar and this in spite of the fact that, as we shall see, it displays interesting and, relative to the two limit cases, novel and illuminating dynamic features. So, we feel this exposition is justified. Of course, there is some work on price-quantity dynamics, e.g. Arrow and Hurwicz (1960), which is relevant. More directly related to these notes are Morishima (1959), Beckmann-Ryder (1969) and Mas-Colell (1974).

1.5 There is a key aspect to tâtonnement dynamics which needs to be emphasized. Actual production and trade only takes place at equilibrium. Outside of it all production and price "decisions" are to be thought of as tentative plans. Thus, it is better not to visualize the dynamics as engaging the economy in real time. For a criticisim of this and alternative approaches with production and trade out of equilibrium see the recent book by Fisher (1983).

2. The Basic Economic Model

2.1 There are ℓ perfectly divisible commodities and we take the economy as composed of a production and a consumption side.

2.2 The production side is composed of n sectors, each one of which can be thought of as an aggregate of several firms. Every sector j is characterized by a convex and closed set of technically feasible input-output vectors $Y_j \subset R^\ell$. According to customary convention the negative (resp. positive) entries of a vector $y_j \in Y_j$ stand for inputs (resp. outputs). Denote by $y = (y_1,\dots,y_n) \in \prod_j Y_j$ the economy wide vector of productions.

2.3 Except for section 5 we shall be interested in the more particular production model where every sector produces only one output (this is called the no joint production model). Without loss of generality we assume that every sector produces a different good. Choosing indices appropriately we can view the j-sector as producing the j good and we can express its technology by a concave production function $g_j\colon R^\ell_+ \to R_+$. We assume that $m < \ell$, i.e., there are non producible factors of production.

2.4 An important particular case is when the technology exhibits constant returns to scale, i.e. if $y_j \in Y_j$ then $\lambda y_j \in Y_j$ for any $\lambda > 0$. In the no joint production model this translates into the homogeneity of degree one of the production functions g_j.

2.5 Every commodity has a price. We fix the price of the ℓ-th commodity (to be thought of as, say, labor services) to be equal to one. The price vector for the first $\ell - 1$ commodities is denoted p. Given p we let $\hat{p} = (p,1) \in R^{\ell}$.

2.6 Given y_j and p the profit (or loss) of the j-sector is simply $\pi_j(y_j,p) = \hat{p} \cdot y_j$. Given y and p the overall vector of profits is $\pi(p,y) = (\hat{p}\cdot y_1,\ldots,\hat{p}\cdot y_m) \in R^m$.

2.7 The demand side of the economy is given to us in a highly reduced form by means of an excess demand function $f(p,\pi) \in R^{\ell-1}$ which assigns net demands (positive entries) or supplies (negative entries) for the first $\ell - 1$ commodities to every $\ell - 1 + m$ vector of prices and profits of the different production sectors $\pi \in R^m$. The excess demand of the ℓ-th commodity is implicitly taken to be $\sum_{j=1}^{m} \pi_j - p\cdot f(p,\pi)$. The complete excess demand system, inclusive of the ℓ-th commodity, is denoted $\hat{f}(p,\pi)$. Of course, it satisfies $\hat{p}\cdot\hat{f}(p,\pi) = \sum_{j=1}^{m} \pi_j$.

2.8 An excess demand function satisfies the <u>Representative Consumer Hypothesis</u> (RC) if, for every p, π, $f(p,\pi)$ could have been generated by a consumer maximizing a utility function $u(z)$ subject to a budget constraint $\{z: p\cdot z \leq \sum_{j=1}^{m} \pi_j\}$.

2.9 An excess demand function f satisfies the <u>Weak Axiom of Revealed Preference</u> (WA) if <u>whenever</u> $f(p,\pi) \neq f(p',\pi')$ <u>and</u> $\hat{p}\cdot\hat{f}(p',\pi') \leq \sum_j \pi_j$ <u>we have</u> $\hat{p}'\cdot\hat{f}(p,\pi) > \sum_j \pi_j$, i.e. if $f(p,\pi)$ is "revealed preferred" to $f(p',\pi')$ then $f(p',\pi')$ cannot be revealed preferred to $f(p,\pi)$. Obviously, the RC Hypothesis implies the WA but the converse need not be the case (except for $\ell = 2$). In fact, as an hypothesis predicated on observed demand behaviour RC is pretty implausible as its satisfaction depends on the fulfillment of delicate integrability conditions. The same cannot be said of the WA. The WA has a clear economic interpretation as a sort of Generalized Law of Demand (more on this later) and while its fulfillment in the aggregate is known to be restrictive it is, at least, a robust property (for the appropriate notions of perturbations). It is just possible that, as an empirical matter, it may hold. A good background reference for all of this is Shafer-Sonnenschein (1982).

2.10 It is time to define the concept of Walrasian equilibrium. Neglecting the possibility of zero prices a pair (p,y) will constitute an equilibrium if demand is equal to supply and every firm maximizes profits. Formally:

Definition: The pair (p,y) constitutes an equilibrium if:

(I) $\hat{f}(p,\pi(p,y)) = \sum y_j$, and

(II) $\hat{p}\cdot y_j \geq \hat{p}\cdot z$ for all $z \in Y_j$ and j.

2.11 Let $F(p,y) = f(p,\pi(p,y))$. Assuming the F is C^1 denote by $S(p,y)$ the $(\ell - 1) \times (\ell - 1)$ matrix $\partial_p F(p,y)$. Consider the property:

(NQD). The matrix $S(p,y)$ is negative quasidefinite, i.e. $v\cdot S(p,y)v < 0$ for $v \neq 0$.

Under NQD the diagonal entries of $S(p,y)$ are negative. Hence, the Law of Demand holds at (p,y) for the first $(\ell - 1)$ commodities in the sense that demand increases if price decreases (y remains fixed but profit income is adjusted when p changes). Suppose that the Law of Demand were to hold at (p,y) for any possible choice of coordinates (i.e. for any way to define composite commodities among the first $(\ell - 1)$). It can be checked that this Generalized Law of Demand is precisely the NQD condition.

2.12 Suppose that (p,y) is an equilibrium. Then the WA implies the slightly weaker version of NQD where the strict inequality is replaced by a weak one. Conversely, NQD implies the WA in a neighborhood of (p,y). Thus, roughly speaking, in a vicinity of equilibrium the WA and NQD amount to the same condition. See Khilstrom, Mas-Colell and Sonnenschein (1976) for all this.

3. Dynamics

3.1 We will now formalize the dynamic laws proposed by Walras for the determination of an equilibrium. The situation studied by Walras was one of no joint production and constant returns. The no joint production aspect does indeed make matters conceptually simpler. Hence, we shall follow his example in this respect. Section 5 contains comments on the general case.

3.2 We first introduce some notation and reformulate the notion of equilibrium for the no joint production case. Let $x \in R^m$ be the vector of gross productions for the m outputs. Given p and x_j denote by $C_j(p,x_j)$ the minimum cost of producing x_j. Assuming that $C_j(\cdot)$ is differentiable we put $c_j(p,x_j) = \partial_{x_j} C_j(p,x_j)$ and $c(p,x) = (c_1(p,x_1),\ldots,c_m(p,x_m))$. Neglecting the possibility of zero production the maximization of profits by sector j is equivalent to the condition $p_j = c_j(p,x_j)$. Denote $p_M = (p_1,\ldots,p_m)$. Given p and x_j let $y_j(p,x_j) \in R^{\ell-1}$ (resp. $\hat{y}_j(p,x_j) \in R^{\ell}$) be the cost minimizing plan for the first $\ell - 1$ commodities (resp. for all of them). Put $y(p,x) = \sum_j y_j(p,x_j)$ and accordingly for $\hat{y}(p,x)$. The equilibrium conditions (i) and (ii) then take the form:

(I) $F(p,\hat{y}(p,x)) - y(p,x) = 0$ (Demand = Supply)

(II) $p_M - c(p,x) = 0$ (Maximum Profits)

3.3 In part II, section 3, of the <u>Eléments</u> Walras proposes as a counterpoint of (I) and (II) two dynamic principles for an economy which at a tentative (p,x) is not in equilibrium:

(I') If the planned demand of a commodity is larger (resp. smaller) than the planned supply then the tentative price increases (resp. decreases). This is the "loi de l'offre et la demande".

(II') If the tentative price of a commodity is larger (resp. smaller) than the (marginal) cost then the tentative planned production increases (resp. decreases). This is the "loi du prix de revient".

Neither production nor trade does actually take place until equilibrium has been reached. Thus the term "tâtonnement" dynamics. For the purposes of local analysis and given the equilibrium conditions (I) and (II) it is now fairly clear how to formalize the dynamic principles (I') and (II') by means of differential equations (the use of differential equations for the study of Walrasian dynamics goes back to Samuelson (1947)). The state space is constituted by the price and quantity variables (p,x). The dynamic equations are:

$$\text{(I')} \quad \dot{p} = K(F(p,\hat{y}(p,x)) - y(p,x))$$

$$\text{(II')} \quad \dot{x} = Q(p_M - c(p,x))$$

where K and Q are positive diagonal matrices of speeds of adjustment. Economic considerations do not give many clues about the values of K and Q. It is therefore important that positive results do not depend too precisely on them.

3.4 Suppose that around an equilibrium we can use equation (II) to solve for productions as function of prices, i.e., $x(p)$ (a salient situation where this cannot be done is the constant returns case). Substituting $x(p)$ for x in (I') we then obtain a <u>pure price dynamics</u> of the form $\dot{p} = G(p)$. This is the type of tâtonnement dynamics which has been most extensively studied (see Hahn (1982) for a survey). It can legitimately be considered as the limit of the general dynamics (I')-(II') obtained by letting quantitites adjust much faster than prices.

3.5 Suppose that around an equilibrium we can use equation (I) to solve for prices as a function of productions, i.e. $p(x)$. Substituting $p(x)$ for p in (II') we then obtain a <u>price quantity (or Marshallian) dynamics</u> of the form $\dot{x} = G(x)$. The symmetry with the pure price dynamics is not quite complete. There is at least one important difference. The price quantity dynamics cannot always be legitimately considered as the limit of the general dynamics (I')-(II') obtained by letting prices adjust much faster than quantities. For it to be so a further and substantial requirement is needed, namely that for x fixed the dynamic systems (I') must have $p(x)$ as a locally asymptotically stable equilibrium (the corresponding condition for the pure price dynamics can be proved to be automatically satisfied).

4. Local Stability

4.1 To analyze the local asymptotic stability of (I')-(II') we shall assume that the system is C^1 in a neighborhood of a fixed reference equilibrium $(\bar{p},\bar{x})$. We proceed by analyzing the first order approximation to (I')-(II') at $(\bar{p},\bar{x})$.

4.2 Some facts from the duality theory of production (see Diewert (1982) for a survey) will be very helpful. Let $\beta_j(p,x_j)$ be the maximum profits of sector j if production must equal x_j, i.e. $\beta_j(p,x_j) = p_j x_j - C_j(p,x_j)$. Put $\beta(p,x) = \sum \beta_j(p,x_j)$. The function β is convex in p, concave in x and, assuming enough differentiability in the relevant region, $\partial_p \beta(p,x) = y(p,x)$. Hence, $\partial_p y(p,x)$ is positive semidefinite (p.s.d.). Clearly, $\partial_x \beta(p,x) = p_M - c(p,x)$ and therefore

$$\partial_p (p_M - c(p,x)) = \partial_{x,p} \beta(p,x) = (\partial_{p,x} \beta(p,x))^T = (\partial_x y(p,x))^T$$

where T denotes matrix transposition. Finally, note that $-\partial_x c(p,x) = \partial_x (p_m - c(p,x)) = \partial_{x,x} \beta(p,x)$ is negative semidefinite (n.s.d.).

4.3 At $(\overline{p},\overline{x})$ profits are maximal given $\overline{p}$. Hence, $\partial_{\hat{y}} \pi(\overline{p},\hat{y}(\overline{p},\overline{x})) = 0$. Using this and the equalities of the last paragraph the Jacobian matrix of the system (I')-(II') at $(\overline{p},\overline{x})$, denoted J, is easily seen to be the $(\ell - 1 + m) \times (\ell - 1 + m)$ matrix

$$J = \begin{bmatrix} K & 0 \\ 0 & 0 \end{bmatrix} \begin{bmatrix} A & -B \\ B & C \end{bmatrix}$$

where: $A = S(\overline{p},\hat{y}(\overline{p},\overline{x})) - \partial_p y(\overline{p},\overline{x})$

$B = (\partial_x y(\overline{p},\overline{x}))^T$

$C = -\partial_x c(\overline{p},\overline{x})$

The matrix C is n.s.d. In the constant returns case $C = 0$. From now on we shall assume that B has maximal rank m. This is an extremely weak and economically sensible hypothesis. It is automatically satisfied if, for example, outputs are not required (or not "too much") for the production of other outputs. Under the NOD hypothesis on the demand function (see section 2) the matrix A will be negative quasidefinite (n.q.d.).

4.4 Suppose that the NOD hypothesis is satisfied and B has maximal rank. Then J has the form $J = LE$ where L is a positive diagonal matrix and E is nonsingular and negative quasisemidefinite (i.e. $E + E^T$ is n.s.d.). These two properties of E are straightforwardly verified. Clearly, any eigenvalue of J

will then have negative real part. Hence, we have shown:

Proposition 1: If at the equilibrium $(\overline{p},\overline{x})$ the NQD condition on demand is satisfied and $\partial_x y(\overline{p},\overline{x})$ has full rank then $\overline{p},\overline{x}$ is locally asymptotically stable for any speeds of adjustment K, Q.

Trivial examples for $\ell = 2$ exhibiting violations of the Law and Demand show that the NQD condition cannot be dispensed with (see section 8). Remember from section 2 the interpretation of the NQD condition as a generalized, coordinate-free, version of the Law of Demand.

4.5 Observe that the matrix E has a sort of skew-symmetric structure. Hence even if A is n.q.d. and, therefore, J a stable matrix, some of the eigenvalues of J will typically exhibit non-zero imaginary parts, i.e. trajectories will converge to equilibrium but they will do so in a spiraling manner with prices and quantities systematically overshooting their equilibrium values. This can best be illustrated in a limit degenerate case where NQD does not hold with strict inequality and the system is stable but not asymptotically stable. Let $\ell = 2$ and suppose that every unit of output can be produced with a unit of input (hence there are constant returns). For a region around $p = 1$ the demand of output is constantly equal to one. Hence an equilibrium is $(\overline{p},\overline{x}) = (1,1)$ and with unitary speed of adjustmenet the dynamic system (I')-(II') reduces to

$$\begin{cases} \dot{p} = 1 - x \\ \dot{x} = p - 1 \end{cases}$$

which has the phase diagram of figure 1(a).

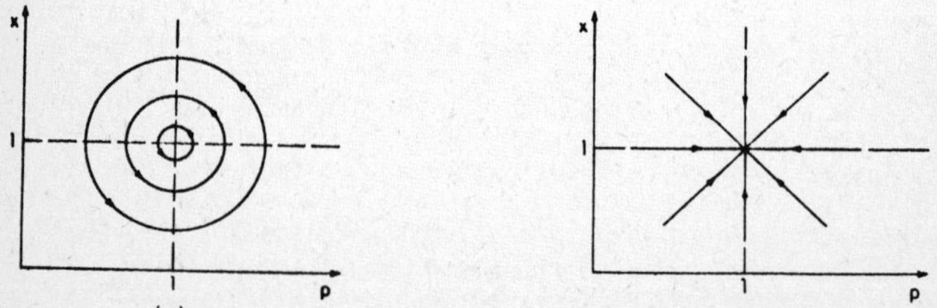

(a) (b)

4.6 Finally, a comment on a peculiarity of the constant returns case that we view as somewhat paradoxical. It appears most clearly for $m = \ell - 1$. Suppose first that C is nonsingular but very small. Equivalently, in a neighborhood of equilibrium we can solve (II) for the competitive "supply function" $x(p)$ and the price effects matrix $\partial x(p)$ is positive definite and very large. In this situation the pure price dynamics will be stable whether or not the NOD condition is satisfied (the price effects from the production side will dominate the possible perverse ones from the consumption side). This is well reflected in the dynamical system (I')-(II'): _If Q is sufficiently large relative to K then it is immediately verified that the system is locally asymptotically stable._ Now consider the constant returns case. From the economic point of view this is the limit situation where the production price effects are infinitely large relative to the consumption effects (in fact, $x(p)$ is not even defined. The production surface has become flat). Hence it could be thought that, with even more reason, the previous underlined statement will remain valid. But this is not so. Suppose, for example, that A is positive definite. Then the matrix in J is completely unstable (i.e. all eigenvalues have positive real parts) for any speeds of adjustment. Mathematically the source of the qualitative discontinuity is clear: the matrix C becomes singular at constant returns. Nevertheless, from the economic viewpoint the discontinuity is surprising. All this will again be illustrated in Section 8.

5. Local stability with general production

5.1 A key difficulty for the treatment of the general joint production case is how to formulate the profit maximization equilibrium condition (II) in a manner that lends itself to the specification of Walras' second dynamic principle. When, as in sections 3 and 4, every sector produces only one output, and input use is instantaneously adjusted to be cost minimizing, there is for every sector a single profit improving direction. Hence, except for speeds of adjustments, the dynamics of the system are completely determined by the requirement that every output moves in the profit maximizing direction. This ceases to be so if there is joint production (or, for that matter, if input used is not instantaneously adjusted).

5.2 The most general version of the second principle could be formulated as follows. Suppose that $p(t)$ and $y(t) \in Y_1, \ldots, Y_m$ are differentiable trajectories of prices and production plans. Then we shall call $p(t), y(t)$ <u>admissible</u> if, for all t, :

(I') $\dot{p}(t) = K(F(p, y(t)) - y(t))$

(II") for all j, $p(t) \cdot \dot{y}_j(t) > 0$, with equality if and only if $y_j(t)$ maximizes profits on Y_j for $p(t)$.

In rigour condition (II") should be strengthened to require that every trajectory $y_j(t)$ not be sluggish, i.e. if at $p(t)$ the potential profit improvement is significant then $p(t) \cdot \dot{y}_j(t)$ should be significantly positive.

5.3 It is a disappointing fact that even under the NOD condition an equilibrium need not be locally asymptotic stable under the dynamic restrictions (I'), (II"). In other words, there are admissible trajectories starting arbitrarily close to equilibrium and diverging from it. In this paragraph we describe an example in the setting of the limiting pure quantity dynamics (this is not restrictive). There are two outputs $x = (x_1, x_2)$ and one input. Every unit of output 1 or 2 can be produced with a unit of input. Although the technologies for the two outputs can be separated they have to be thought of as being under the same management. Without loss of generality the outputs are measured as deviations from equilibria (so that $x = 0$ is an equilibrium) and output prices $p = (p_1, p_2)$ as deviations from unit cost (so that at equilibrium $p = 0$). For productions x let $p(x)$ be the market clearing prices (with the price of the input fixed at one). The NOD condition translates into $\partial p(x)$ being n.q.d. in a neighbourhood of the origin. In the example production always takes place at the efficiency frontier. There is no difficulty in guaranteeing that $p(\ )$ can be extended to the interior of the production set in a manner consistent with NOD.

Let $p(x) = \begin{bmatrix} -3 & 5 \\ -5 & -3 \end{bmatrix} x \equiv Ax$. The matrix A is n.q.d.

Consider now $\dot{x} = \begin{bmatrix} 1 & 1 \\ -1 & 1 \end{bmatrix} x \equiv Bx$ (or, equivalently, $\dot{x} = BA^{-1}p$).

Then $A^TB = \begin{bmatrix} 2 & 8 \\ -8 & 2 \end{bmatrix}$ is p.q.d. Hence $p(x) \cdot \dot{x} = x \cdot A^TBx > 0$ at all $x \neq 0$. So, any solution trajectory $x(t)$ is profit improving. But the eigenvalues of B are $1 \pm i$ and so, all the solutions to the linear system $\dot{x} = Bx$ are unstable. A glance at figure 2 may help to understand what is happening.

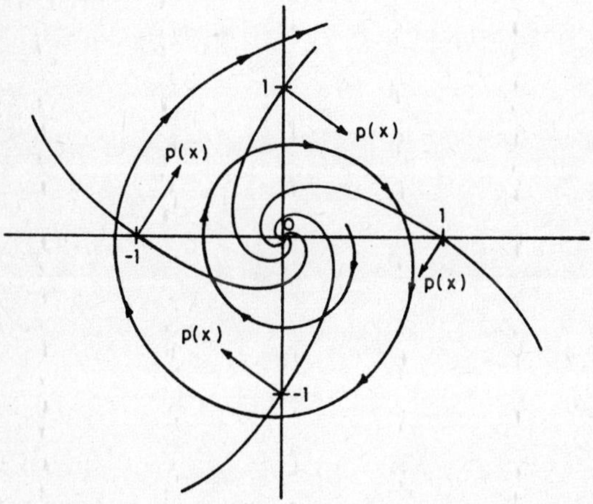

Figure 2

5.4 In the context of the previous examples (except for the particular numerical values) is there a more restrictive dynamics on $x(t)$ than (II") guaranteeing local stability? Clearly the answer is yes. Just take $\dot{x} = Qp(x)$ where Q is positive definite (e.g. a diagonal positive matrix). Then

$$V(x) = p(x) \cdot Qp(x)$$

provides a Lyapunov function. This, of course, agrees with the (II') dynamics.

5.5 It will be mentioned in Section 7 that if demand satisfies the Representative Consumer hypothesis then the pure quantity dynamics of the system (I')-(II') is stable. The contrast with the situation of the two previous paragraphs is clear and it illustrates well that there is a price to pay for relaxing the RC hypothesis to the WA. In order to obtain local stability one must, at the very least, tighten the specification of Walras' second dynamic principle from (II") to something like (II'). The precise form of this more restricted dynamics in the general join production case we do not know. A final observation: it is instructive to see in figure 2 why the RC hypothesis is violated. Under RC the matrix A would have to be symmetric and the field of perpendiculars to $p(x)$ would draw a family of closed curves from the inside of which $x(t)$ would not escape (in other words, the utility function of the RC serves as a Lyapunov function).

5.6 The observations of the previous paragraph on the (I')-(II") dynamics and the RC hypothesis referred only to the pure quantity dynamics, i.e. to K large. For the general case we do not know if this dynamics is locally stable. More formally (but not absolutely precisely):

Problem 1: Determine if under the RC hypothesis any non-sluggish and admissible for (I'), (II") trajectory $(p(t),y(t))$ must coverge to equilibrium provided it starts near enough to it.

6. Different Dynamics

6.1 In this section we take a brief glimpse at price-quantity dynamics which cannot be considered as Walrasian in nature because they do not attempt to model plausible behaviour of competitive markets. The purpose of the section is merely to make the point that price-quantity dynamics does not end with Walras' dynamic principles.

6.2 Suppose there was a planner that had to devise a dynamic system to reach equilibrium. Would he come up with Walras' principles (I')-(II')? It is unlikely. If one forgets about the underlying competitive market economics the system (I')-(II') has to appear as a peculiar one because of its indirectness. Indeed, prices react to quantities and quantities to prices. This indirectness is, incidentally, the source of the skew symmetric structure of the matrix J and therefore of the spiraling trajectories. Our planner would, more likely, first think of a <u>direct</u> method where quantities produced react to demand and prices move to match marginal costs. The contrast between the indirect and the direct approach is most striking as applied to the example in 4.5. For the same data a direct dynamics would be

$$\begin{cases} \dot{p} = 1 - p \\ \dot{x} = 1 - x \end{cases}$$

which has the phase diagram of figure 1b).

6.3 Is there anything general in the stability of the previous example for the direct method? First of all let us formalize the latter. Suppose that we are in the no joint production world of section 3 and 4. To take the simplest case assume also that $m = \ell - 1$, i.e. there is a single nonproducible factor of production. Then we can define the dynamics of the direct method by

$$(I^*) \qquad \dot{p} = K(c(p,x) - p)$$

$$(II^*) \qquad \dot{x} = Q(F(p,\hat{y}(p,x)) - y(p,x))$$

The Jacobian matrix of the system (I^*)-(II^*) at the equilibrium $(\overline{p},\overline{x})$ is

$$J^* = \begin{bmatrix} K & 0 \\ 0 & Q \end{bmatrix} \begin{bmatrix} -B & -C \\ A & -B \end{bmatrix}$$

where the matrices A, B and C are as in 4.3. We shall make a further hypothesis on the matrix $B = (\partial_x y(\overline{p},\overline{x}))^T$ which is economically natural and quite standard in the input-output analysis of production (e.g. Nikaido (1968)): <u>B^T has positive diagonal and negative off-diagonal entries. Moreover, B is a productive, i.e. there is a strictly positive vector v such that $B^T v$ is a strictly positive vector.</u> In words, the production structure is such that, assuming cost minimization, an increase in the production of an output leads to a net surplus of the output and to an increase in the use of every input (remember that input use is measured in negative units). Also, there is some way to increase the production of every output that leads to a positive net surplus for each of them. It is well known (e.g. Nikaido (1968)) that any matrix with the properties of B (as, for example, KB) is positive quasidefinite. This immediately yields the following result:

Proposition 2: Suppose that:

(i) there is no joint production and a single nonproducible factor of production;

(ii) the matrix $(\partial_x y(\overline{p},\overline{x}))$ has a positive diagonal, negative off-diagonal entries and is productive; and

(iii) there are constant returns to scale, i.e., $C = 0$.

Then the Jacobian matrix J^* of the system (I*)-(II*) is stable. This is true independently of the particular matrix A.

The conditions of this proposition are precisely the hypothesis of the famous Non-Substitution Theorem (see, for example, Nikaido (1968)) asserting that equilibrium prices can be determined independently of the demand side of the economy. It is interesting that the stability of the Non-Substitution equilibrium with independence of the demand side follows for (I^*)-(II^*) but not, as we saw in 4.6, for (I')-(II'). If we depart from the hypothesis of the proposition by, for example, allowing $C \neq 0$, it is entirely possible, however, for (I^*)-(II^*) to be unstable even if the matrix A is symmetric negative definite (hence not even the RC hypothesis guarantees the stability of (I^*)-(II^*) in the non-constant returns case). As an example let $\ell - 1 = 2$, $K = Q = I$ and put

$$J^* = \begin{bmatrix} -20 & 16 & 20 & -4 \\ 1 & -2 & -4 & 1 \\ -20 & -5 & -20 & 16 \\ -5 & -2 & 1 & -2 \end{bmatrix}$$

Note that, for $v = (0,-1,1,1)^T$, $J^*v = v$. Hence, J^* has a real, positive eigenvalue.

6.4 The general setting for the comparative study of the properties and domains of stability of systems such as (I')-(II') or (I^*)-(II^*) is an abstract theory of decentralized adjustment mechanisms (indeed, a system such as (I^*)-(II^*), although not market-like, seems intuitively as decentralized as (I')-(II')). The formulation of such a theory has been rigorously initiated by Jordan (1982) (see, also, Saari-Simon (1978)).

6.5 It is important not to lose sight that Walras' dynamics (I')-(II') deal with planned production and tentative prices. It does not take place in real time. There is, for example, something strange in thinking of an actual expansion of production in a situation that may be of excess supply. Real time dynamics opens up a host of new mathematical and economic problems. This is not the place to go into them. There is an extensive literature. See Hahn (1982), Fisher (1983) and their references.

7. Brief Comments on Global Stability

7.1 Once the local stability of the system has been studied it is almost unavoidable to ask about the global stability of the price quantity dynamics. It is important to keep in mind, however, that the global analysis is more difficult to interpret than the local. In the first place, the farther we are from equilibrium the less confidence we can have in precisely formulated dynamic laws. In the second place, the tatonnement dynamics is not a real system taking place in real time. Remember that there is not trade out of equilibrium. Perhaps we can attach some meaning to a globally convergent dynamics but a limit cycle, say, lacks any real significance. The point is that either the tatonnement works by taking us to equilibrium and then we have a theory or it does not and then we don't. Because of all this our observations on global stability will be cursory and brief.

7.2 Suppose that the Weak Axiom is satisfied, the equilibrium is unique and there is no joint production. Assume further (this is only a minor regularity strengthening) that the pure price and the pure quantity dynamics are well defined for the system (I')-(II'), i.e. for the system with constant speeds of adjustment.

Then both dynamics are globally stable. In fact, the Euclidean distance to equilibrium serves in both cases as a Lyapunov function. This is standard for the pure price dynamics (see Hahn (1982)) and it is entirely analagous for the pure quantity case.

7.3 Maintaining the hypothesis of the previous paragraph suppose that, in addition, the RC hypothesis holds. Can the results be improved? Yes, to the extent of allowing for variable speeds of adjustment and, more generally, for weak versions of the dynamic principles such as (II") for the quantity case. With a RC there is an obvious candidate for a Lyapunov function: the utility function itself. The contrast between the WA and the RC hypothesis in the analysis of global stability seems to be completely parallel to the one drawn in Section 5 for local stability.

7.4 In contrast to the two limit cases of pure price and pure quantity dynamic it is our impression that even in the most favourable situation, i.e. no joint production, constant speed of adjustment dynamics and RC Hypothesis (and, we could add, $\ell = 2$) the global stability of system (I')-(II') is not guaranteed. But this could be wrong because we have no formal example. So, we leave this as:

Problem 2: *Determine if under the RC Hypothesis the system (I')-(II') is globally stable, or find a counterexample.*

8. Brief Discussion of the One Input-One Output Case

8.1 In this section we will quickly discuss the particular case where: (i) there is only one output, i.e. $\ell = 2$, and (ii) demand is independent of profit income. Both hypotheses facilitate phase diagram analysis. A thorough examination has been carried out by Beckman and Ryder (1969). The (I')-(II') dynamics now takes the form:

$$(I') \quad \dot{p} = F(p) - x$$

$$(II') \quad \dot{x} = q(p - c(x))$$

where x, p are real numbers and, without loss of generality, the speed of adjustment of the price equation is fixed to equal one. In accord with (ii), demand $F(p)$ depends only on p. It is worth mentioning that this is compatible with the Representative Consumer Hypothesis (or the Weak Axiom, there is no distinction for $\ell = 2$) if and only if $F(p)$ is a decreasing function. For simplicity we always assume that $F(p) = 0$ for any sufficiently large p and that (I')-(II') have a single rest point, see figure 3.

8.2 As it should be, the local analysis of (I')-(II') yields the familiar conclusions. The Jacobian matrix at equilibrium is:

$$J = \begin{bmatrix} a & -1 \\ q & -qc \end{bmatrix}$$

where a, c are, respectively, the slopes of demand and cost. We have $c > 0$ and, because equilibrium is unique, $ac < 1$, see figure 3. From trace $J_q = a - qc$ and $\det J_q = q(1 - ac)$ we can reach the following conclusions about the local dynamics of (I')-(II'):

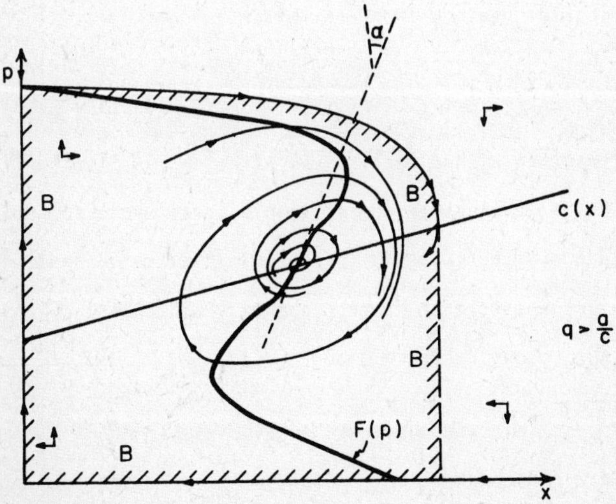

FIGURE 3

(i) If $a < 0$, e.g. there is a Representative Consumer, then the equilibrium is locally stable. For fixed a it goes from a stable node to a stable spiral point as c decreases.

(ii) If $a > 0$ then the local stability depends on q. At low q the system if locally unstable. At $q^* = \frac{a}{c}$ it undergoes a Hopf bifurcation towards stability. Indeed, det $J_q > 0$ for any $q > 0$ but trace $J_q \lessgtr 0$ according to if $q \gtrless q^*$ (see Hassard-Kazarinoff-Wan (1981) for the Hopf bifurcation). Note that if $c = 0$, e.g. there are constant returns, then $q^* = \infty$ and the system is always unstable.

8.3 Some brief words on the global dynamics of (I')-(II') which, incidentally, we take to be defined on the boundary of R^2_+ in the natural way. The key observation, due to Beckmann and Ryder (1969), is that the system has an absorbing, bounded, simply connected region. Region B in figure 3 will do. In the figure the upper boundary of the region is the part above $c(\cdot)$ of any trajectory starting at a $(0,p)$ with $F(p) = 0$. If the system is locally unstable, e.g. $a > 0$, $q < q^*$, then this and Poincaré-Bendixon theory (see Hartman (1964)) yield the existence of a stable limit cycle. This cycle which is obtained from a mixture of local and global considerations and which is always stable should not be confused with the cycle obtained from Hopf bifurcation theory. The existence and stability of the latter is entirely controlled by local information on the demand and cost functions at equilibrium. Thus, it is perfectly possible, and as likely as the contrary, that the higher derivatives of demand and cost at equilibrium force the existence of an unstable (resp. stable) Hopf cycle for some values of $q > q^*$ (resp. $q < q^*$). The existence of an absorbing region does then still imply that there must be at least another stable (Poincare-Bendixon) cycle. The possibility is illustrated in figure 3.

Summing up: except in two cases there is nothing simple about the global dynamics of even the simplest demand and supply model. The two cases are: (i) the demand function is decreasing on its entire domain, or (ii) the cost function is strictly increasing (i.e. $\frac{dc(x)}{dx} > \varepsilon > 0$ for all x) and the speed of adjustment q is high enough. The system is globally stable in both these cases (thus, in figure 3 if q is large the intermediate region of instability disappears). The stability proofs are not difficult to work out.

References

Arrow, K. and L. Hurwicz (1958), "On the stability of the competitive equilibrium", I, Econometrica, 26.

Arrow, K. and L. Hurwicz (1960), "Decentralization and Computation in resource allocation", in R. Pfouts, ed., Essays in Economics and Econometrics, The University of North Carolina Press.

Beckmann, M. and H. Ryder (1969), "Simultaneous Price and Quantity Adjustment in a Single Market", Econometrica, 37.

Diewert, E. (1982), "Duality Approaches to Microeconomic Theory", Chapter 12, Vol. II, in K. Arrow and M. Intriligator, eds., Handbook of Mathematical Economics, North Holland Press.

Fisher, F. (1983), Disequilibrium Foundations of Equilibrium Economics, Econometric Society Monographs in Pure Theory, Cambridge University Press.

Hahn, F. (1982), "Stability", chapter 16, Vol. II, in K. Arrow and M. Intriligator eds., Handbook of Mathematical Economics, North Holland Press.

Hartman, P. (1964), Ordinary Differential Equations, John Wiley.

Hassart, B., N. Kazarinoff, and Y. Wan (1981), Theory and Applications of Hopf Bifurcation, London Mathematical Society Lecture Notes Series, 41, Cambridge University Press.

Jordan, J. (1982), "The Informational Requirements of Local Stability in Decentralized Allocation Mechanisms", University of Minnesota Department of Economics Discussion Paper No. 82-166, September.

Khilstrom, R., A. Mas-Colell and H. Sonnenschein (1976), "The Demand Theory of the Weak Axiom of Revealed Preference", Econometrica, Vol. 44, No. 5.

Mas-Colell, A. (1974) "Algunas Observaciones Sobre la Teoría del Tâtonnement de Walras en Economias Productivas", Anales de Economía, 21-22, Madrid.

Morishima, M. (1959), "A reconsideration of the Walras-Cassel-Leontief Model of General Equilibrium", in Mathematical Methods in the Social Sciences, K. Arrow, S. Karlin, P. Suppes, ed. Stanford University Press.

Nikaido, H. (1968), Convex Structures and Economic Theory, Academic Press.

Novshek, W. and H. Sonnenschein (1984), "Quantity adjustment in an Arrow-Debreu-McKenzie Type Model", this volume.

Saari, D. and C. Simon (1978), "Effective Price Mechanisms", Econometrica, Vol. 46.

Samuelson, P., (1947), Foundations of Economic Analysis, Harvard University Press.

Shafer, W. and H. Sonnenschein (1982), "Market Demand and Excess Demand Functions", Chapter 14, Vol. II of K. Arrow and M. Intriligator, eds. Handbook of Mathematical Economics, North Holland Press.

Walras, L. (1926), Elements d'Economie Politique Pure, Edition definitive, Paris. There is an English Translation: Elements of Pure Economics, R. Irwin, 1954.

A PRICE ADJUSTMENT MODEL WITH INFINITESIMAL TRADERS

by

H. Jerome Keisler

Department of Mathematics
University of Wisconsin
Madison, Wisconsin 53706

Introduction

In this paper we develop a general probabilistic model for the movement of prices in an exchange economy with a large number of agents. The model is a non-tatonnement process; that is, trading takes place even when the price is not at equilbrium. However, prices will move rapidly towards an equilibrium value, and most trades will take place when prices are close to equilibrium.

The model may be briefly described as follows. There is a finite set of commodities, a central market which sets prices, and a large finite set of agents who trade with the central market. Time is divided into small intervals of equal length. The process may start after a sudden change in the economy, with prices out of equilibrium. At each time interval, one agent is chosen at random and makes a trade with the central market. The trade is determined by the agent's demand function applied to his current commodity vector and the current price. The price is then adjusted by a price adjustment function, which also depends on the agent's commodity vector and the current price. The price is adjusted by an amount which is small but is much larger than the reciprocal of the number of agents.

The main result shows that under certain stability assumptions, with large probability the price vector will move on a path which is close to its expected value. Moreover, the price will at first move very rapidly towards a temporary equilibrium and will then move slowly. The reason for this is that the price is adjusted on the basis of the actions of a sample of agents which is small compared to the whole economy but is still large enough to be statistically significant.

The model is highly flexible and can be given a variety of economic interpretations by appropriate choices of the demand and price adjustment functions. Some of the possibilities are indicated in this paper by examples. Section 2 contains an example of a pure exchange economy, and an exchange economy with continuous production by the central market. Section 3 has an example in which different agents trade with different frequencies, a model in which the agents make use of their knowledge of prices at previous visits to the market, a model with finitely many markets, each with its own price vector, and a model with continuous consumption and production.

The theorems will be stated precisely, but no proofs will be given in this paper. The results are new theorems in probability theory whose proofs will appear in Keisler [8]. The exact formulation of the theorems uses notions from nonstandard analysis. The set of agents is a hyperfinite set (an infinite set which has many properties of finite sets). Time is divided into infinitesimal intervals, and prices are adjusted at each trade by an amount which is infinitesimal but whose product with the number of agents is infinite. The results hold with probability one in the Loeb measure, which is a standard probability measure obtained in a natural way by counting the elements of hyperfinite sets. Section 1 contains a simple form of the main result, which is appropriate for exchange economies. Section 3 has a more general form of the theorem and examples of economic interpretations.

Much of this paper can be read without a detailed knowledge of nonstandard analysis. However, several introductory sources on the subject are becoming available; see references [3], [6], [7], [10], [11]. Nonstandard exchange economies have been studied extensively in the literature from the standpoint of equilibrium theory, beginning with Brown and Robinson [2]. Expositions of standard equilibrium and price adjustment theories can be found in references [1], [4], and [5].

I wish to thank Robert Anderson, Donald Brown, Sergio Fajardo, Kenneth Judd, Thomas Kurtz, Lucinda Lewis, Peter Loeb, Hugo Sonnenschein, Keith Stroyan, and Frank Watternburg for helpful discussions at various stages of this work.

This research was supported in part by the National Science Foundation, the Institute for Advanced Study, and the University of Wisconsin.

1. An Exchange Economy

We shall first introduce an exchange process in a finite economy, and then pass to the hyperfinite (i.e. nonstandard) setting.

By a finite exchange process we mean the following. Let A be a finite set of agents and let d be a positive integer which stands for the number of commodities. We divide time into intervals of length $\Delta t = 1/\#(A)$, where $\#(A)$ is the number of agents. Think of A as a large finite set, whence Δt is small. Let T be the set of multiples of Δt ,

$$T = \{0,\Delta t,2\Delta t,\ldots,\} .$$

We use R for the set of real numbers and N for the set of positive integers.

At time $t = 0$ there is an initial price $p(0) \in R^d$ and commodity allocation $C(a,0) \in R^d$ for each $a \in A$. Each agent has a type $X(a) \in R$ which remains fixed. The price and allocation will change randomly with time according to a Markov process determined by an excess demand function

$$f(x,c,p) : R \times R^d \times R^d \to R^d ,$$

a price adjustment function

$$g(x,c,p) : R \times R^d \times R^d \to R^d ,$$

and a price adjustment speed $1/\varepsilon$. Each agent of type x has the excess demand function $f(x,\cdot,\cdot)$ whose arguments are the commodity vector c and price vector p . ε and $\Delta t/\varepsilon$ are small.

We are now ready to describe the Markov process. At each time $t \in T$, an agent $\omega(t) \in A$ is selected at random, independently of t . Formally, the set A has the counting measure where each agent has weight $\Delta t = 1/\#(A)$, and the sample space is the space $\Omega = A^T$ with the product measure. This measure is called the measure of independent sampling (with replacement). The agent $\omega(t)$ trades with the central market at time t , while the other agents are idle. Thus at time t the commodity vectors change according to the rule

$$C(a,t+\Delta t,\omega) - C(a,t,\omega) = \begin{cases} f(X(a),C(a,t,\omega),p(t,\omega)) & \text{if } a = \omega(t) \\ 0 & \text{otherwise.} \end{cases}$$

The price at time t changes with the rule

$$p(t+\Delta t,\omega) - p(t,\omega) = g(X(a),C(a,t,\omega),p(t,\omega))\ \varepsilon^{-1}\Delta t$$

where $a = \omega(t)$. We emphasize that $C(a,t,\omega)$ and $p(t,\omega)$ are random, because they depend on $\omega \in A^T$. At time $t = 0$ they are deterministic, $C(a,t,\omega) = C(a,0)$, $p(0,\omega) = p(0)$.

We wish to describe the behavior of this exchange process when A is large and ε, $\Delta t/\varepsilon$ are small. To do this we now pass to the nonstandard setting. A hyperfinite set is a set A such that for some infinite hyperinteger H of the nonstandard universe, there is an internal bijection of $\{1,\ldots,H\}$ onto A. H is called the internal cardinality of A, and is written $H = \#(A)$. (An internal set is a set which belongs to the star of some standard set.)

By a hyperfinite exchange process we mean an exchange process in the nonstandard universe such that d is finite, the set A of agents is hyperfinite, and the price adjustment speed ε^{-1} is such that ε and $\Delta t/\varepsilon$ are infinitesimal. (Note that $\Delta t = 1/\#(A)$ is infinitesimal since A is infinite.) The sample space A^T is the set of all internal functions $\omega : T \to A$ choosing an agent $\omega(t)$ who trades at time t. There is a natural standard probability measure on A^T, called the Loeb measure (Loeb [10]). The Loeb measure is a complete σ-additive probability measure which is generated by the nonstandard independent sampling measure in much the same way that Lebesgue measure is generated by the length of intervals.

The times at which a single agent $a \in A$ trades will be Poisson process with an expected waiting time of one between trades, and these Poisson processes are independent for different $a \in A$. (This construction of a Poisson process is in the original paper of Loeb [9]).

At this point we have made no assumption on the functions f and g. We wish to leave open the possibility of a variety of economic interpretations. The simplest story is a pure exchange economy where $|p(0)| = 1$, $f(x,c,p)$ is the excess demand function for an agent of type x obtained by maximizing his utility function $U(x,c)$ within the budget set at price p, and

$$g(x,c,p) = f(x,c,p) + (1 - |p|)p .$$

In this case prices are kept on the unit sphere and move in the direction of the exchange which is made at time t. The central market has an inventory vector $I(t,\omega)$ which changes by $-f(X(a),C(a,t,\omega),p(t,\omega))$ when $a = \omega(t)$ trades. The price change $p(t,\omega) - p(0)$ is then proportional to the decrease in inventory,

$$p(t,\omega) - p(0) \approx -(I(t,\omega) - I(0)) \cdot \varepsilon^{-1}\Delta t .$$

Thus the central market can set its prices by looking at its inventory.

We introduce a differential equation associated with the exchange process. Given points $p, q \in {}^*R^d$, $p \approx q$ means that p is infinitely close to q, and ${}^o p$ is the standard part of p. ${}^o p$ exists if and only if p is finite. If F is an internal function from the set A of agents into ${}^*R^d$, we often consider the sum $\sum_{a\in A}|F(a)|\Delta t$. This sum is the average value of $F(a)$ over A. F is said to be S-integrable over A if $\sum_{a\in A}|F(a)|\Delta t$ is finite and $\sum_{a\in B}|F(a)|\Delta t \approx 0$ for any internal set $B \subset A$ of Loeb measure zero.

1.1 Definition. The initial differential equation of a hyperfinite exchange process is the standard initial value problem

$$q(0) = {}^o p(0) , \quad q'(s) = {}^o(\textstyle\sum_{a\in A} g(X(a),C(a,0),q(s))\Delta t) ,$$

provided the standard parts exist.

This is the equation which describes the tatonnement process with initial price ${}^o p(0)$ and allocation $C(\cdot,0)$, and price adjustment function g. In an economy where no trading takes place but the price moves in the direction of the average value of $g(X(a),C(a,0),q(s))$ over A, the price would follow this equation.

Let $h(q)$ be a C^1 function from R^d into R^d and let $q_v(s)$ be the unique solution of the initial value problem

(1) $$q(0) = v\ ,\ q'(s) = h(q(s))\ .$$

A point r is said to be an <u>exponentially stable equilibrium</u> of $h(\cdot)$ if $h(r) = 0$ and all the eigenvalues of the Jacobian of $h(\cdot)$ at r have negative real parts. (This implies that for all u in a neighborhood of r, $q_u(s) \to r$ exponentially and uniformly in u as $s \to \infty$). We say that r is an <u>exponentially stable attractor</u> of the initial value problem (1) if r is an exponentially stable equilibrium and for all u in some neighborhood of v, $q_u(s) \to r$ as $s \to \infty$. It is possible for two different initial values to have different exponentially stable attractors.

We now state the first theorem.

1.2 <u>Theorem</u>. Given a hyperfinite exchange process, assume that:

(i) A is hyperfinite and

$$\varepsilon \approx 0\ ,\ \Delta t \varepsilon^{-1} \log(\varepsilon^{-1}) \approx 0\ .$$

(ii) $p(0)$ is finite and $X(\cdot)$ and $C(\cdot,0)$ are S-integrable over A.

(iii) $f(x,c,p)$ and $g(x,c,p)$ are standard functions with finite uniform Lipschitz bounds in x, c, p, and $g(x,c,p)$ is C^1 (continuously differentiable) in x,c, and p.

(iv) The initial differential equation has an exponentially stable attractor r_0.

Then there is a positive $t_1 \in R \cup \{\infty\}$, a standard continuous function $r : [0,t_1) \to R^d$ with $r(0) = r_0$, and for each uniformly Lipschitz function $\phi : R^d \to R$ a standard differentiable function $\overline{\phi} : [0,t_1) \to R$, such that with Loeb probability one:

(a) Whenever $t \approx 0$ in T, $p(t,\omega) \approx q({}^o(t/\varepsilon))$ where q is the solution of the initial d.e.

(b) Whenever $t \in T$ and $0 < {}^o t < t_1$, $p(t,\omega) \approx r(t)$ and $\sum_{a \in A} g(C(a,t,\omega),p(t,\omega)) \approx 0$.

(c) Whenever $t \in T$ and ${}^o t < t_1$, $\sum_{a \in A} \phi(C(a,t\omega))\Delta t \approx \overline{\phi}(t)$.

Discussion. The functions $q(s)$, $r(t)$, and $\overline{\phi}(t)$ are deterministic, that is, they do not depend on the random sequence of agents $\omega(t)$ who trade at any time t. Thus with Loeb probability one, for ${}^{o}t < t < t_1$, $p(t,\omega)$ is infinitely close to its expected value, and for each ϕ, the average value of $\phi(C(a,t,\omega))$ over A is infinitely close to its expected value. This average value $\sum_{a\in A} \phi(C(a,t\omega))\Delta t$ describes the distribution of the commodity vectors over agents.

Conclusion (a) of the theorem states that, with Loeb probability one, the price vector starts out by moving infinitely fast along the tatonnement path $q(s)$. For instance, $p(0) \approx q(0)$, $p(\varepsilon,\omega) \approx q(1)$, $p(2\varepsilon,\omega) \approx q(2)$. It follows that for $t \approx 0$ and t/ε infinite, $p(t,\omega) \approx r_0 = \lim_{s\to\infty} q(s)$. For noninfinitesimal t, conclusion (b) states that $p(t,\omega)$ follows a path $r(t)$ which is continuous in t. Moreover, the price vector is infinitely close to a "temporary" equilibrium point of the price adjustment function g. The equilibrium is temporary because $C(a,t,\omega)$ and hence the equilibrium price change with t.

Each agent type x has an excess demand function $f(x,\cdot,\cdot)$ and price adjustment function $g(x,\cdot,\cdot)$. Although the numerical value of x has no direct interpretation, it does impose a restriction on f and g when there are infinitely many agent types, since f and g must be Lipschitz in x.

The theorem as stated only says that t_1 is some positive extended real number. There is a stronger form of the theorem, not stated in this paper, which characterizes t_1 and the functions $r(t)$ and $\overline{\phi}(t)$ by a system of differential equations in a Banach space.

In the case that there are only finitely many types of agents and the functions f and g are linear in c for each agent type, the expected behavior of the hyperfinite exchange process can be explicitly described by a finite system of differential equations. This is the content of the next theorem.

1.3 Theorem. Suppose a hyperfinite exchange economy satisfies the assumptions of Theorem 1.2 and in addition:

(v) There are only finitely many agent types, that is, the function $x(\cdot)$ has finite range $\{x_1,\dots,x_n\}$.

(vi) For each agent type x and price vector p, the functions $f(x,c,p)$ and $g(x,c,p)$ are linear in c.

Let m_j be the measure of the set of agents of type x_j,

$$m_j = {}^{o}(\#\{a : X(a) = x_j\}/\#(A)) ,$$

and let $c_j(0)$ be the initial average commodity vector

$$c_j(0) = {}^{o}(\textstyle\sum_{X(a)=x_j} C(a,0)\Delta t) .$$

Then the initial differential equation takes the form

$$q(0) = {}^{o}p(0) , \quad q'(s) = \textstyle\sum_{j=1}^{n} g(x_j,c_j(0),q(s))m_j .$$

Moreover, there is a positive $t_1 \in R \cup \{\infty\}$ such that with Loeb probability one, for all $t \in T$ with $0 < {}^{o}t < t_1$, the price and average commodity vectors satisfy

$$p(t,\omega) \approx r(t) , \quad \sum_{\substack{a\in A \\ X(a)=x_j}} C(a,t,\omega)\Delta t \approx c_j(t)$$

where $r(t)$, $c_j(t)$ are solutions of the standard system of equations

$$r(0) = \lim_{s \to \infty} q(s) ,$$

$$c_j'(t) = f(x_j,c_j(t),r(t))m_j ,$$

$$\textstyle\sum_{j=1}^{n} g(x_j,c_j(t),r(t))m_j = 0 .$$

Discussion. The hypothesis $\Delta t\varepsilon^{-1} \log \varepsilon^{-1} \approx 0$ can be replaced in this case by the weaker hypothesis $\Delta t\varepsilon^{-1} \approx 0$. The reason things are simpler for f and g linear in c is that the average value of a linear function of $C(a,t,\omega)$ over A equals the linear function of the average value. In particular examples one can solve the equations in Theorem 1.3 by using the last equation to eliminate $r(s)$ and then solving a system of differential equations in $c_j(s)$, $j = 1,\ldots,n$. We shall now illustrate this with two simple examples.

2. Examples

2.1. In this example there are two types of agents, $X(a) = 1$ and $X(a) = 2$, with exactly half of the agents in each type. There are two commodities, and we denote a commodity vector c by $c = (y,z)$, and a price vector p by $p = (u,v)$. The agents have Cobb-Douglas utility functions

$$U(1,y,z) = yz^{\alpha}, \quad U(2,y,z) = yz^{\beta}$$

where α and β are constant positive real numbers. Let $a = \frac{1}{1+\alpha}$, $b = \frac{1}{1+\beta}$. The excess demand functions which maximize the utility functions subject to the budget constraint $p \cdot \Delta c = 0$ are

$$f(1,c,p) = a\langle -\alpha y + \frac{vz}{u}, \frac{\alpha uy}{v} - z\rangle ,$$

$$f(2,c,p) = b\langle -\beta y + \frac{vz}{u}, \frac{\beta uy}{v} - z\rangle .$$

Let the price adjustment rule g be

$$g(x,c,p) = f(x,c,p) + (1 - |p|)p .$$

Take $\varepsilon \approx 0$ such that $\Delta t \varepsilon^{-1} \log \varepsilon^{-1}$. Suppose the initial price $p(0)$ is on the unit sphere in the positive orthant, and the initial commodity allocation $C(a,0)$ is in the positive orthant. For $j = 1,2$ let

$$C_j(t,\omega) = \sum_{X(a)=j} C(a,t,\omega)\Delta t = \langle Y_j(t,\omega), Z_j(t,\omega)\rangle .$$

Thus $Y_j(t,\omega)$ is half the average y holding for agents of type j. Let $y_j(0) = {}^oY_j(0)$, $z_j(0) = {}^oZ_j(0)$.

By Theorem 1.3, with probability one, for $t \approx 0$ the price $p(t,\omega)$ will move infinitely rapidly along the solution path of the initial d.e. and approach an equilibrium value $r = (u,v)$. Solving $g(1,c_1,r) + g(2,c_2,r) = 0$ for r, we obtain

$$\frac{v}{u} = \frac{a\alpha y_1(0) + b\beta y_2(0)}{az_1(0) + bz_2(0)}, \quad |r| = 1 .$$

The price path will be on the unit circle $|p(t)| \approx 1$. Then when $0 < {}^ot < t_1$,

$p(t,\omega)$ will remain infinitely close to the constant value r while $Y_j(t,\omega)$ and $Z_j(t,\omega)$ will be infinitely close to the solution of the differential equations

$$y_1'(t) = \frac{1}{2}\,a(-\alpha y_1(t) + \frac{vz_1(t)}{u}),\ y_1(0) = {}^oY_1(0)\ ,$$

$$z_1'(t) = \frac{1}{2}\,a(\frac{\alpha u y_1(t)}{v} - z_1(t))\ ,\quad z_1(0) = {}^oZ_1(0)\ ,$$

and similarly for y_2, z_2. The reason that $r(0) = r$ remains constant in this example is that the average commodity vectors $y_j(t)$, $z_j(t)$ move so that the equilibrium value with respect to the price adjustment function g stays at r. When ${}^ot > 0$, the second and later trades by an agent will all be infinitesimal, and trading dies down after most agents have made their first trade. We shall see later that t_1 is ∞ in this example, so the equations hold for all finite t.

2.2. We now modify our first example to give an example where the price does not stay infinitely close to a constant value when ${}^ot > 0$. In this example the agent types and excess demand function f are the same as in Example 2.1. However, the central market is continually producing the second commodity, which results in a different price adjustment rule. The central market is able to use h^2 units of commodity y to produce h units of commodity z, for any $h \geq 0$. It chooses h so as to maximize the profit

$$-uh^2 + vh$$

at a price $p = (u,v)$. This maximum occurs at

$$h = v/2u\ .$$

It adds the quantity h of commodity z which is produced to its inventory and takes out the equivalent quantity of y at price p, $\frac{v}{u}h$. The net change in inventory is therefore

$$\langle -\frac{v}{u}h, h\rangle = \langle -\frac{1}{2}\left(\frac{v}{u}\right)^2, \frac{1}{2}\frac{v}{u}\rangle\ .$$

The appropriate price adjustment rule is

$$g(x,c,p) = f(x,c,p) + \langle \tfrac{1}{2}\left(\tfrac{v}{u}\right)^2, -\tfrac{1}{2}\tfrac{v}{u} \rangle + (1 - |p|)p \ .$$

The new term pushes the price of the first commodity up and the price of the second down, and is orthogonal to p.

This time the price vector will move infinitely fast when $t \approx 0$ to a temporary equilibrium value $r(0)$. For ${}^{o}t > 0$ the price will be infinitely close to a moving temporary equilibrium value $r(t)$. Solving

$$g(1,c_1(t),r(t)) + g(2,c_2(t),r(t)) = 0$$

for $r(t) = (u(t),v(t))$, we have

$$\frac{v(t)}{u(t)} = -w(t) + \sqrt{w(t)^2 + 2(a\alpha y_1(t) + b\beta y_2(t))}\ ,$$

$$w(t) = az_1(t) + bz_2(t)\ , \quad |r(t)| = 1\ .$$

$y_j(t)$ and $z_j(t)$ will move so that $v(t)/u(t)$ changes with t, with the equations

$$y_1'(t) = 1/2\ a[-\alpha y_1(t) + \frac{v(t)z_1(t)}{u(t)}]\ ,$$

$$z_1'(t) = 1/2\ a[\frac{\alpha u(t)y_1(t)}{v(t)} - z_1(t)]\ ,$$

and similarly for y_2, z_2. Again, it turns out that t_1 is infinite and the equations hold for all finite t.

3. General Exchange Processes

In this section we state a more general form of Theorem 2.2. and give a variety of economic interpretations. The notion of a hyperfinite exchange process will be generalized in several ways. First, we allow the commodity dimension to be different from the price dimension, and absorb the agent type into the commodity vector. Thus the processes of Section 1 have commodity vectors of dimension $d + 1$, the last component being the agent type. As another example, the price vector could have dimension $d - 1$, with the dth commodity taken as a numeraire which has no price. Furthermore, instead of a single excess demand function f, one of a finite set of excess demand functions $f_1,\dots,f_j$ is chosen at random at each time. Similarly, one of a finite set of price adjustment functions is chosen at random. Also, the excess demand functions and price adjustment functions depend on the time t as well as on c and p.

A <u>(general)</u> <u>hyerpfinite</u> <u>exchange</u> <u>process</u> is specified by finite positive integers k, d, and j for the commodity and price dimensions and the number of excess demand and price adjustment functions, a hyperfinite set A of agents, a price adjustment speed $1/\varepsilon$, standard functions

$$f_i : R^k \times R^d \times [0,\infty) \to R^k , \quad i = 1,\dots,j ,$$
$$g_i : R^k \times R^d \times [0,\infty) \to R^d , \quad i = 1,\dots,j ,$$

and an S-integrable initial allocation

$$C(\cdot,0) : A \to {}^*R^k$$

and finite initial price $p(0) \in {}^*R^d$. Δt and T are as before, but now the sample space is

$$\Omega = (A \times J)^T$$

where $J = \{1,\dots,j\}$, with the counting measure on $A \times J$ and the Loeb measure generated by the nonstandard independent sampling measure on $(A \times J)^T$. Let $\omega(t) = \langle a(t),j(t)\rangle$. Thus at each time $t \in T$, an element $a(t) \in A$ and an element $j(t) \in J$ are chosen independently.

The commodity vectors and price vector change at time t according to the rules

$$C(a,t+\Delta t,\omega) - C(a,t,\omega) = \begin{cases} f_{j(t)}(C(a,t,\omega),p(t,\omega),t) & \text{if } a = a(t) , \\ 0 & \text{otherwise} \end{cases}$$

and

$$p(t+\Delta t,\omega) - p(t,\omega) = g_{j(t)}(C(a,t,\omega),p(t,\omega),p(t,\omega),t)\cdot\varepsilon^{-1}\Delta t$$

where $a = a(t)$.

Let g be the average of the functions $g_1,\ldots,g_j$; that is,

$$g(c,p,t) = \frac{1}{j} \sum_{i=1}^{j} g_i(c,p,t) .$$

The <u>initial differential equation</u> is

$$g(0) = {}^{o}p0 , \quad g'(s) = {}^{o}(\sum_{a\varepsilon A} g(c(a,0),q(s),0))\Delta t .$$

<u>3.1. Theorem.</u> Given a general hyperfinite exchange process, assume that:

(i) A is hyperfinite and

$$\varepsilon \approx 0 , \quad \Delta t\, \varepsilon^{-1} \log(\varepsilon^{-1}) \approx 0 .$$

(ii) $p(0)$ is finite and $c(\cdot,0)$ is S-integrable over A .

(iii) For each $i \varepsilon J$, $f_i(c,p,t)$ and $g_i(c,p,t)$ are standard functions which are continuous in t and uniformly Lipschitz in c,p, and $g_i(c,p,t)$ is C^1 in c,p,

(iv) The initial differential equation has an exponentially stable attractor r_0 .

Then the conclusions of Theorem 1.2 hold, with the extra argument t in the last equation

$$\sum_{a\varepsilon A} g(C(a,t,\omega),p(t,\omega),t) \approx 0 .$$

We conclude with a discussion of some economic interpretations of the extra parameters in Theorem 3.1.

The dependence of the excess demand function f_i and price adjustment function g_i on the random choice $i \varepsilon J$ can be used in several ways.

3.2. The agents and market can employ mixed strategies in choosing the excess demand and price adjustment.

3.3 The exchange process can depend on outside random events.

3.4 Different agent types can have different expected waiting times between trades (so that some agents trade more frequently than others).

As an illustration, we shall modify Example 2.1 so that agents of type one trade 3 times as often as agents of type two. Let $j = 3$. For $i = 1,2,3$, let $f_i(1,c,p)$ be as before,

$$f_i(1,c,p) = a\langle -\alpha y + \frac{vz}{u} , \frac{\alpha uy}{v} - z\rangle .$$

Let $f_1(2,c,p)$ be as before, but $f_2(2,c,p) = f_3(2,c,p) = 0$. That is,

$$f_i(2,c,p) = \begin{cases} b \langle -\beta y + \frac{vz}{u} , \beta \frac{uy}{v} - z\rangle & \text{if } i = 1 \\ 0 & \text{if } i = 2,3 . \end{cases}$$

Let $g_i(x,c,p) = f_i(x,c,p) + (1 - |p|)p$, as before. For $t \approx 0$ the price $p(\omega,t)$ will again move infinitely fast and approach the temporary equilibrium value $r(0) = \langle u(0),v(0)\rangle$ such that $|r(0)| = 1$ and

$$\frac{v(0)}{u(0)} = \frac{a\alpha y_1(0) + \frac{1}{3} b\beta y_2(0)}{az_1(0) + \frac{1}{3} bz_2(0)} .$$

However, this time the expected price will continue to move by a noninfinitesimal amount when ${}^{o}t > 0$, and will be infinitely close to a differentiable function $r(t)$ with probability one. Intuitively, this is because the percentage of agents of type 1 who have not traded will decrease faster than the percentage of traders of type 2 who have not traded. It turns out that $t_1 = \infty$, so the price is close to its expected value for all finite times. Moreover, the expected price and the distribution of commodities approach limits as $t \to \infty$.

3.5 In this model we interpret the hyperfinite exchange process by an economy which has j different markets, each with its own price vector. At each time t, an agent $a(t) \in A$ and a market $j(t) \in J$ are chosen at random, and $a(t)$ visits market $j(t)$. There are n actual commodities. The price space has dimension $d = nj$, with one n-dimensional price vector for each of j markets. The commodity space has dimension $k = 1 + n + nj$. At each time t, the state $C(a,t,\omega)$ of an agent a contains one component for the agent type, n components for his commodity vector, and a record of the price vector at his last visit to each of the j markets. When agent a visits market i, he learns the current price at that market only. The excess demand function f_i chooses a new commodity vector depending on the type, present commodity vector, record of old prices in each market, and current price in the ith market. f_i also updates the price record in the ith market, and leaves other price records fixed. The price adjustment function g_i changes the price vector for the ith market and leaves the other prices fixed. With this framework, it would be natural to make further assumptions on how the agents take advantage of price differences, and show that in certain cases the prices will become close to each other.

3.6 In this model, suggested by R.M. Anderson, the agents have excess demands which depend on t and maximize expected future utilities given their knowledge of previous price behavior. There is an exchange economy with one central market and d actual commodities. The price space has dimension d, and the commodity space has dimension $(1 + d)(1 + k)$. At each time t, the state $C(a,t,\omega)$ of an agent contains one component for the agent type, d components for the agent's commodity vector, and a record of the price vectors and times for each of the last k visits of the agent to the market. (If there are fewer than k previous visits, fill the extra components with zeros.) Each agent type x has a utility function for future commodity streams and a measure on all possible price paths. The demand function $f(x,c,p,t)$ of an agent of type x is obtained as follows. The agent type does not change. The commodity vector changes so as to maximize, within the budget set, the expected future utility conditioned on the stream of k previous prices and times, and the present price and time. The price record components are updated in the obvious way, discarding the earliest value to make room for the present value. The price adjustment function $g(x,c,p,t)$ may (for example) be the commodity vector components of $f(x,c,p,t)$, so that prices reflect inventory.

3.7 The dependence of f and g on time allows us to introduce consumption and production into the exchange process. The following process with consumption and production can be represented as a hyperfinite exchange process. Each agent a has an agent type $X(a) \in {}^*R$ and a commodity vector $\overline{C}(a,t,\omega) \in {}^*R^d$. There is a price vector $p(t,\omega) \in {}^*R^d$. For each agent type x there is an excess demand function $\overline{f}(x,\overline{c},p)$, and a consumption function $h(x,t)$ which represents the rate of income (positive) and consumption (negative) at time t . The commodity vector $\overline{C}(a,t,\omega)$ changes with the rule

$$\overline{C}(a,t+\Delta t,\omega) - \overline{C}(a,t,\omega) =$$

$$\begin{cases} h(X(a),t)\Delta t + \overline{f}(X(a),\overline{C}(a,t,\omega),p(t,\omega)) & \text{if } a = \omega(t) \\ h(X(a),t)\Delta t & \text{otherwise.} \end{cases}$$

There is also a production function $\ell(p,t)$ which represents the net rate of production feeding into the market at time t . The market adjusts prices in the direction opposite to its change in inventory. The rule for price adjustment is thus

$$p(t+\Delta t,\omega) - p(t,\omega) = [-\ell(p(t,\omega),t) + \overline{f}(X(a),\overline{C}(a,t,\omega),p(t,\omega\varepsilon))]\frac{1}{\varepsilon}\,\Delta t$$

where $a = \omega(t)$.

Assume that $\overline{f}$ is uniformly Lipschitz and C^1 , and h and ℓ are continuous in t and uniformly Lipschitz in x and p . We may interpret this process as a hyperfinite exchange process as follows. The new commodity vector is

$$C(a,t,\omega) = \overline{C}(a,t,\omega) - \sum_{s=0}^{t-\Delta t} h(X(a),t)\Delta t .$$

This is the initial allocation plus the net sum of trades. The new excess demand function is

$$f(x,c,p,t) = \overline{f}(x,c + \textstyle\int_0^t h(x,t)dt,p) .$$

The new price adjustment function is

$$g(x,c,p,t) = -\ell(p,t) + f(x,c,p,t) .$$

Then f and g are uniformly Lipschitz and C^1 in x,c,p and continuous in t , and $C(a,t,\omega)$, $p(t,\omega)$ change by the previous rules (treating the agent type as an extra coordinate of c).

References

1. Arrow, K.J. and Hahn, F.H. General Competitive Analysis. Holden-Day, 1971.

2. Brown, D.J. and Robinson, A. Nonstandard Exchange Economies. Econometrica 43 (1975), 41-55.

3. Cutland, N.J. Nonstandard Measure Theory and its Applications. To appear, Bull. London Math. Soc.

4. Debreu, G. Theory of Value. Yale Univ. Press, 1959.

5. Hahn, F. Stability. Ch. 16 in Handbook of Mathematical Economics, Vol. II, ed. by K. Arrow and M. Intrilligator, North-Holland, 1982.

6. Keisler, H.J. Foundations of Infinitesimal Calculus. Prindle, Weber, and Schmidt, 1976.

7. ________. An Infinitesimal Approach to Stochastic Analysis. Amer. Math. Soc. Memoirs, to appear.

8. ________. Infinitesimal Stochastic Difference Equations. To appear.

9. Loeb, P.A. Conversion from Non-standard to Standard Measure Space. Trans. Amer. Math. Soc. 211 (1975), 113-122.

10. ________. An Introduction to Nonstandard Analysis and Hyperfinite Probability Theory, in Probabilistic Analysis and Related Topics, Vol. 2, ed. by A.T. Barucha-Reid, Academic Press, 1979, pp. 105-142.

11. Stroyan, K.D. and Bayod, J.M. Foundations of Infinitesimal Stochastic Analysis. North-Holland, to appear.

A REVISED VERSION OF SAMUELSON'S CORRESPONDENCE PRINCIPLE: APPLICATIONS OF RECENT RESULTS ON THE ASYMPTOTIC STABILITY OF OPTIMAL CONTROL TO THE PROBLEM OF COMPARING LONG RUN EQUILIBRIA

W.A. Brock

Department of Economics
University of Wisconsin
Madison, Wisconsin 53706

Section 1: Introduction

The purpose of this article is to discuss some recent results on the global asymptotic stability of optimal control and show how they may be used with profit in the problem of comparing long run equilibria.

To be more specific, in Section 1 we shall study optimal control problems of the form

$$\begin{aligned} &\text{maximize } \int_0^\infty e^{-\rho t}\, \pi\,(x(t),\dot{x}(t),\alpha)\, dt \\ &\text{s.t. } x(0) = x_o \text{ given} \end{aligned} \tag{1}$$

where $\pi(x(t),\dot{x}(t),\alpha)$ is instantaneous payoff at time t, which is assumed to be a function of the state of the system at time t, $x(t)$, the rate of change of the state $\frac{dx}{dt} \equiv \dot{x}(t)$ and a vector of parameters, α. Here $x(t) \in R^n$, $\dot{x}(t) \in R^n$, $\alpha \in R^m$ and $\rho > o$. As in Rockafellar [35] the maximum in (1) is taken over the set of absolutely continuous functions $x(\cdot)$ such that $x(0) = x_o$.

If $\pi(\cdot,\cdot,\alpha)$ is strictly concave in (x,x) then there is at most one optimum path $x(t,x_o,\alpha)$ for each x_o, α. If the optimum exists for each (x_o,α) then there is a function

$$h: R^n \times R^m \to R^n$$

called the "optimal policy function" such that

$$\dot{x}(t,x_o,\alpha) = h[x(t,x_o,\alpha),\alpha] \tag{2}$$

Furthermore, h does not depend upon x_o or on t due to the time stationarity of (1).

What we shall discuss in this paper is a set of sufficient conditions on π and ρ which imply that there is a unique steady state $\overline{x}(\alpha)$ such that for all x_o

$$x(t,x_0,\alpha) \to \overline{x}(\alpha), \quad t \to \infty . \tag{3}$$

Property (3) is called global asymptotic stability and is abbreviated: G.A.S.. The discussion of sufficient conditions on π for (3) to hold will be terse because this is covered in detail by my survey paper [7]. It will be helpful to the reader if he has a copy of [7] while reading this essay.

After a brief discussion of sufficient conditions on π and ρ for G.A.S. we shall take up the problem of comparing long run equilibria. This problem is known by most readers as "comparative statics" or "comparative dynamics" and is the main concern of this article. Furthermore, something called "Samuelson's Correspondence Principle" is supposed to play a role in the exercise.

Before we indicate how sufficient conditions for G.A.S. in optimal control problems are related to Samuelson's Correspondence Principle and since this principle plays a central role in this essay, let us remind readers how it is described in the Foundations and of some criticism that it has received.

Samuelson's Correspondence Principle (CP)

Samuelson, in the Foundations [36], considered the system of equations

$$0 = E(\rho,\alpha) \tag{4}$$

where

$$E: R^n \times R^m \to R^n$$

is a system of excess demand functions for $n + 1$ goods as a function of the price vector $(p_1,\ldots,p_n)$ and the parameter vector $(\alpha_1,\ldots,\alpha_m)$. Note that there are only n independent equations by Walras' Law. The $(n + 1)$th good is a numeraire. Equations (4) describe a competitive equilibrium where excess demand equals zero (we are assuming no free goods). Now (4) is an equilibrium system. It tells us what the equilibrium price is but it does not tell us how the economic system gets to equilibrium.

Samuelson proposed the adjustment mechanism

$$\dot{p}_i = g_i(E_i(p,\alpha)),\ i = 1,2,\dots,n$$
$$p_i(o) = p_{i_o} \quad \text{given},\ i = 1,2,\dots,n \tag{5}$$

where

$$g_i(0) = 0\ ,\ g_i(E_i) > 0,\ \text{for}\ E_i > 0,\ \text{and}\ g_i(E_i) < 0,\ \text{for}\ E_i < 0\ .$$

Mechanism (5) corresponds to the intuitive idea that price increases when excess demand is positive and vice versa.

After introducing (5) Samuelson studied its asymptotic stability and enunciated his Correspondence Principle: the hypothesis of asymptotic stability of (5) together with a priori information on $\partial E/\partial\alpha$ gives rise to useful restrictions on

$$\partial\overline{p}/\partial\alpha$$

where $\overline{p}(\alpha)$ is the equilibrium price (assumed locally unique) as a function of α. Samuelson applied his principle to other problems as well as general equilibrium but we shall concentrate on the equilibrium problem (4) here for illustrative purposes.

I have deliberately stated the Correspondence Principle as a methodological principle rather than as a precise theorem in order to capture Samuelson's basic idea. Research of Quirk-Saposnik [34], et al has shown that it is not possible in general to use the hypothesis of asymptotic stability of (5) together with sign information on $\partial E/\partial\alpha$ to get comparative statics information on $\partial E/\partial\alpha$.

For example, look at the case where α is one dimensional. Without loss of generality assume $g_i(E_i) = E_i$. Differentiate (4) totally with respect to α and solve for $\partial\overline{p}/\partial\alpha$,

$$\partial\overline{p}/\partial\alpha = -\left(\frac{\partial E}{\partial p}\right)^{-1} \frac{\partial E}{\partial\alpha}\ . \tag{6}$$

The hypothesis that all eigenvalues of $\partial E/\partial p$ have negative real parts contains n restrictions and a priori sign restrictions on $\frac{\partial E}{\partial\alpha}$ contain n more restrictions. But there are n^2 elements in $\partial E/\partial p$. Since Sonnenschein's theorem [39] shows that the axioms of Arrow-Debreu-McKenzie general equilibrium theory are general enough to allow <u>any continuous function</u> from $R^n \to R^n$ to be an excess demand function for some $n + 1$ goods general equilibrium system, it comes as no surprise that examples of higher dimensional systems satisfying all of the restrictions listed above could be created that give arbitrary signs to $\partial\bar{p}/\partial\alpha$. Yet, in such examples, $\partial E/\partial p$ was a stable matrix and $\partial E/\partial\alpha$ had apriori sign restrictions.

These findings led to a lot of research on the correspondence principle (Quirk-Saposnik [34]) that concluded that a priori sign information on $\partial E/\partial\alpha$ plus stability assumed on $\partial E/\partial p$ gave sign restrictions on $\partial\bar{p}/\partial\alpha$ from (6) if the system (6) was low dimensional and/or if $\partial E/\partial p$ "had a lot of zeroes in it."

This was discouraging enough. But while the Quirk-Saposnik type of research was going on the very mechanism (5) came under attack as a description of adjustment. The papers by Gordon and Hines [18] and Phelps and Winter in [32] come to mind. Gordon and Hines argued that speculative activity would destroy any such mechanism (5). They also asked "Whose maximizing behavior does such a mechanism describe?" They argued that it is mechanical and not based on self interested behavior. Phelps and Winter in their article in [32] developed the beginnings of an alternative disequilibrium dynamics.

After the "Phelps Volume" [31] was published there were several attempts in the literature to rationalize mechanisms of the type (5) but no consensus seems in sight. Hence, the epitaph of the correspondence principle was written by Arrow and Hahn [2, p. 321] in their chapter on comparing equilibria: "It "isn't"."

Shortly after the Arrow Hahn book was published the Sonnenschein-Mantel-Debreu theorem [39], [28], and [17] appeared. This result showed that any continuous function $E(p)$ could be an excess demand function for some economy populated by people with perfectly well behaved utility functions.

In view of the SMD result it seems that the CP is sure to fail to be of much use if one insists on the generality of abstract general equilibrium theory. Nevertheless, the CP in some form lurks in the "underworld" of economists of a more practical bent.

I will offer here a version of the CP that I think is somewhat immune to the criticisms listed above. Return now to the optimal control problem (1) together with the dynamics of the solution (2). Many intertemporal equilibrium systems studied in the literature: optimal economic growth, (re: Journal of Economic Theory Symposium Volume Feb., 1976) adjustment cost models in the neoclassical theory of investment (re: Lucas [23], Treadway [40], and Mortensen [29]), perfect foresight models (re: Brock [4], Lucas and Prescott [24]), to name a few, can be fitted into (1). For example, the device of describing general intertemporal equilibrium as the solution to a problem of maximizing a discounted sum of consumer surplus is used in an economically interesting class of equilibrium models in modern capital theory. These are covered by (1). See [24] and [38] for a development of this idea.

Let

$$0 = h(x(\alpha),\alpha) \tag{7}$$

play the role of (4) and let (2) play the role of (5) in the CP.

Revised Correspondence Principle: For problems of type (1) whose solution generates the "equilibrium disequilibrum" adjustment process (2) the hypotheses of linear asymptotic stability (L.A.S.) of the solution $\overline{x}(\alpha)$ to (7) with respect to (2) together with a priori economically natural structural assumptions on $\pi(x,\dot{x},\alpha)$ leads to useful comparative statics information on $\partial\overline{x}/\partial\alpha$.

The revised CP is the main subject of this essay.

Turn now to a closely related idea. Arrow and Hahn [2], in their chapter on comparing equilibria gave little credence to the hope that the hypothesis of L.A.S. alone of equilibria of (5) would yield useful restrictions on $\partial\overline{p}/\partial\alpha$. They did show, however, how sufficient conditions for L.A.S. or G.A.S. of (5) such as "all goods are gross substitutes" yield useful restrictions on $\partial\overline{p}/\partial\alpha$. This is a "Correspondence Principle of sorts" in that stability hypotheses are closely linked to the problem of getting useful restrictions on $\partial\overline{p}/\partial\alpha$.

We shall investigate the same idea for (1) and (2) in this article.

Problem: What restrictions do the various sufficient conditions for L.A.S. or G.A.S. of a steady state $\overline{x}$ of (2) together with the natural structure of $\pi(x,\dot{x},\alpha)$ impose on $\partial\overline{x}/\partial\alpha$?

In Section 3, we obtain the following result for

$$\pi = p\ f(x,\dot{x}) - \alpha_1' x - \alpha_2' \dot{x} \tag{8}$$

where f is concave in $(x,\dot{x})$. Here $a'b$ denotes the scalar product of the vectors a and b. Let

$$H^o(q,x) = \sup_{\dot{x}} [p\ f(x,\dot{x}) - \alpha_1 x - \alpha_2 \dot{x} + q'\dot{x}] ,$$

and let $(\overline{x},\overline{q})$ be a steady state of (2) where $\overline{q}$ is the costate variable at steady state $\overline{x}$. Consider the three hypotheses:

(i) $H^o_{qx} = 0$, at $(\overline{q},\overline{x})$;

(ii) $Q \equiv \begin{bmatrix} H^o_{qq} , & \rho/2\ I_n \\ \rho/2\ I_n , & -H^o_{xx} \end{bmatrix}$ is positive definite at $(\overline{q},\overline{x})$;

(iii) $R \equiv H^{o^{-1}}_{qq} H^o_{qx}$ is negative quasidefinite at (q,x)

where H^o_{qx}, H^o_{qq} H^o_{qx} is the usual notation for second order partial derivatives and I_n denotes the $n \times n$ identity matrix. Any of these three hypotheses are sufficient for the G.A.S. of $\overline{x}(\alpha)$ (re [7]).

<u>Theorem</u>: For π given by (8) any of the hypotheses (i), (ii), (iii) imply that

$$\frac{\partial \overline{x}}{\partial \alpha_1} , \frac{\partial \overline{x}}{\partial \alpha_2} , \frac{\partial \overline{x}}{\partial \beta} \tag{9}$$

are all negative quasidefinite. Here $\beta \equiv \alpha_1 + \rho\alpha_2$.

<u>Remark</u>: If (8) describes instantaneous profit for a competitive one product firm then

$$\overline{x}(\alpha_1,\alpha_2)$$

is the long run or steady state demand function for x. The quantity $\beta \equiv \alpha_1 + \rho\alpha_2$ is rent and

$$\frac{\partial \overline{x}}{\partial \beta}$$

negative quasi definite says that the "demand for $\overline{x}$ is downward sloping".

This is a nontrivial result because long run demands $\overline{x}(\alpha)$ generated by optimization problems like (1) may not slope downward due to dynamic interactions (cf. Mortensen [29, p. 664]).

The paper is organized as follows: Section One contains the introduction. Section Two develops abstract comparative statiscs results that will be used later. Section Three develops the result that was described above.

In Section Four we show that the three G.A.S. hypotheses described above imply

$$B(\rho) \equiv q' \frac{d\overline{x}}{d\rho} < 0 .$$

The latter quantity

$$q' \frac{d\overline{x}}{d\rho}$$

is a measure of capital deepening introduced by Burmeister and Turnovsky [12]. The Burmeister-Turnovsky article relates the negativity of $B(\rho)$ to the "Cambridge" controversy in capital theory.

Section Five provides a modified proof of part of a theorem of Mortensen [29]. His theorem relates the hypothesis of L.A.S. of the optimal steady state $\overline{x}$ to qualitative information on

$$\frac{\partial\overline{x}}{\partial\alpha} .$$

Section Six closes with a summary.

Notations. Equations will be numbered consecutively in each section. The section number of an equation will be given only when necessary. Partial derivatives will be denoted by subscripts as in (i)-(iii) above. Upper bars will be dropped from equilibrium quantitites whenever it is possible to do so without causing confusion. We say that an $n \times n$ matrix A is negative quasidefinite if $x'Ax < 0$ for all $x \neq 0$. We reserve the term "negative definite" for the case when A is symmetric and $x'Ax < 0$ for all $x \neq 0$. The symbol A' denotes the transpose of matrix A. Also $\dot{x}$ is short for dx/dt.

Before we begin we would like to point out that a paper by Burmeister and Long [14] attacks a somewhat similar question. They are interested in the implications of the L.A.S. hypothesis for the comparison of steady states under changes in ρ. We focus on the formulation of "equilibrium disequilibrium" mechanisms $\dot{x} = h(x,\alpha)$ and the extension of Samuelson's Correspondence Principle to such mechanisms. To our knowledge Burmeister-Long [14] and Mortenson [29] are the first to explicitly formulate questions of the type: What are the implications of the L.A.S. hypothesis on the optimal steady states of a control problem for the problem of comparing steady states? The reformulation of Samuelson's Correspondence Principle proposed in Brock [5] has been studied by Magill-Scheinkman [27] and Magill [26]. Araujo-Scheinkman [1], and McKenzie [30] contain related results. Let us get into the substance of the paper.

Section 2: Abstract Results on Comparing Optimal Steady State

This section will develop abstract results which will be given content in later sections.

Consider the system:

$$\dot{q} = \rho q - H_x^o\,(q,x,\alpha) \tag{1}$$

$$\dot{x} = H_q^o\,(q,x,\alpha)\;,\; x(0) = x_o\;. \tag{2}$$

Equations (1), (2) are necessary for optimality in a large class of problems. The transversality condition,

$$\lim_{t\to\infty} q(t)'\;x(t)\;e^{-\rho t} = 0\;, \tag{3}$$

has been shown to be necessary as well as sufficient for a general class of problems by Benveniste and Scheinkman [3].

A steady state $\overline{x}(\alpha)$ with its associated costate $\overline{q}(\alpha)$ must solve:

$$0 = \rho\overline{q}(\alpha) - H_x^o(\overline{q}(\alpha),\overline{x}(\alpha),\alpha) \tag{4}$$

$$0 = H_q^o(\overline{q}(\alpha),\overline{x}(\alpha),\alpha). \tag{5}$$

The transversality condition (3) is automatically satisfied at a steady state $\overline{x}(\alpha)$, $\overline{q}(\alpha)$. Hence equations (4) and (5) characterize optimal steady states.

Totally differentiate both sides of (4), (5) with respect to α (drop upper bars to ease typing) to obtain

$$0 = \rho q_\alpha - H^o_{xq} q_\alpha - H^o_{xx}\, x_\alpha - H^o_{x\alpha} \tag{6}$$

$$0 = H^o_{qq}\, q_\alpha + H^o_{qx}\, x_\alpha + H^o_{q\alpha} \tag{7}$$

Premultiply (6), (7) by the matrix (x'_α, q'_α) to obtain

$$(x'_\alpha, q'_\alpha)\begin{bmatrix} H_{x\alpha} - \rho q_\alpha \\ -H^o_{q\alpha} \end{bmatrix} = -x'_\alpha\, H^o_{xx} x_\alpha + q'_\alpha\, H^o_{qq} q_\alpha - x'_\alpha H^o_{xq} q_\alpha + q'_\alpha H^o_{qx} x_\alpha\ . \tag{8}$$

The R.H.S. of (8) is nonnegative quasidefinite because H^o is convex in q and concave in x, and the crossproduct terms cancel. This can be seen immediately by premultiplying and post multiplying R.H.S. of (8) by a vector $a \varepsilon R^m$. Recall that $\alpha \varepsilon R^m$.

Add $\rho x'_\alpha q_\alpha$ to both sides of (8) to get for $a \varepsilon R^m$

$$a'(x', q')\begin{bmatrix} H^o_{x\alpha} \\ -H^o_{q\alpha} \end{bmatrix} a = a'(q_\alpha, x_\alpha)'\; Q(\alpha)(q_\alpha, x_\alpha)a \tag{9}$$

where

$$Q(\alpha) \equiv \begin{bmatrix} H_{qq} & \rho/2\; I_n \\ \rho/2\; I_n & -H^o_{xx} \end{bmatrix}$$

The matrix $Q(\alpha)$ plays a central role in the stability hypotheses of Brock-Scheinkman [10], Magill [25], and Rockafeller [35]. Magill, for example, shows that if $Q(\alpha)$ is positive definite at the steady state $(x(\alpha_o), q(\alpha_o))$ then $x(\alpha_o)$ is locally asymptotically stable. Brock and Scheinkman [10] differentiate the function $V = \dot{q}'\,\dot{x}$ with respect to t along solutions of (1) and (2) and show that $\frac{dV}{dt} = (\dot{q}, \dot{x})' > 0$ so that the positive definiteness of $Q(\alpha)$ implies that V acts like a Lyapunov function. Hence the global positive definiteness of Q implies G.A.S.

In the spirit of the correspondence principle we have an abstract "comparative statics" result:

Theorem 1. If $Q(\alpha)$ is positive semi definite at $x(\alpha_0)$, $q(\alpha_0)$ then for all $a \varepsilon R^m$

$$a'(x'_\alpha, q'_\alpha)\begin{bmatrix} H^0_{x\alpha} \\ -H^0_{q\alpha} \end{bmatrix} a \geq 0 \tag{11}$$

at $x(\alpha_0)$, $q(\alpha_0)$

Proof: Obvious from (9).

Theorem 1 will be a useful tool when we turn to a problem where α enters the Hamiltonian with a specific structure. Also notice that except for "hairline" cases $Q(\alpha)$ is always positive definite when $\rho = 0$.

Turn now to another abstract result. Solve (7) for q_α in terms of x_α:

$$q_\alpha = -H^{0^{-1}}_{qq} H^0_{qx} x_\alpha - H^{0^{-1}}_{qq} H^0_{q\alpha} \tag{12}$$

Insert (12) into (6) to get

$$0 = -(\rho - H^0_{xq}) H^{0^{-1}}_{qq} H^0_{qx} x_\alpha - (\rho - H^0_{xq}) H^{0^{-1}}_{qq} H^0_{q\alpha} - H^0_{xx} x_\alpha - H^0_{x\alpha} . \tag{13}$$

Equation (13) will play a central role in the comparative statics analysis of the Lucas-Treadway-Mortensen model of optimal accumulation of capital by a profit maximizing firm under adjustment cost which will be carried out in the sequel.

For the case where the Hamiltonian is separable in q and x i.e. $H^0_{xq} = H^0_{qx} = 0$, equations (12) and (13) give us

$$q_\alpha = -H^{0^{-1}}_{qq} H^0_{q\alpha} \tag{14}$$

$$0 = -\rho H^{0^{-1}}_{qq} H^0_{q\alpha} - H^0_{xx} x_\alpha - H^0_{x\alpha} . \tag{15}$$

Section 3: Applications to Adjustment Cost Models

Consider the model

$$\text{maximize} \int_0^\infty e^{-\rho t} \pi(x, \dot{x}, \alpha) dt \quad \text{s.t.} \quad x(0) = x_0 \tag{1}$$

where

$$\pi(x,\dot{x},\alpha) = f(x,\dot{x}) - \alpha_1'x - \alpha_2'\dot{x} \ . \tag{2}$$

This model was studied by Lucas [23], Mortensen [29], and Treadway [40] among others. We shall calculate the quantities H^o_{qq}, H^o_{qx}, H^o_{xx}, etc. for this model. Here, as elsewhere, subscript notation will be used for partial derivatives. The function π will be assumed to be twice continuously differentiable and concave in $(x,\dot{x})$, and all optimum paths will be assumed to be interior to all natural boundaries throughout this article. We use here the convention that if we write A^{-1}, for example, we take it for granted that it is assumed that A^{-1} exists. Now put $\alpha \equiv (\alpha_1,\alpha_2)$ and

$$H^o(q,x,\alpha) \equiv \underset{u\varepsilon R^n}{\text{maximum}} \{f(x,u) - \alpha_1'x - \alpha_2'u + q'u\} \tag{3}$$

Let

$$u^o(q,x,\alpha_2) \tag{4}$$

denote the optimum choice of u in (3). Note that u^o does not depend upon α_1. Since

$$f_u(x,u^o) = \alpha_2 - q \tag{5}$$

$$f_{ux} + f_{uu}\,u^o_x = 0,\ u^o_x = -f^{-1}_{uu}\,f_{ux} \tag{6}$$

$$f_{uu}\,u^o_q = -I_n\ ,\ u^o_q = -f^{-1}_{uu} \tag{7}$$

$$f_{uu}\,u^o_{\alpha_2} = I_n\ ,u^o_{\alpha_2} = f^{-1}_{uu} \tag{8}$$

$$u^o_{\alpha_1} = 0 \tag{9}$$

From the above equations the formulae below follow quickly.

$$H^o_x = f_x(x,u^o) - \alpha_1,\ H^o_{xx} = f_{xx} + f_{xu}\,u^o_x = f_{xx} - f_{xu}\,f^{-1}_{uu}\,f_{ux} \tag{10}$$

$$H^o_{x\alpha_1} = f_{xu}\,u^o_{\alpha_1} - I_n = -I_n\ ,\ H^o_{x\alpha_2} = f_{xu}\,u^o_{\alpha_2} = f_{xu}f^{-1}_{uu} \tag{11}$$

$$H^o_{xq} = f_{xu}\,u^o_q = -f_{xu}\,f^{-1}_{uu} \tag{12}$$

$$H_q^o = u^o \ , \ H_{qq}^o = u_q^o = -f_{uu}^{-1} \tag{13}$$

$$H_{qx}^o = u_x^o = -f_{uu}^{-1} f_{ux} \tag{14}$$

$$H_{q\alpha_1}^o = u_{\alpha_1}^o = 0 \ , \ H_{q\alpha_2}^o = u_{\alpha_2}^o = f_{uu}^{-1} \tag{15}$$

Let us examine some of the abstract results obtained in the previous section. We record (2.13) here for convenience and analyze it first.

$$0 = -(\rho I_n - H_{xq}^o) H_{qq}^{o^{-1}} H_{qx}^o x_\alpha - (\rho I_n - H_{xq}^o) H_{qq}^{o^{-1}} H_{q\alpha}^o - H_{xx}^o x_\alpha - H_{x\alpha}^o . \tag{16}$$

Examine (16) for $\alpha = \alpha_1$. By (11) and (15) we get

$$0 = -(\rho I_n - H_{xq}^o) H_{qq}^{o^{-1}} H_{qx}^o x_{\alpha_1} - H_{xx}^o x_{\alpha_1} + I_n . \tag{17}$$

Premultiply both sides of (17) by x_{α_1}' and manipulate to get

$$0 = -\rho x_{\alpha_1}' H_{qq}^{o^{-1}} H_{qx}^o x_{\alpha_1} + x_{\alpha_1}' H_{xq}^o H_{qq}^o H_{qx}^o x_{\alpha_1} - x_{\alpha_1}' H_{xx}^o x_{\alpha_1} + x_{\alpha_1}' . \tag{18}$$

Since x_{α_1} is an $n \times n$ matrix, equation (18) is an $n \times n$ matrix equation. Pre and post multiply (18) by the $n \times 1$ vector a to get

$$\begin{aligned} 0 = -\rho(x_{\alpha_1} a)' &\underset{(?)}{H_{qq}^{o^{-1}}} H_{qx}^o (x_{\alpha_1} a) + (H_{qx}^o x_{\alpha_1} a)' \underset{(+)}{H_{qq}^{o^{-1}}} (H_{qx}^o x_{\alpha_1} a) \\ &- \underset{(+)}{(x_{\alpha_1} a)' H_{xx}^o (x_{\alpha_1} a)} + \underset{(?)}{a' x_{\alpha_1}' a} . \end{aligned} \tag{19}$$

Notice that we used $H_{qx}^{o'} = H_{xq}^o$ here. The signs in parentheses are signs of each term in equation (19).

We now arrive at

<u>Theorem 1</u> If $\rho > 0$ and $H_{qq}^{o^{-1}} H_{qx}^o$ is negative quasisemidefinite at the steady state $x(\alpha)$ then x_{α_1} is negative quasisemidefinite.

Proof: We must show that for all vectors a

$$a' x_{\alpha_1} a \leq 0. \tag{20}$$

But

$$(x_{\alpha_1} a)' H^{o^{-1}}_{qq} H^o_{qx}(x_{\alpha_1} a) < 0$$

by hypothesis. The other two terms of (19) are nonnegative by convexity of H^o in q and concavity of H^o in x. Hence

$$a'\dot{x}'_{\alpha_1} a < 0 .$$

But

$$a'\dot{x}'_{\alpha_1} a = a'\dot{x}_{\alpha_1} a$$

This ends the proof.

Theorem 1 is a typical example of a comparative statics result that may be derived from a G.A.S. hypothesis. The assumption that

$$R \equiv H^{o^{-1}}_{qq} H^o_{qx}$$

is negative quasidefinite is just the sufficient condition for G.A.S. reported in Brock-Scheinkman [11] and Magill [25]. We digress in order to sketch how R negative quasidefinite implies L.A.S..

Brock and Scheinkman [11] show that the hypothesis that $H^{o^{-1}}_{qq} H^o_{qx} \equiv R$ is negative quasidefinite implies the local asymptotic stability of the optimal solution (2.2) of (3.1), which we record here for convenience

$$\dot{x} = h(x,\alpha),\ x(0) = x_o$$

for $x_o = \overline{x}$. They do this by putting $V = \dot{x}'\, G\dot{x}$, $G \equiv H^{o^{-1}}_{qq}$ and calculating

$$\begin{aligned} \dot{V} &= \ddot{x}'G\dot{x} + \dot{x}'\, G\ddot{x} + \dot{x}'\, \dot{G}\, \dot{x} \\ &= 2\,\dot{q}'\dot{x} + \dot{x}'[R + R']\dot{x} + \dot{x}'\dot{G}\,\dot{x} \\ &< 2\,\dot{q}'\dot{x} + \dot{x}'\dot{G}\dot{x}\ . \end{aligned}$$

Now $\dot{G} = 0$ at steady states and $\dot{q}'\dot{x} < 0$ because

$$q(x(t)) = W_x(x(t))\ ,\ \dot{q} = W_{xx}\dot{x},\ \dot{q}'\dot{x} = \dot{x}'W_{xx}\dot{x} < 0$$

Therefore

$$\dot{V} < 0$$

and V is a Lyapunov function.

Recall that $W(x_o) \equiv \text{maximum} \int_0^\infty e^{-\rho t} \pi(x,\dot{x},\alpha)\, dt$ s.t. $x(o) = x_o$, is concave in x_o provided that π is concave in $(x,\dot{x})$ which we assume. Hence, $\dot{x}'W_{xx}\dot{x} \leq 0$ if it exists. See Brock [7] and, especially Brock and Scheinkman [11] for details.

Thus we see that the negative quasidefiniteness of R plays a central role as a sufficient condition for L.A.S.. It turns out to be very powerful in analyzing a large class of adjustment cost models of Lucas-Mortensen-Treadway type. See [11] and [38] for the details. We now turn back now to more discussion of x_α.

Notice that the $n \times n$ matrix x_{α_1} is not necessarily symmetric but our result gives sufficient conditions for it to be negative quasisemidefinite, i.e.,

$$a'x_{\alpha_1} a \leq 0 \tag{21}$$

for all $a \in R^n$. Since α_1 is the vector of wage rates for x, (21) says that the long run factor demand curve $x(\alpha)$ is "downward sloping" in a generalized sense. We turn to similar results about x_{α_2}.

Replace α by α_2 in (16) above and use (11), (15) to obtain

$$0 = -(\rho I_n - H^o_{xq}) H^{o^{-1}}_{qq} H^o_{qx} x_{\alpha_2} - (\rho I_n - H^o_{xq}) H^{o^{-1}}_{qq} f^{-1}_{uu} - H^o_{xx} x_{\alpha_2} \tag{22}$$
$$- f_{xu} f^{-1}_{uu}$$

Now by (13)

$$H^{o^{-1}}_{qq} = -f_{uu}$$

so that

$$(\rho I_n - H^o_{xq}) H^{o^{-1}}_{qq} f^{-1}_{uu} = -(\rho I_n - H^o_{xq}) . \tag{23}$$

Also

$$-f_{xu} f_{uu}^{-1} = H_{xq}^{o} \tag{24}$$

by (14). Hence by (23) and (24)

$$-(\rho I_n - H_{xq}^{o}) H_{qq}^{o^{-1}} f_{uu}^{-1} - f_{xu} f_{uu}^{-1} = \rho I_n - H_{xq}^{o} + H_{xq}^{o} = \rho I_n . \tag{25}$$

Thus (22) simplifies down to

$$0 = -\rho H_{qq}^{o^{-1}} H_{qx}^{o} x_{\alpha_2} + H_{xq}^{o} H_{qq}^{o^{-1}} H_{qx}^{o} x_{\alpha_2} + \rho I_n - H_{xx}^{o} x_{\alpha_2} . \tag{26}$$

Now follow the argument from equation (17) leading up to Theorem 1 to obtain

Theorem 2: If $\rho > 0$ and $H_{qq}^{o^{-1}} H_{qx}^{o}$ is negative quasisemidefinite, then x_{α_2} is negative quasisemidefinite:

It is worthwhile and instructive to obtain Theorem 2 in a different manner. Look at the steady state equations:

$$0 = \rho q - H_x^{o} = \rho q + \alpha_1 - f(x) \tag{27}$$

$$0 = H_q^{o} = u^{o} \tag{28}$$

$$0 = \alpha_2 - q - f_u . \tag{29}$$

From (27), (28) and (29) we find that steady state x must satisfy

$$0 = \rho\alpha_2 + \alpha_1 - \rho f_u (x,0) - f_x (x,0) . \tag{30}$$

Put

$$\beta = \rho\alpha_2 + \alpha_1$$

and differentiate (30) totally w.r.t. β to get

$$0 = I_n - \rho f_{ux} x_\beta - f_{xx} x_\beta \tag{31}$$

$$x_\beta = (f_{xx} + \rho f_{ux})^{-1} . \tag{32}$$

Now obviously

$$x_{\alpha_1} = x_\beta , x_{\alpha_2} = \rho x_\beta . \tag{33}$$

Hence if $\rho > 0$ and x_{α_1} is negative quasisemidefinite then so also is x_{α_2}, which gives another proof of theorem 2.

We close this discussion of the implications of the negative quasidefiniteness of $H^{o^{-1}}_{qq} H^{o}_{qx}$ to the problem of comparing long run equilibria in the Lucas-Treadway-Mortensen (LTM) model by noticing how equations (17), (18), (19) utilize the special structure of H^o as a function of α to "force" the discovery of $H^{o^{-1}}_{qq} H^{o}_{qx}$ as the central quantity to determine the sign of

$$a' x_{\alpha_1} a .$$

It is fascinating to note that the negative quasi definiteness of $H^{o^{-1}}_{qq} H^{o}_{qx}$ is a very expeditious G.A.S. hypothesis for the LTM model as well as playing a central role in determining the sign of $x_{\alpha_1}, x_{\alpha_2}$. See [11] for the details. We now turn to the comparative statics implications of the separability of the Hamiltonian in (q,x).

Separability of H^o occurs when $H^o_{xq} = 0 = H^o_{qx}$ for all (q,x), α. Record (2.14), (2.15) for convenience.

$$q_\alpha = -H^{o^{-1}}_{qq} H^o_{q\alpha} \tag{34}$$

$$0 = -\rho H^{o^{-1}}_{qq} H^o_{q\alpha} - H^o_{xx} x_\alpha - H^o_{x\alpha}. \tag{35}$$

Replace α by α_1 in (35), and use (11) and (15) to obtain

$$0 = -H^o_{xx} x_{\alpha_1} + I_n . \tag{36}$$

Hence,

<u>Theorem 3</u>: If $H^o_{xq} = 0$ for all x, q, α then if $\rho > 0$

$$x_{\alpha_1} , x_\beta , x_{\alpha_2}$$

are all negative quasisemidefinite and symmetric.

<u>Proof</u>: The matrix x_{α_1} is negative quasi semi definite and symmetric from (36). Equation (33) gives the rest of the theorem. This ends the proof.

The separability of the Hamiltonian is Scheinkman's [38] G.A.S. hypothesis. Again we see the intimate connection between a G.A.S. hypothesis and strong comparative statics results.

Let us use the abstract results (2.8) and (2.9) to get some more comparative statics for the L.M.T. model. We record (2.8) and (2.9) for convenience.

$$(x_\alpha', q_\alpha')\begin{bmatrix} H^o_{x\alpha} - \rho q_\alpha \\ \\ -H^o_{q\alpha} \end{bmatrix} = \begin{matrix} - x_\alpha' H^o_{xx} x_\alpha + q_\alpha' H^o_{qq} q^\alpha \\ - x_\alpha' H^o_{xq} q_\alpha + q_\alpha' H^o_{qx} x_\alpha \end{matrix} \tag{37}$$

$$\begin{aligned} x_\alpha' H^o_{x\alpha} - q' H^o_{q\alpha} = \rho x_\alpha' q_\alpha - x_\alpha' H^o_{xx} x_\alpha x_\alpha + q_\alpha' H^o_{qq} q_\alpha \\ - x_\alpha' H^o_{xq} q_\alpha + q_\alpha' H^o_{qx} x_\alpha \end{aligned} \tag{38}$$

Notice that (38) is the same as (2.9) and (38) trivially follows from (37).

Replace α by α_1 in (37), use $H^o_{x\alpha_1} = -I_n$, $H^o_{q\alpha_1} = 0$ from (11), (15) for the L.M.T. model to obtain

$$\begin{aligned} -x_{\alpha_1}' - \rho x_{\alpha_1}' q_{\alpha_1} = -x_{\alpha_1}' H^o_{xx} x_{\alpha_1} + q_{\alpha_1}' H^o_{qq} q_{\alpha_1} - \\ - x_{\alpha_1}' H^o_{xq} q_{\alpha_1} + q_{\alpha_1}' H^o_{qx} x_{\alpha_1} . \end{aligned} \tag{39}$$

Pre and post multiply both sides of (39) by $a \in R^n$ to obtain

$$-a'x_{\alpha_1}' a - \rho a'x_{\alpha_1}' q_{\alpha_1} a = -a'x_{\alpha_1}' H^o_{xx} x_{\alpha_1} a + a'q_{\alpha_1}' H^o_{qq} q_{\alpha_1} a. \tag{40}$$

Notice that the cross product terms cancel to give R.H.S. (40). From (40)

$$-a' x_{\alpha_1}' a = (q_{\alpha_1} a, x_{\alpha_1} a)' Q(\alpha) (q_{\alpha_1} a, x_{\alpha_1} a) \tag{41}$$

where

$$Q(\alpha) \equiv \begin{bmatrix} H^o_{qq} & \rho/2 \, I_n \\ \rho/2 \, I_n, & -H^o_{xx} \end{bmatrix} .$$

We can now prove

Theorem 4: (i) The matrix

$$x'_{\alpha_1} + \rho\, x'_{\alpha_1} q_{\alpha_1}$$

is negative quasisemidefinite. (ii) If $Q(\alpha)$ is positive semi definite then

$$x_{\alpha_1}\,,\; x_\beta\,,\; x_{\alpha_2}$$

are all negative quasisemidefinite.

Proof: Part (i) follows immediately from (40) because H^0 is convex in q and concave in x. To obtain part (ii) first note from (41) that $Q(\alpha)$ positive semi definite implies directly that x_{α_1} and hence x_{α_1} is negative quasisemidefinite. That x_β and x_{α_a} are negative quasi semi definite follows directly from equation (33). This ends the proof.

Once again we see that a G.A.S. hypothesis, viz $Q(\alpha)$ positive semi definite, yields strong comparative static results. Furthermore, when $\rho = 0$ Theorem 4 (ii) shows us that $x_{\alpha_1}, x_\beta, x_{\alpha_2}$, are all negative quasisemidefinite.

Remark. When $\pi = pf(x,\dot{x})^2 - \alpha_1'x - \alpha_2'\dot{x}$ where ρ is product price we may obtain comparative statics results on p by noticing that the choice of optimum path is homogeneous of degree 0 in (p,α_1,α_2). Put $\bar{\alpha}_1 = p^{-1}\alpha_1$, $\bar{\alpha}_2 = o^{-1}\alpha_2$. Then use the results obtained above to obtain qualitative results for $\partial x/\partial p$.

We turn now to the impact on the steady state x when the discount ρ is increased.

Section 4: Relationships Between G.A.S. Hypotheses and Generalized Capital Deepening.

Consider the steady state equations

$$0 = \rho q - H_x^0\,(q,x) \tag{1}$$

$$0 = H_q^0\,(q,x)$$

Burmeister-Turnovsky [15] introduce the measure of capital deepening

$$B(\rho) \equiv q' x_\rho$$

where x_ρ is the derivative of the steady state with respect to ρ: An economy is called "regular" at ρ_0 if

$$B(\rho_0) < 0 .$$

The motivation for introducing $B(\rho)$ is discussed in detail in [15]. It is a measure of sorts for the impact on the steady state capital stock constellation when the interest rate ρ changes in a growth model.

It turns out that the following Theorem may be proved.

<u>Theorem</u>: All of the following G.A.S. hypotheses at $q(\rho_0)$, $x(\rho_0)$ are sufficient for $B(\rho) < 0$ at $\rho = \rho_0 > 0$: (i) Q is positive semi definite, (ii) $H^{o^{-1}}_{qq} H^o_{qx}$ is negative quasi semi definite, or (iii) $H^o_{xq} = 0$.

Proof: We demonstrate (i) first. Differentiate (1) totally w.r.t. ρ to obtain

$$0 = \rho q_\rho + q - H^o_{xq} q_\rho - H^o_{xx} x_\rho \tag{2}$$

$$0 = H^o_{qq} q_\rho + H^o_{qx} x_\rho . \tag{3}$$

Premultiply (2) by x'_ρ to get

$$0 = \rho x'_\rho q_\rho + x'_\rho q - x'_\rho H^o_{xq} q_\rho - x'_\rho H^o_{xx} x_\rho . \tag{4}$$

Premultiply (3) by q'_ρ to get

$$0 = q'_\rho H^o_{qq} q_\rho + q'_\rho H^o_{qx} x_\rho . \tag{5}$$

Add (4) and (5) to get

$$0 = \rho x'_\rho q_\rho + x'_\rho q - x'_\rho H^o_{xx} x_\rho + q'_\rho H^o_{qq} q_\rho = (q_\rho, x_\rho)' Q(q_\rho, x_\rho) + x'_\rho q. \tag{6}$$

It follows immediately from (6) that (i) implies

$$x'_\rho q = q' x_\rho < 0 .$$

In order to derive the second result first solve (3) for q_ρ in terms of x_ρ and, second, insert the solution into (2) to get equations (7) and (8) below.

$$q_\rho = -H^{o^{-1}}_{qq} H^o_{qx} x_\rho , \tag{7}$$

$$0 = -\rho H^{o^{-1}}_{qq} H^o_{qx} x + q + H^o_{xq} H^{o^{-1}}_{qq} H^o_{qx} x_\rho - H^o_{xx} x_\rho \tag{8}$$

Premultiply both sides of (8) by x'_ρ to obtain

$$0 = \rho x'_\rho H^{o^{-1}}_{qq} H^o_{qx} x_\rho + x'_\rho q + x'_\rho H^o_{xq} H^{o^{-1}}_{qq} H^o_{qx} x_\rho - x'_\rho H^o_{xx} x_\rho . \tag{9}$$

Now

$$x'_\rho H^o_{xq} H^{o^{-1}}_{qq} H^o_{qx} x_\rho = (H^o_{qx} x_\rho)' H^{o^{-1}}_{qq} (H^o_{qx} x_\rho > 0$$

since H^o is convex in q. Also

$$-x'_\rho H^o_{xx} x_\rho > 0$$

because H^o is concave in x. Hence from (9) either (ii) or (iii) is sufficient for

$$q'x_\rho < 0 .$$

This ends the proof.

Remark. Parts (i) and (ii) of this theorem are due to Brock and Brumeister [8] and M. Magill [25] respectively.

A fascinating discussion of the implications of the L.A.S. hypothesis in the problem of comparing equilibria when ρ changes and the relation of this problem to the Cambridge Controversy in Capital Theory as well as the "Hahn Problem" is contained in Burmeister and Long [14].

This concludes the presentation of results that we have obtained on the implications of sufficient conditions on $\pi(x,\dot{x},\alpha)$ and ρ for the G.A.S. of optimal paths for qualitative results on steady states. Notice that all of the results are of the following character: A G.A.S. hypothesis and a hypothesis about how α enters H^o is placed upon the Hamiltonian $H^o(q,x,\alpha)$ of the system to obtain results on comparing steady states. This suggests that a general theory of comparing steady states is waiting to be discovered. This is so because "Hamiltonian like" constructs are very general. For example, such a construct can be invented for dynamic games where some arguments enter in a passive way and are determined by equilibrium forces in much the same way as competitive prices are determined and other arguments enter in an active way and are determined in much the same way as Cournot oligoply models determine output levels. See Brock [61 for a development in general "Hamiltonian" terms of this class of dynamic industrial organization games which are due to Edward Prescott and his students at Carnegie. The paper of Dechert [19] locates sufficient conditions for the equilibria of such games to be representable as the Euler equation of some variational problem.

Furthermore, the analysis of Cass and Shell [16] neatly develop, with a duality emphasis, the Hamiltonian formalism of modern growth theory for both descriptive and optimal growth models. A "Hamiltonian like" formalism underlies virtually any dynamic model that has a recursive structure. Hence results such as those obtained in this article which depend upon hypotheses placed upon the Hamiltonian alone should extend to more general models (re. [6]).

Turn now to the development of results on comparing equilibria that depend only on the L.A.S. hypothesis of the steady state x.

Section 5: Example of Use of the Natural Structure of a Dynamic Model and the L.A.S. Hypothesis to Get Strong Comparative Statics Results

This section presents a simplified proof of a theorem of Mortensen. Return to the adjustment cost model of Lucas-Treadway and Mortensen.

$$\text{maximize } \int_0^\infty (Pf(x,\dot{x}) - \alpha_1'x - \alpha_2'u)\, e^{-\rho t} . \tag{1}$$
$$\text{s.t. } x(o) = x_o,\ \dot{x} = u$$

Assume P, α_1, α_2 are time independent. Write the necessary conditions for optimality in Euler equation form,

$$\frac{d}{dt}(f_u - \alpha_2) = f_x - \alpha_1 + \rho(f_u - \alpha_2) \ . \tag{2}$$

Let $\bar{x}$ be a steady state and let $x_o = \bar{x} + \Delta x_o$. Under very general conditions (See Magill [25]) equation (2) may be approximated thusly for small Δx_o.

$$\frac{d}{dt}(f_{uu}\ \Delta u + f_{ux}\ \Delta x) = f_{xu}\ \Delta u + f_{xx}\ \Delta x + \rho\ f_{ux}\ \Delta x + \rho\ f_{uu}\ \Delta u \tag{3}$$

$$\Delta\dot{x} = \Delta u \ , \ \Delta x(o) = \Delta x_o \ . \tag{4}$$

Here (3) was obtained from (2) by expansion in a Taylor series at $(\bar{x},0)$ and using the equations of steady state to cancel off the first order terms. All second derivatives are evaluated at the steady state $(x,u) = (\bar{x},0)$.

Now if f is strictly concave in $(x,\dot{x})$ we saw before that there is a policy function $h(x,P,\alpha)$ such that optimum trajectories satisfy

$$\dot{x} = h(x,P,\alpha),\ x(0) = x_o \tag{5}$$

Linearize h around the steady state $\bar{x}$ to get

$$\Delta\dot{x} = h_x(\bar{x};P,\alpha)\ \Delta x,\ \Delta x(o) = \Delta x_o \ . \tag{6}$$

Equations (3), (4), and (6) describe the same trajectory. Therefore the matrix $M \equiv h_x(\bar{x};p,\alpha)$ must solve a quadratic matrix equation that is generated by (3). I.e.

$$BM^2 + (C - C' - \rho B)M = A + \rho C \tag{7}$$

where

$$B = f_{uu}\ ,\ C = f_{ux}\ ,\ C' = f_{xu}\ ,\ A = f_{xx}\ . \tag{8}$$

Equation (7) is obtained by plugging

$$\Delta\dot{x} = M\ \Delta x,\ \Delta\ddot{x} = M\Delta\dot{x} = M^2\Delta x \tag{9}$$

into (3) and equating coefficients.

Equation (7) is difficult to solve for the optimal adjustment matrix M except in the one dimensional case. But, nonetheless, we can say a good deal about M in terms of A, B, C, ρ.

For instance, we know that for $f(x,\dot{x})$ strictly concave there is just one steady state $\bar{x}$ and it is G.A.S. for the case $\rho = 0$ where the maximum is interpreted in the sense of the overtaking ordering (cf. Brock and Haurie [9] and references). Scheinkman's [38] result tells us that, except for hairline cases, if $\rho > 0$, and ρ is small enough then G.A.S. will hold. Hence, we know, except for hairline cases that M is a stable matrix when ρ is small.

We may also employ the G.A.S. hypotheses listed above to find conditions on A, B, C, ρ that guarantee that M is a stable matrix. See the Brock "Survey" paper [7] where this exercise is carried out in detail.

In this section we are interested in the following: What restrictions does the stability of M imply on the comparison of steady states? This question is more in the spirit of the Revised Correspondence Principle which asserts that stability of M will generate comparative statics results. This brings us to Mortensen's Theorem.

Theorem (Mortensen [29]). Assume B is negative definite. If M is a stable matrix then $\bar{x}_\beta$, $\frac{\partial h}{\partial \beta}(\bar{x}; p,\alpha_1,\alpha_2)$, $\beta \equiv \alpha_1 + \rho\, \alpha_2$ are both symmetric and negative definite iff C is symmetric. Moreover, the characteristic roots of M are all real if C is symmetric.

Proof: See Mortensen [29]. We need to develop formulae for later use. First, by direct use of the steady state equations

$$\bar{x}_\beta = (A + \rho C)^{-1} \;, \; \frac{\partial h}{\partial \beta}(\bar{x};p,\alpha_1,\alpha_2) = -M(A + \rho C)^{-1} \tag{10}$$

Second, the following lemma is needed for later developments.

Lemma: At any steady state, if the quadratic approximation (3) is valid then

$$M'B - BM = C - C' \tag{11a}$$

$$A + \rho C = (M' - \rho I_n)BM. \tag{11b}$$

Proof of the Lemma: Equation (11b) follows directly from (11a) and (7). So we only need to establish (11a) only. Write the necessary conditions of optimality in Hamiltonian form:

$$\dot{q} = \rho q - H_x^o (q,x) \tag{12}$$

$$\dot{x} = H_q^o (q,x), \; x(0) = x_o \tag{13}$$

$$\lim_{t\to\infty} e^{-\rho t} q(t)'x(t) = 0 . \tag{14}$$

In order to see that (14) is necessary for optimality and is the correct transversality condition in general see Benveniste and Scheinkman [3].

Following Magill [25] look at the necessary conditions for optimality of the linear quadratic approximation to (1) written in Hamiltonian form.

$$\Delta\dot{q} = \rho\Delta q - H_{xq}^o \, \Delta q - H_{xx}^o \, \Delta x \tag{15}$$

$$\Delta\dot{x} = H_{qx}^o \, \Delta x + H_{qq}^o \, \Delta q \tag{16}$$

$$\lim_{t\to\infty} e^{-\rho t} \Delta q'(t) \, \Delta x(t) = 0 \tag{17}$$

Here the matrices in (15) and (16) are evaluated at steady state $(\overline{q},\overline{x})$ and Δx, Δq are deviations from steady state.

Now suppose that

$$\Delta q = W \, \Delta x \tag{18a}$$

for some matrix W. The intuition behind this is compelling. For if $R(x_o) \equiv \text{maximum} \int_0^\infty e^{-\rho t} \pi(x,u,\alpha) \, dt$, s.t. $x(0) = x_o$, $\dot{x} = u$ and if R is twice continuously differentiable at $x_o = \overline{x}$, then (18a) holds, where $W = \frac{\partial^2 R}{\partial x^2} (\overline{x})$. This is so because by definition of q

$$q = \frac{\partial R}{\partial x} .$$

Hence

$$\Delta q = \frac{\partial^2 R}{\partial x^2} \Delta x = W \, \Delta x$$

for the linear approximation.

Turn back to (16),

$$\dot{\Delta x} = H^o_{qx}\ \Delta x + H^o_{qq}\ \Delta q = H^o_{qx}\ \Delta x + H^o_{qq}\ W\ \Delta x = M\ \Delta x\ . \tag{18b}$$

Hence

$$M = H^o_{qx} + H^o_{qq} W. \tag{19}$$

Now calculate

$$M'B - BM$$

from (19).

$$M'B - BM = (H^o_{xq} + W\ H^o_{qq})\ B - B\ (H^o_{qx} + H^o_{qq}\ W) \tag{20}$$

But

$$B \equiv f_{uu},\ H^o_{qq} = -\ f^{-1}_{uu},\ H^o_{xq} = -f_{xu}\ f^{-1}_{uu},\ H^o_{qx} = -f^{-1}_{uu}\ f_{ux}$$

from (3.13), (3.12), and (3.14).

Thus

$$M'B - BM = H^o_{xq}\ f_{uu} - f_{uu}\ H^o_{qx} = -f_{xu} + f_{ux} = C - C'\ . \tag{21}$$

Remark. Notice that the proof of the lemma did not assume $\overline{x}$ was L.A.S. or G.A.S. What is needed for the proof is that the linear quadratic approximation to (1) be valid, and that $R(x)$ be twice continuously differentiable. A sufficient condition for both is that $f(x,\dot{x})$ be quadratic in $(x,\dot{x})$. See Magill [25] for a discussion of the linear quadratic approximation. Hence, in particular, the result (21) holds for all problems whre $f(x,\dot{x})$ is quadratic and concave in $(x,\dot{x})$. Mortenson does not need to assume that $\overline{x}$ is L.A.S. to get (21), when $f(x,\dot{x})$ is quadratic in $(x,\dot{x})$.

Examine the following equalities which follow directly from (11b)

$$A + \rho C = M'BM - \rho BM \tag{22a}$$

$$-(A + \rho C)M^{-1} = \rho B - M'B. \tag{22b}$$

Notice that by (11a) both $A + \rho C$ and $(A + \rho C)M^{-1}$ are symmetric provided that

$C = C'$. Hence by (10) it follows that $\bar{x}_\beta$ and $\frac{\partial h}{\partial \beta}$ are both symmetric since the inverse of a symmetric matrix is symmetric.

Remark: The only part of Mortensen's theorem that needs the L.A.S. of $\bar{x}$ is the negative definiteness of $\bar{x}_\beta$ and $\frac{\partial h}{\partial \beta}$. The symmetry of $\bar{x}_\beta$ and $\frac{\partial h}{\partial \beta}$ as well as the reality of the characteristic roots of M require only the symmetry of C alone.

Mortensen's theorem is an excellent example of how the indigenous structure of the adjustment cost model interplays with the L.A.S. hypothesis to produce strong qualitative results.

Corollary

(i) $H^{o^{-1}}_{qq} \, H^{o}_{qx} = f_{ux} \equiv C'$

(ii) If C is negative quasidefinite then $\bar{x}$ is L.A.S. and both $\bar{x}_\beta$, $\frac{\partial h}{\partial \beta}(\bar{x}, P, \alpha_1, \alpha_2)$ are negative quasidefinite.

Proof: The first formula follows directly from

$$H^{o}_{qq} = -f^{-1}_{uu}, \; H^{o}_{qx} = -f^{-1}_{uu} f_{ux} , \tag{23}$$

and $C \equiv f_{xu}$. Here equations (23) are recorded from (3.13), (3.14) for convenience.

Now C is negative quasidefinite iff C' is. Hence the negative quasi definiteness of C is simply the sufficient condition for G.A.S. reported in Brock-Scheinkman [10] and Magill [25]. We now turn to the task of showing that $\bar{x}_\beta$ and $\frac{\partial h}{\partial \beta}$ are negative quasidefinite. Look at 22a, b. Since for any $a \in R^n$

$$a'(M'B - BM)a = a'(C - C')a = 0 ,$$

and $\bar{x}_\beta$, $\frac{\partial h}{\partial \beta}$ are negative quasidefinite iff $A + \rho C$, $-(A + \rho C)M^{-1}$ are negative quasidefinite, by (22a) and (22b) we need only show that BM is positive quasi definite in order to finish the proof. Recall that

$$\bar{x}_\beta = (A + \rho C)^{-1}, \; \frac{\partial h}{\partial \beta} = - [(A + \rho C)M^{-1}]^{-1} . \tag{24}$$

In order to see that BM is positive quasidefinite, calculate

$$BM = f_{uu}(H^o_{qq} W + H^o_{qx}) = -W - H^{o^{-1}}_{qq} H^o_{qx} . \qquad (25)$$

The first equality follows from (23) and the second follows because

$$f_{uu} = -H^{o^{-1}}_{qq} .$$

Now W is negative semidefinite by concavity of the state valuation function of the associated linear quadratic approximation of the original problem around the steady state $\overline{x}$ (Magill [25]). Hence the R.H.S. of (25) is positive quasidefinite. This ends the proof.

Remark: Some additional structure on the problem above and beyond the stability of M is needed in order to get the negative quasisemidefiniteness of $\overline{x}_\beta$. This is so because Mortensen [29, p. 663] provides a two dimensional example where M is stable, C is not symmetric, and

$$\frac{\partial \overline{x}_2}{\partial \beta_2} > 0$$

The reader is advised to look at Magill and Scheinkman [27] where for the case of (1) a complete characterization of the local behavior of (5) near steady states is given under the assumption that the matrix f_{xx} is symmetric.

Furthermore if P, α_1, α_2 in (1) were determined endogenously by the device of maximizing a discounted sum of consumer net producer surplus, the revised correspondence principle could be developed in price space rather than in quantity space as is done here. In that way an "equilibrium disequilibrium" price adjustment process is derived that replaces the ad hoc Walrasian tatonnement. The methods developed in this paper can be used to show how structural properties of the Hamiltonian of the discounted consumer net producer surplus problem translates into a correspondence principle for the equilibirum price adjustment process derived thereby. This question has been studied by Magill-Scheinkman [27], and Magill [26].

Section 6: Summary, Conclusions, and Suggestions for Future Research

This article has shown how a Samuelson type of "Correspondence Principle" can be developed for a class of an optimal control problems that arise in modern capital theory. More particularly we have shown how three sufficient conditions for the global asymptotic stability of an optimal steady state that have been obtained recently by researchers imply comparative statics results on the optimal steady state when they are combined with specific structural hypotheses on the Hamiltonian of the optimal control problem.

Furthermore, we have modified a result of Mortensen to point out how the L.A.S. hypothesis alone on the optimal steady state implies strong comparative statics results when combined with certain structural assumptions on the Hamiltonian.

The purpose of this article has been to show that a version of Samuelson's Correspondence Principle can be developed for the recursive equilibrium systems typical of the modern "equilibrium-disequilibrum dynamics" that is somewhat immune to the criticism leveled against the Correspondence Principle in the case of Arrow-Debreu-McKenzie general equilibrium theory. Work by Magill and Scheinkman [27], Magill [26] has gone beyond what is done here in developing the revised correspondence principle.

More work needs to be done in exploring the implications of different G.A.S. hypotheses for comparative statics in the context of the optimal control model studied in this paper as well as more general recursive equilibrium systems before we can have much confidence that the ideas presented in this paper will be of much use for dynamic economics. In particular <u>some</u> structure will have to be replaced upon $\pi(x,\dot{x},\alpha)$ above and beyond concavity in $(x,\dot{x})$. This is so because examples were created in [7] where given arbitrary dynamics $\dot{x} = F(x)$, a $\pi(x,\dot{x},\alpha)$ could be found that generated $x = F(\dot{x})$ as the optimum dynamics. The examples did not make much sense from an economic point of view but they showed that concavity of π in $(x,\dot{x})$ is not enough to get useful restrictions on the optimal dynamics.

FOOTNOTES

0. This paper is a revision and updating of my 1976 paper (Brock [3]). I thank F.R. Chang, A.G. Malliaris and H. Weinberger for help with the editorial work and the catching errors. I also thank the NSF for continual support of my research. None of the above is responsible for errors and opinions expressed in this article.

REFERENCES

[1] Araujo, A.P., and Scheinkman, J.A., "Notes on Comparative Dynamics", in J.R. Green and J.A. Scheinkman (eds.), General Equilibrium, Growth, and Trade: Essays in Honor of Lionel McKenzie. New York, Academic Press, 1979.

[2] Arrow, K. and Hahn, F., General Competitive Analysis, San Francisco, CA., Holden Day, 1971.

[3] Benveniste, L.M. and Scheinkman, J.A., "Duality Theory for Dynamic Optimization Models of Economics: The Continuous Time Case", Journal of Economic theory, Vol. 27, Number 1, June 1976, 1-19.

[4] Brock, W., "On Models of Expectations That Arise Form Maximizing Behavior of Economic Agents Over Time", Journal of Economic Theory, Vol. 5, No. 3, December 1972, pp. 348-376.

[5] Brock, W., "Applications of Recent Results of the Asyptotic Stability of Optimal Control to the Problem of Comparing Long Run Equilibria", Report 7652, Center for Mathematical Studies in Business and Economics, The University of Chicago, December 1976.

[6] Brock, W., "Differential Games with Active and Passive Variables", in Mathematical Economics and Game Theory: Essays in Honor of Oskar Morgenstern, R. Henn and O. Moeschlin (eds.), Springer Verlag, Berlin, 1977, 345.

[7] Brock, W., "The Global Asymptotic Stabilty of Optimal Control: A Survey of Recent Results", in M.D. Intriligator (ed.) Frontiers of Quantitative Economics. Volume 3A, Amsterdam, Elsevier-North Holland Publishing Co., 1977, pp. 207-237.

[8] Brock, W. and Burmeister, E., "Regular Economies and Conditions for Uniqueness of Steady States in Optimal Multisector Economic Models", International Economic Review, Vol. 17, No. 1, February 1976, pp. 105-120.

[9] Brock, W. and Haurie, A., "On Existence of Weakly Optimal Trajectories Over an Infinite Time Horizon", Mathematics of Operations Research, Vol. 1, No. 4, November, 1976, 337-346.

[10] Brock, W. and Scheinkman, J.A., "Global Asymptotic Stability of Optimal Growth Systems with Applications to the Theory of Economic Growth" Journal of Economic Theory, Vol. 12, No. 1, february 1976, pp. 164-190.

[11] Brock, W. and Scheinkman, J.A., "The Global Asymptotic Stability of Optimal Control with Applications to Dynamic Economic Theory", in J. Pitchford and S. Turnovsky (eds.), Applications of Control Theory to Economic Analysis, Amsterdam, Elsevier-North Holland Publishing Company, 1977.

[12] Burmeister, E. and Graham, D.A., "Multi-sector Economic Models with Continuous Adaptive Expectations", Review of Economic Studies, Vol. 41, No. 3, July 1974, pp. 323-336.

[13] Burmeister, E. and Graham, D.A., "Price Expectations and Global Stability in Economic Systems", Automatica, Vol. 11, 1975, pp. 487-497.

[14] Burmeister, E. and Long, V.N., "On Some Unresolved Questions in Capital Theory: An Application of Samuelson's Correspondence Principle", The Quarterly Journal of Economics, Vol. 91, No. 2, May 1977, pp. 289-314.

[15] Burmeister, E. and Turnovsky, S.J., "Capital Deepending Response in an Economy with Heterogeneous Capital Goods", American Economic Review, Vol. 62, No. 5, December 1972, pp. 842-853.

[16] Cass, D. and Shell, K., "The Structure and Stability of Competitive Dynamical Systems", Journal of Economic Theory, Vol. 12, No. 1, February 1976, pp. 31-70.

[17] Debreu, G., "Excess Demand Functions", Journal of Mathematical Economics, Vol. 1, No. 1, March 1974, pp. 15-21.

[18] Gordon, D. and Hynes, A., "On the Theory of Price Dynamics", in E.S. Phelps, (ed.), Microeconomic Foundations of Employment and Inflation Theory, New York, W.W. Norton & Company, Inc., 1970, pp. 369-393.

[19] Dechert, W.D., "Optimal Control Problems From Second Order Difference Equations", Journal of Economic Theory, Vol. 19, No. 1, October 1978, 56-63.

[20] Hahn, F.H., "Equilibrium Dynamics with Heterogeneous Capital Goods", The Quarterly Journal of Economics, Vol. 80, No. 4, November 1966, pp. 633-46.

[21] Hestenes, Magnus R., Calculus of Variations and Optimal Control Theory, New York, John Wiley & Sons, 1966.

[22] Liviatan, N. and Samuelson, P.A., "Notes on Turnpikes: Stable and Unstable", Journal of Economic Theory, 3 (Dec. 1969), 454-75. Reprinted in Robert C. Merton, ed., The Collected Scientific Papers of Paul A. Samuelson, Volume III, Cambridge, AM: The MIT Press, 1972.

[23] Lucas, R.E., "Optimal Investment Policy and the Flexible Accelerator", International Economic Review, Vol. 8, No. 1, February 1967, pp. 78-85.

[24] Lucas, R.E. and Prescott, E., "Investment Under Uncertainty", Econometrica, Vol. 39, No. 5, September 1971, pp. 659-682.

[25] Magill, Michael J.P., "Some New Results on the Local Stability of the Process of Capital Accumulation", Journal of Economic Theory, Vol. 15, No. 1, June 1977, pp. 174-210.

[26] Magill, Michael J.P., "The Stability of Equilibrium", International Economic Review, Vol. 20, No. 3, October 1979, pp. 577-597.

[27] Magill, M.J.P. and Scheinkman, J.A., "Stability of Regular Equilibria and the Correspondence Principle for Symmetric Variational Problems", International Economic Review, Vol. 20, No. 2, June 1979, pp. 297-315.

[28] Mantel, R., "On the Characterization of Aggregate Excess Demand", Journal of Economic Theory, Vol. 7, No. 3, March 1974, pp. 348-353.

[29] Mortensen, D.T., "Generalized Costs of Adjustment and Dynamic Factor Demand Theory", Econometrica, Vol. 41, No. 4, July 1973, pp. 657-665.

[30] McKenzie, Lionel W., "Optimal Economic Growth and Turnpike Theorems", Social Science Working Paper 267, California Institute of Technology, May 1979. To appear in The Handbook of Mathematical Economics, edited by Arrow and Intriligator.

[31] Phelps, E.S., Macroeconomic Foundations of Employment and Inflation Theory, New York, W.W. Norton & Company, Inc. 1970.

[32] Phelps, E.S. and Winter, S.G., "Optimal Price Policy Under Atomistic Competition", in E.S. Phelps, (ed.), Microeconomic Foundations of Employment and Inflation Theory, New York, W.W. Norton & Company, Inc., 1970, pp. 309-337.

[33] Pontryagin, L.S. and Associates, The Mathematical Theory of Optimal Processes, New York, Interscience, 1962.

[34] Quirk, J. and Saposnik, R., Introduction to General Equilibirum Theory and Welfare Economics, New York, McGraw-Hill, 1968.

[35] Rockafellar, R.T., "Saddle Points of Hamiltonian Systems in Convex Lagrange Problems Having a Non-Zero Discount Rate", Journal of Economic Theory, Vol. 12, No. 1, February 1976, pp. 71-113.

[36] Samuelson, P.A., Foundations of Economic Analysis. Cambridge, MA: Harvard University Press, 1947.

[37] Scheinkman, J.A., On Optimal Steady States of n-sector Growth Models When Utility is Discounted, J. Econ. Theory, 12 (1976), 11-30.

[38] Scheinkman, J.A., "Stability of Separable Hamiltonians and Investment Theory", Review of Economic Studies, 45 (October, 1978), 559-570.

[39] Sonnenschein, H., "Market Excess Demand Functions", Econometrica 40, 549-563.

[40] Treadway, A.B., The Rational Multivariate Flexible Accelerator, Econometrica 39 (1971), 845-855.

DYNAMIC IMPLICATIONS OF THE FORM OF THE BUDGET CONSTRAINT

Truman F. Bewley
Department of Economics
and the
Cowles Foundation
Yale University
New Haven, CT 06520

A subject much discussed in economics is the effect of having more or fewer markets. The markets in question are usually markets for insurance, for loans or for goods to be delivered in the future. One of the effects of having more such markets is to give consumers more flexibility in the use of their financial power. I will try to convince you that such flexibility can have a substantial effect on the dynamic behavior of an economy.

The importance of such financial flexibility may be illustrated by considering a model which represents the equilibrium behavior of a growing economy. Imagine that there are finitely many immortal individuals who all come into the world at once. There are two commodities, labor and a produced good which may be consumed or used in the production process. Each consumer starts with a certain amount of this good and has a certain amount of labor to offer in every period. Production is organized by a firm. Trading may be thought of in two different ways. We may imagine that all trading is done in the first period and is done in forward committments to receive or deliver the good or labor. Or we can imagine that trading is done each period in the good and labor for current delivery and that people always know all future prices. Trading is made in exchange for some unit of account, there being a different unit of account each period. There is a market for one-period loans in every perjod, in which current a unit of account is exchanged for a promise to deliver a unit of account in the following period. The interest rate on these loans makes all units of account commensurable.

There follows a formal description of such a model. There are I consumers, and the utility function of consumer i is

$$\sum_{t=0}^{\infty} (1+\rho)^{-t} u_i(c_t),$$

where c_t is consumption in period t. I assume that the discount rate on future utility, ρ, is the same for all consumers. Consumer i's supply of labor in period t is L_{it}. His supply of the produced good in period 0 is y_{i0}. He is able to afford any stream of consumption $(c_0, c_1, \ldots\ldots)$ which satisfies the constraint

$$\sum_{t=0}^{\infty} p_t c_t \leq p_0 y_{i0} + \sum_{t=0}^{\infty} w_t L_{it} ,$$

where p_t is the price of the produced good in period t and w_t is the wage of labor for that period. Prices are in terms of the period zero unit of account. Each consumer chooses the affordable consumption stream which maximizes his utility function. The firm has production function

$$y_{t+1} = f(k_t, L_{t+1}) ,$$

where y_t, k_t, and L_t are the period t output, input of produced good, and input of labor, respectively. The firm maximizes profits, which amounts to choosing k_t and L_{t+1} for each t so as to maximize

$$p_{t+1} f(k_t, L_{t+1}) - p_t k_t - w_{t+1} L_{t+1} .$$

The economy is in equilibrium if prices are such that the maximizing behavior of consumers and the firm lead to commodity balance. That is,

$$L_t = \sum_{i=1}^{I} L_{it} , \text{ for all } t,$$

$$\sum_i y_{i0} = k_0 + \sum_i c_{i0} , \text{ and}$$

$$y_t = k_t + \sum_i c_{it} , \text{ for } t > 0.$$

Suppose that aggregate labor supply, $\sum L_{it}$, is constant. If sufficient regularity conditions are imposed on the u_i and f, then an equilibrium converges in the sense that the c_{it}, k_t, $(1 + \rho)^{-t} p_t$, and $(1 + \rho)^{-t} w_t$ converge as t goes to infinity. (See Brock and Mirman, Section 2). This is the well-known turnpike theorem, which is interpreted as giving some coherence to optimal growth paths.

In the above model, it was assumed that consumers had an unlimited capacity to borrow and lend. If we go to the opposite extreme and assume that consumers have no way to move purchasing power between periods, then the model collapses as a model of capital accumulation. Consumers would never be able to save and the capital stock would always be zero. An intermediate hypothesis is that consumers can accumulate assets, but cannot borrow. In this case, one can have cyclically fluctuating equilibria.

Imagine that trading takes place in each period and that the unit of account is always the produced good of the current period. There are two prices in each period t, the wage w_t, and the interest rate on wealth held from period t to $t + 1$, call it r_t. Wealth may be thought of as shares in the capital stock of the firm or as loans to the firm. The wealth or assets of consumer i in period t, denoted A_{it}, is defined inductively by the equations

$$A_{i0} = w_0 L_{i0} + y_{i0} - c_{i0} \quad \text{and}$$

$$A_{i,t+1} = (1 + r_t)A_{it} + w_{t+1}L_{i,t+1} - c_{i,t+1} \text{, for } t \geq 0.$$

Consumer. i can afford the consumption stream $(c_0, c_1, \ldots)$ if $A_{it} \geq 0$, for all t.

Imagine an example with two consumers. Consumer 1 has labor supply 1 in odd periods and none in even periods. Consumer 2 has labor supply 1 in even periods and none in odd periods. Suppose that future utility is discounted at a rate exceeding the interest rate. Then, we can imagine that consumers would save from periods when they earn wages to periods when they do not, but would save nothing from a period without earnings to the next period. Such savings behavior disconnects successive periods in a way that makes cycles possible.

In order to see the cycle, notice that if the interest rate from period t to $t + 1$ is r_t, then the capital stock k_t in period t satisfies

$$\frac{\partial f}{\partial k}(k_t, 1) = 1 + r_t \text{ ,}$$

since the return on capital must equal that on savings. This equation makes k_t a non-increasing function of r_t; call it $k(r_t)$. The consumer who labors in period t will earn a wage equal to

$$w_t = \frac{\partial f}{\partial L}(k(r_{t-1}),1) ,$$

If he saves only during periods when he works, his saving will be a function of r_{t-1} and r_t; call it $A(r_{t-1},r_t)$. The interest rate is determined by the equation $A(r_{t-1},r_t)) = k(r_t)$. This difference equation can be such that it has cyclic solutions. A cycle of period 2 is illustrated in the diagram below. In the diagram, r_e and r_o represent the interest rate in even and odd periods, respectively. A fully specified example is given in the appendix.

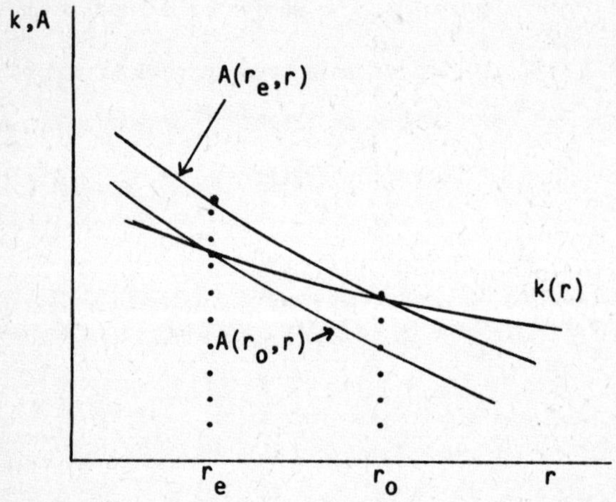

In order to see why cycles may occur, let us return to the first model in which all trading is done in period zero. Since there is only one unit of account and each consumer has only one budget constraint, the marginal value of the unit of account corresponding to purchases in any period is constant. That is, for each consumer i, there is $\lambda_i > 0$ such that

$$(1 + \rho)^{-t} \frac{du_i}{dc}(c_{it}) \leq \lambda_i p_t , \text{ for all } t,$$

with equality if $c_{it} > 0$. This means that the equilibrium maximizes the function

$$\sum_{t=0}^{\infty} (1 + \rho)^{-t} \sum_{i=1}^{I} \lambda_i^{-1} u_i(c_{it}) ,$$

provided the u_i are concave. Since the equilibrium maximizes such a function, it is possible to use a simple argument to prove that the equilibrium converges. (See section 2 of Brock and Mirman (3).)

In the case of the example without borrowing, there is no common unit of account, but we might be able to choose the units of account for each period so that their marginal utility is nearly constant. This would be possible if the ratio of the marginal utilities of units of account for the two consumers were nearly constant. In the example, this ratio fluctuates.

There is a way to guarantee that this ratio would move only slowly even if borrowing were impossible. Suppose that the model were such that the equilibrium real rate of return on capital were always non-negative. This could be guaranteed by introducing a technology for storing the produced good without loss. Suppose also that each consumer's discount rate on future utility, ρ, were nearly zero. The first order conditions for utility maximization imply that

$$\frac{du_i}{dc}(c_{it}) \geq \frac{1 + r_t}{1 + \rho}\,\frac{du_i}{dc}(c_{i,t+1}) \geq (1 + \rho)^{-1}\,\frac{du_i}{dc}(c_{i,t+1}).$$

Since ρ is nearly zero, $\frac{du_i}{dc}(c_{it})$ is nearly non-increasing in t and hence can fluctuate only slowly, apart from possible occasional decreases. This in turn implies that consumption, interest rates, and production can fluctuate only slowly or occasionally. What is going on behind the scenes is that because the interest rate is close to or larger than the consumer's discount rate on future utility, consumers accumulate enough assets so as to smooth fluctuations in their income. The asset accumulation by individuals has a steadying effect on the whole economy.

The process of allowing the consumers' discount rate on utility to go to zero corresponds to shortening the length of time periods. The lower bound of zero on the real rate of return may be thought of as being provided by money and a stable monetary policy. Thus, if one imagines that fluctuations in technology, resource supplies and tastes are short-term or rapid and if monetary policy is "stabilizing", then in an economy with no borrowing, consumer behavior would be such as to stabilize the dynamic behavior of equilibrium, and the equilibrium would not look very different from that of an economy with trading forward indefinitely into the future.

APPENDIX

There are two commodities, labor and a produced good. Inputs of produced good, k, in period t and of labor, L, in period $t + 1$ produce output in period $t + 1$ according to the production function

$$f(k,L) = 2k + 4L - k^2/2L \ .$$

This function is increasing over the range of values occurring in the equilibrium to be defined.

There are two consumers. Consumer 1 has a supply of one unit of labor in odd periods and none in even periods. Consumer 2 has a supply of one unit of labor in even periods and none in odd periods. The utility function of each consumer is of the form

$$\sum_{t=0}^{\infty} 2^{-t} u(c_t) \ ,$$

where c_t is the consumption of the produced good in period t. u is any increasing, concave, real-valued function defined on the non-negative numbers and satisfying the following conditions:

$$\frac{du}{dc^-}(3/4) = 80 \ , \ \frac{du}{dc^+}(3/4) = 20 \ , \ \frac{du}{dc}(2\ 5/8) = 17, \text{ and } \frac{du}{dc}(4\ 5/8) = 16.$$

Notice that u has a kink at $3/4$.

It is easily checked that the following is an equilbrium with no borrowing. The interest rate is 1/2 from even to odd periods and is -1/2 from odd to even periods. In odd periods, output is 4 7/8, the input of produced good into production for the next period is 3/2, the consumption of person 1 is 2 5/8, and the consumption of person 2 is 3/4. Consumer 1 has all the assets at the end of the period. In even periods, output is 5 7/8, the input of produced good is 1/2, the consumption of person 1 is 3/4 and that of person 2 is 4 5/8. Person 2 has all the assets at the end of the period.

In the equilibrium, the consumers always consume 3/4 when they have no labor. They save when they labor and save nothing when they do not. The savings function is, then $(0.75)(1 + r)^{-1}$. The capital invested as a function of r is $1 - r$. The two solutions of the equation $(0.75)(1 + r)^{-1} = 1 - r$ are the equilibrium interest rates.

REFERENCES

Brock, William and Leonard Mirman, "Optimal Economic Growth and Uncertainity; the Discounted Case," Journal of Economic Theory 4 (1972), 479-513.

COMPARATIVE STATICS FOR MULTIDIMENSIONAL OPTIMAL STOPPING PROBLEMS

W.A. Brock* and M. Rothschild**

Department of Economics*
University of Wisconsin, Madison
Madison, Wisconsin 53706

Department of Economics**
University of California, San Diego
La Jolla, California 92093

INTRODUCTION

The problem of choosing a stopping time τ to maximize $E[X(t)e^{-rt}]$ where $X(t)$ is a real valued stochastic process is analyzed in [1]. Motivation for this problem comes from economics. Briefly, $X(t)$ is the intrinsic value of an asset. The same asset's market value is

$$V(x) = \sup_{\tau \varepsilon T} \{E[x(\tau)e^{-r\tau} \,|X(0) = X]\}.$$

where T is the set of all nonanticipating stopping times.

The problem is to determine the market value and the optimal stopping rule and, in particular, to analyze how these change as the parameters of the problem change. In [1] most attention is paid to the case where $X(t)$ is a stationary diffusion process with instantaeous drift $b(x)$ and instantaneous variance $\sigma^2(x)$. However, [1] also treats the case where $X(t)$ is a discrete time Markov process. For the diffusion case, the results in [1] are about as complete as we would hope for. However, the restriction to one dimensional diffusion processes is limiting. In this paper we show how the methods of [1] may be used to analyze the problem of choosing a stopping rule to maximize $E[R(X(\tau))^{-r\tau} \,|X(0) = X]$ where $X(t)$ is a vector valued random process and $R(X)$ is the reward which the owner of the asset reaps if he stops the asset's growth and sells it when the state variable is X. For example, suppose the asset is a tree and the two components of X are the number of board feet in the tree and the current price of lumber. In this case we will have $R(x_1,x_2) = x_1x_2$. Alternatively, we might suppose that X is a forest with many trees which, because of economies of scale in the lumbering process, must all be cut down together. Then we will have $R(X) = \sum X_i$.

We treat both diffusions and discrete time processes. We show how, for each case, the results and techniques of [1] may be generalized in a relatively straightforward way.

1. DIFFUSIONS

Suppose the current state of an asset is given by a d-dimensional vector X which evolves according to the stochastic differential equation

$$dX = f(X)dt + G(X)dW \tag{1.1}$$

where W is an m-dimensional Wiener process, $f(\cdot)$ a d-dimensional vector and $G(\cdot)$ a d by m matrix.

For simplicity suppose that the process must stop if X ever leaves the compact set D. Let $\tau(D)$ be the first time $X(t)$ leaves D. Let T be the set of all stopping times and let

$$\mathcal{J} = \{\tau \in T : \tau = \tau \wedge \tau(D) \quad \text{for some} \quad \tau \in T\}$$

then the market value is

$$V(X) = \sup_{\tau \in \mathcal{J}} E[R(X(\tau))e^{-r\tau} \mid X(0) = X].$$

Standard results [4] imply that subject to regularity conditions, the optimal stopping rule is characterized as follows: there is an open (relative to D) set $\underline{C}$ (called the continuation region) such that on $\underline{C}$, V satisfies the partial differential equation

$$rV = V_x f + \frac{1}{2} \operatorname{tr} [GG'V_{xx}] .$$

The optimal stopping rule is to stop on the first exit from $\underline{C}$. If $X \in \Gamma(\underline{C}) \setminus \Gamma(D)$, where Γ denotes the boundary, then

$$R_x(X) = V_x(X), \; R(X) = V(X) .$$

On $\underline{C}$, $V(X) > R(X)$. On the stopping set, $\underline{S} = D \setminus C$, $V(X) = R(X)$.

<u>Proposition 1</u>: Let τ be the optimal stopping rule and define $\tau^*(t) = t \wedge \tau$ then $V(X(\tau^*(t))e^{-r\tau^*(t)})$ is a martingale.

Proof: Clearly, we only need prove this for $t < \tau$; if $X(t) \in \underline{C}$, then Ito's lemma implies

$$d(V e^{-rt}) = e^{-rt}[-rV + V_x f(x) + \frac{1}{2} \operatorname{tr} GG'V_{xx}]dt + e^{-rt} V_x G\, dW$$
$$= e^{-rt} V_x G\, dW .$$

Since the Ito integral is a martingale, $E[V(X(t))e^{-rt}|X(0) = X] = V(X)$. This generalizes the result in [1] which states that $V(X(\tau^*(t))e^{-r\tau^*(t)}$ is a martingale.

COMPARATIVE STATICS

In [1] it was shown that when the state variable X was one dimensional, and thus f and G in (1.1) were scalars, one could analyze the effects of changes in f and G by using the following principle: If V is increasing at X_0, an increase in mean, $f(X)$, in a small neighborhood of X_0 will increase $V(\cdot)$ everywhere and cause the continuation region to expand; if V is convex near X_0 a local increase in variance (that is in $G(X)$) near X_0 will have the same effects. If V is decreasing and concave near X_0, a local increase in mean or in variance will decrease V and cause the continuation region to contract. We now show how these results can be generalized.

Let X be given by the vector diffusion (1.1). Since the instantaneous mean of the diffusion process X is the vector $f(X)$, an increase in mean is an increase in all of the components of $f(X)$. The analogue of the instantaneous variance of X is the matrix $G(X)G'(X)$. We define an increase in variance as a change to a matrix $H(X)$ such that $H(X)H'(X) - G(X)G'(X)$ is positive definite.

Let J be an open set in the continuation region and suppose $\eta(X)$ is a function from R^d to R such that $\eta(X)V_x(X) > 0$ for $X \in J$ and $\eta(X) = 0$ for $X \notin J$. Let $\delta(X)$ be a R^d to $R^{d\times m}$ function such that $\delta(X) = 0$ for $X \notin J$ while if $X \in J$,

$$G(X)\delta'(X) + \delta(X)G'(X) \quad \text{is nonnegative definite,} \tag{1.2a}$$

and

$$\delta(X)\delta'(X) \quad \text{is positive definite.} \tag{1.2b}$$

Now consider the asset which evolves according to

$$dX = (f(X) + \alpha\eta(X))dt + (G(X) + \alpha\delta(X))dW \tag{1.3}$$

If $\alpha > 0$, this asset has a greater mean and a larger variance on J than does the asset which evolves according to (1.1). Let $\hat{V}^{\alpha}$ be the value of the asset which evolves according to (1.3) and is stopped optimally.

<u>Theorem 1</u>: Suppose that for $X \varepsilon J$, $\eta V_X > 0$ and V_{XX} is positive definite. Then there is an $\varepsilon > 0$ such that if $0 \leqslant \alpha < \varepsilon$,

$$\hat{V}^{\alpha}(X) > V(X) \quad \text{for} \quad X \varepsilon J ;$$

$$\hat{V}^{\alpha}(X) \geqslant V(X) \quad \text{for} \quad X \not\varepsilon J .$$

Proof: The proof depends on a simple result in matrix algebra

<u>Lemma</u>. If U, A are positive definite symetric square matrices of the same order then $tr(AU) > 0$.

Proof: Let $U = C' \Lambda C$ where Λ is a diagonal matrix of the eigenvalues of U. Since A is non-negative definite, there is a matrix B such that $A = BB'$. Then

$$tr(AU) = tr(BB'C' \Lambda C) = tr(B'C' \Lambda CB) = tr(G \Lambda G') = tr(\Lambda G'G) = \sum_i \lambda_i g_i' g_i ,$$

where g_i is the ith row of the matrix $G' = CB$ and λ_i is the ith eigenvalue of U. Since U is positive definite and $CB \neq 0$ the conclusion follows.

Proof of Theorem 1: Let V^{α} be the value of the asset which evolves according to (1.3) but which is stopped whenever it leaves <u>C</u>. Since this is not the optimal stopping rule for an asset which evolves according to (1.3), $\hat{V}^{\alpha}(X) \geqslant V^{\alpha}(X)$. Let $Z(X) = V^{\alpha}(X) - V(X)$. Note that

$$rZ(X) - Z_x f(X) - \frac{1}{2}\,\mathrm{tr}(G(X)G'(X)Z_{xx}(X)) = Q(X) \tag{1.4}$$

where

$$Q(X) = \alpha[\eta(X)V_x^\alpha(X) + \mathrm{tr}(H(X)V_{xx}^\alpha(X))]$$

and

$$H(X) = G(X)\delta'(X) + \delta'(X)G(X) + \alpha\delta(X)\delta'(X).$$

Now $Q(X) = 0$ for $X \not\in J$. We will prove that

$$Q(X) > 0 \quad \text{for} \quad X \in J \,. \tag{1.5}$$

It is relatively straightforward to adapt arguments from Krylov [3, Lemma 6 on page 25, pages 38 and 41] to show that $V_x^\alpha(x)$ and $V_{xx}^\alpha(x)$ are continuous in α. (A proof is available from the authors upon request.) Since $V_x^\alpha(x)$ and $V_{xx}^\alpha(x)$ are continuous functions of α, there is an $\varepsilon > 0$ such that $\eta V_x^\alpha(x) > 0$ and $V_{xx}^\alpha(X)$ is positive definite for $\alpha < \varepsilon$ and $x \in J$. Since H is positive definite the Lemma implies (1.5).

To prove the theorem it will suffice to prove that

$$Z(X) \geq 0 \quad \text{for} \quad X \in \underline{C} \,.$$

For $X \in \Gamma(\underline{C})$, $Z(X) = 0$. Suppose there is an X in the interior of $\underline{C}$ such that $Z(X) < 0$. Then there is an $\tilde{X} \in \underline{C}$ such that Z has a local minimum at $\tilde{X}$ and $Z(\tilde{X}) < 0$. At $\tilde{X}$, $Z_x(\tilde{X}) = 0$ and therefore (1.4) implies

$$Z(\tilde{X}) = r^{-1}[Q(\tilde{X}) + \frac{1}{2}\,\mathrm{tr}(G(\tilde{X})G'(\tilde{X})Z_{xx}(\tilde{X}))]$$

However, at a local min, Z_{xx} is positive semidefinite so that the Lemma implies $Z(\tilde{X}) \geq 0$. This contradiction completes the proof.

Note that since $V^\alpha(X) \geq V(X)$ for all $x \in \underline{C}$, the continuation region for the process with the larger mean and variance is larger than (or at least as large as) the continuation region for the process which evolves according to (1.1).

<u>Remark</u>. In the scalar case examined in [1] we were able to use the analogue of Theorem 1 to obtain comparative statics results about the effects of local changes

in means and variances in a wide variety of cases. This was because we showed that V was always increasing and we found conditions, which were easy to interpret and to verify, which determined whether V was locally convex or concave. In the multidimensional case we have not found Theorem 1 so useful because we have not found ways to determine the characteristics of V. The strongest results we have obtained is: if R is strictly convex then

$$\mathrm{tr}(GG'V_{xx}) > \mathrm{tr}(GG'R_{xx}) > 0 \tag{1.6}$$

on the free boundary of $\underline{C}$. Hence V_{xx} cannot be negative definite on the free boundary of $\underline{C}$. This is much weaker than the analogous result in the scalar case. In [1] we showed that if the reward R is convex then the value V is convex at the free boundary of $\underline{C}$.

Inequality (1.6) follows from two facts. First on the free boundary of C we must have

$$-rR + R_x f + \frac{1}{2}\,\mathrm{tr}(GG'R_{xx}) < 0 \,. \tag{1.7}$$

If not, it would pay to continue the process a little longer (cf. Miroshnichenko [4]) which contradicts the defintion of the free boundary of $\underline{C}$. Second, the standard smooth pasting conditions of optimal stopping imply that, on the free boundary of $\underline{C}$ we must have

$$rV = rR, \; V_x = R_x \,. \tag{1.8}$$

Relations (1.7) and (1.8) together with

$$-rV + V_x f + \frac{1}{2}\,\mathrm{tr}(GG'V_{xx}) = 0$$

on $\underline{C}$ imply (1.6).

2. DISCRETE TIME

If we pose the optimal stopping problem in discrete time, we are able to get somewhat more useful comparative statics results. Thus, in this section we will study the problem of finding the optimal time to stop a process whose state follows a one-dimensional discrete time continuous state space Markov process $\{X_n\}$. The objective is to maximize the expected discounted reward. The discount factor is denoted by

$$\beta = \frac{1}{1+r}$$

where r is the rate of interest.

This problem is a special case of the general optimal stopping problem studied by Chow-Robbins-Siegmund [2] and Sirjaev [5]. We shall follow the notation of Chow-Robbins-Siegmund, abbreviated CRS, as closely as possible in what follows.

We are interested in "comparative dynamics" results in this article. In order to obtain such results for the "infinite horizon" problem we will first obtain results for N period problems by the method of backward induction. Second we will take N to infinity in order to extend results to the infinite horizon case.

Following CRS, put

$$V_n^N(X_n) \equiv \sup_{n \leq \tau \leq N} E\{\beta^{\tau-1} R(X_\tau) | X_n\} \ . \tag{2.1}$$

Here the supremum is taken over all stopping times τ that are measurable (i.e., the event $\{\tau = k\}$ depends only upon $\{X_i\}_{i \leq k}$). Here $V_n^N(X_n)$ is the value function of an N period problem starting at n. Obviously

$$V_N^N(X_N) = \beta^{N-1} R(X_N) \tag{2.2}$$

$$V_n^N(X_n) = \sup\{\beta^{n-1} R(X_n), E[V_{n+1}^N(X_{n+1}) | X_n]\} \tag{2.3}$$

$$V_n^N(X) \leq V_n^{N+1}(X), \quad n = 1,2,\ldots; \quad N = 1,2\ldots \ . \tag{2.4}$$

Let

$$V_n^\infty(X) \equiv \lim_{N \to \infty} V_n^N(X) \tag{2.5}$$

which exists by (2.4).

CRS give sufficient conditions for

$$V_n^\infty(X) = V_n(X) \equiv \sup_{n \leq \tau < \infty} E\{\beta^{\tau-1} R(X_\tau) | X_n = X\}. \quad (2.6)$$

We refer the reader to CRS for sufficient conditions for existence of an optimal stopping time τ_n^N for problem (2.1) with $n \geq 1$, $N < \infty$. We are concerned with the case $n = 1$, $N = \infty$. Put $\tau_1^\infty \equiv \tau$. It turns out that τ is of the form

$$\text{Stop at the first time } n \text{ such that } \beta^{n-1} R(X_n) \geq E\{V_{n+1}(X_{n+1}) | X_n\} \text{ .} \quad (2.7)$$
$$\text{continue otherwise.}$$

Let

$$C_n^N = \{X | \beta^{n-1} R(X) < E[V_{n+1}^N(X_{n+1}) | X]\} \text{ .}$$

The set C_n^N is the continuation region for an N period problem starting at date n.

Since we have nothing new to say about existence of an optimal stopping time or the equivalence and finiteness of the quantities $V^\infty(X)$, $V_n(X)$ we shall simply assume such properties in what follows. The reader is referred to CRS [3] and Sirjaev [5] for a complete discussion.

Consider the special case (in which all processes of the form $X_{n+1} = \underline{F}(X_n, \varepsilon_{n+1})$ may be written)

$$X_{n+1} - X_n = f(X_n, n + 1) + G(X_n, n + 1)\varepsilon_{n+1} \quad (2.8)$$

where $\{\varepsilon_n\}_{n=1}^\infty$ is independent, identically distributed, with mean zero and variance unity. Here F and G are arbitrary functions from R^2 to R. That is, f is a function of the current state, X_n, and time, $n + 1$, as is the current variance G^2. Equation (2.8) is a discrete time version of the continuous time diffusion process as studied in section 1. However, since the time dependence in (2.8) is completely arbitrary, for the one dimensional case, the formulation here is considerably more general than that of section 1.

It is natural to ask the following questions.

What happens to V_n^N, V_n if $G(\cdot,t)$ is increased at date t? What happens to the boundary of C_n^N when $G(\cdot,t)$ is increased at date t, $n \leq t \leq N$? Here X_n^N is in the boundary of C_n^N if

$$\beta^{n-1}R(X_n^N) = E\{V_{n+1}^N(X_{n+1})|X_n = X_n^N\}. \qquad (2.9)$$

In the one dimensional case C_n^N-boundary points X_n^N are called critical numbers. Critical numbers must satisfy (2.9).

Critical numbers are useful. If they are unique they have the interpretation:

$$\begin{aligned} &\text{stop if } X_n \geq X_n^N \\ &\text{continue if } X_n < X_n^N . \end{aligned} \qquad (2.10)$$

The following theorem may be established.

<u>Theorem 1</u>. Suppose that $R(\cdot)$, each component of $F(\cdot,n)$, and $G(\cdot,n)$ are non-negative, non-decreasing and convex for each $n = 1,2,\ldots$. Then for all N, n

$$V_n^N(\cdot) \text{ are convex non-decreasing} \qquad (2.11)$$

Suppose, that, in addition,

$$G_1(\cdot,t) \leq G_2(\cdot,t) \quad \text{and} \quad G_1(\cdot,s) = G_2(\cdot,s) \quad \text{for} \quad s \neq t \qquad (2.12)$$

Then

$$V_{n,1}^N(\cdot) \leq V_{n,2}^N(\cdot) , \quad \text{for} \quad n < t \qquad (2.13)$$

$$V_{n,1}^N(\cdot) = V_{n,2}^N(\cdot) , \quad \text{for} \quad n \geq t \qquad (2.14)$$

where

$$F(X,n) \equiv X + f(X,n) . \qquad (2.15)$$

Note that the conclusion to this theorem is considerably stronger than the conclusion of Theorem 1.1, but that the hypotheses are stronger and the result is restricted to the one dimensional case. We give an intuitive explanation before the formal proof.

We establish the theorem by backward induction. The idea is simple: First we show that V_{n+1}^N convex non-decreasing implies V_n^N is convex non-decreasing. Trivially, $V_N^N(X) = \beta^{N-1}R(X)$ is convex non-decreasing. Second, an increase in $G(X,t)$ induces a mean preserving spread at t. Hence the expected value of V_{n+1}^N doesn't decrease provided V_{n+1}^N is convex. Let us go on to the details.

Proof: Trivially $V_N^N(X) = \beta^{N-1}R(X)$ is convex non-decreasing. We claim that V_{n+1}^N convex non-decreasing implies V_n^N is convex non-decreasing. Now

$$V_n^N(X) = \max\{\beta^{n-1}R(X), E\{V_{n+1}^N[F(X,n+1) + G(X,n+1)\varepsilon_{n+1}]|X\}\}. \qquad (2.16)$$

Since the max operator preserves convexity and monotonicity, all we must show is that

$$E\{V_{n+1}^N[F(X,n+1) + G(X,n+1)\varepsilon_{n+1}]|X\}$$
$$\equiv \int_\varepsilon V_{n+1}^N\,[F(X,n+1) + G(X,n+1)\varepsilon]d\mu(\varepsilon) \qquad (2.17)$$

is convex non-decreasing in X.

Let $X_1 \leq X_2$. Then

$$\int_\varepsilon V_{n+1}^N[F(X_1,n+1) + G(X_1,n+1)\varepsilon]d\mu(\varepsilon) \qquad (2.18)$$

$$\leq \int_\varepsilon V_{n+1}[F(X_2,n+1) + G(X_1,n+1)\varepsilon]d\mu(\varepsilon) \qquad (2.19)$$

$$\leq \int_\varepsilon V_{n+1}[F(X_2,n+1) + G(X_2,n+1)\varepsilon]d\mu(\varepsilon)\,, \qquad (2.20)$$

The first inequality follows because V_{n+1}^N, $F(\cdot,n+1)$ are non-decreasing. The second inequality follows because $G(X_1,n+1) \leq G(X_2,n+1)$ and V_{n+1}^N is convex. Hence $V_n^N(X)$ is non-decreasing in X.

To show convexity, let $0 \leq \alpha \leq 1$, X_1, X_2 be given. Then

$$\int_\varepsilon V_{n+1}[F(\alpha X_1 + (1-\alpha)X_2,n+1) + G(\alpha X_1 + (1-\alpha)X_2,n+1)\varepsilon]d\mu(\varepsilon)$$

$$\leq \int_\varepsilon V_{n+1}[\alpha F(X_1,n+1) + (1-\alpha)F(X_2,n+1) + G(\alpha X_1 + (1-\alpha)x_2,n+1)\varepsilon]d\mu(\varepsilon) \qquad (2.21)$$

$$< \int_\varepsilon V_{n+1}[\alpha F(X_1,n+1) + (1-\alpha)F(X_2,n+1) + [\alpha G(X_1,n+1) + (1-\alpha)G(X_2,n+1)]]\varepsilon\} d\mu(\varepsilon) \tag{2.22}$$

$$< \alpha \int_\varepsilon V_{n+1}^N[F(X_1,n+1) + G(X_1,n+1)\varepsilon]d\mu(\varepsilon) + (1-\alpha)\int_\varepsilon V_{n+1}[F(X_2,n+1) + G(X_2,n+1)\varepsilon]d\mu(\varepsilon). \tag{2.23}$$

The first inequality follows because $F(\cdot,n+1)$ is convex and V_{n+1}^N is non-decreasing. The second inequality follows from convexity of G and the convexity of V_{n+1}^N. Finally, the last inequality follows directly from convexity of V_{n+1}^N.

Since the max operator preserves convexity and monotonicity, $V_n(\cdot)$ is convex non-decreasing. This establishes part (2.11) of the theorem.

In order to establish the second part look at

$$V_t^N(X) = \max\{\beta^{t-1}R(X), \int_\varepsilon V_{t+1}^N (F(X,t+1) + G(X,t+1)\varepsilon)d\mu(\varepsilon)\} \tag{2.24}$$

$$V_{t-1}^N(X) = \max\{\beta^{t-2}R(X), \int_\varepsilon V_t^N(F(X,t) + G(X,t)\varepsilon)d\mu(\varepsilon)\} . \tag{2.25}$$

The increase in $G(\cdot,\cdot)$ occurs only at date t. Hence from (2.24) obviously V_t^N, V_s^N, $s > t$ all remain unchanged. At date $t-1$, V_{t-1}^N is increased since the increase in $G(\cdot,t)$ induces a "mean preserving spread" at date t. Since the max operator preserves monotonicity V_r^N increases for $r < t-1$. This ends the proof.

The theorem may be established for $N = \infty$ by taking the limit of V_n^N for each fixed n, X. The proof of the theorem also shows that the sets C_n^N increase when G is increased.

The assumption that F, G are convex non-decreasing in X for each n is strong but not vacuous. For the one dimensional case our result covers linear processes with arbitrary time varying non-negative coefficients.

It is easy to establish the following.

Corollary 1. Suppose that $F(\cdot,n)$, $G(\cdot,n)$ are non-decreasing convex for each n. Suppose that

$$F_1(\cdot,t) < F_2(\cdot,t) \tag{2.26}$$

and all other $F(\cdot,n)$ remain unchanged. Then

$$V^N_{n,1}(\cdot) \leq V^N_{n,2}(\cdot)\,, \quad \text{for} \quad n < t \tag{2.27}$$

$$V^N_{n,1}(\cdot) = V^N_{n,2}(\cdot)\,, \quad \text{for} \quad n \geq t\,. \tag{2.28}$$

Proof. Write

$$V^N_n(X) = \max\{\beta^{n-1}R(X), \;\; V^N_{n+1}[F(X,n+1) + G(X,n+1)\varepsilon]d\mu(\varepsilon)\}\,. \tag{2.29}$$

Clearly, if $V_{n+1}(\cdot)$ is non-decreasing then an increase in $F(X,n+1)$ increases $V^N_n(X)$. Hence the rest of the proof proceeds as that of Theorem 1. This ends the proof.

The same kind of analysis used to produce comparative dynamics results for the values V^N_n and the continuation regions C^N_n may be used to develop results for more complicated problems. For example, consider renewal in the one dimensional case. Write

$$V_n(X) = \max\{\beta^{n-1}R(X), \beta^{n-1}R(X) - P\beta^{n-1} + E[V_{n+1}(X_{n+1})|X_n = 0], \tag{2.30}$$
$$E[V^N_{n+1}(X_{n+1})|X_n = X]\}.$$

I.e., the value of a problem with size X at date n with horizon N is the maximum of three options: (i) stop now, don't renew; (ii) stop now, renew at size 0 with renewal cost P; (iii) let it continue one more period.

Since

$$V^N_N(X) = \beta^{N-1}R(X) \tag{2.31}$$

the same CRS backward induction technique may be used to establish Theorem 1 and Corollary 1 for this case.

TIME STATIONARY CASE

More can be said in the case where F, G do not depend upon n. To see this work in current values and let

$$W^N_n(X) = V^N_n(X)/\beta^{n-1}\,, \; W_n(X) = V_n(X)/\beta^{n-1}\,. \tag{2.32}$$

Then (2.3) becomes

$$W_n^N(X) = \max\{R(X), \beta E[W_{n+1}^N(X_{n+1})|X_n = X]\} . \tag{2.33}$$

Furthermore

$$W_n(X) = \max\{R(X), \beta E[W_{n+1}(X_{n+1})|X_n = X]\}. \tag{2.34}$$

Since $\{\varepsilon_n\}_{n=1}^{\infty}$ is i.i.d. (independent and identically distributed) and F, G are time independent, it follows from the definition that $W_n(X)$ does not depend upon n. Hence the time independent case is characterized by the set of solutions to the equation

$$R(X) = \beta \int W(F(X) + G(X)\varepsilon)d\mu(\varepsilon) . \tag{2.35}$$

It is clear from the proofs of Theorem 1.1 and Corollary 1 that under the conditions of these theorems increases in F and G increase W and expand the stopping region.

The results that we have obtained to date for the discrete time case are limited. The assumption that the non-negative matrix function G is non-decreasing and convex in X is strong. In the scalar case it reduces to the usual meaning of non-decreasing and convex.

The assumption that F is non-decreasing and convex is strong. An interesting outstanding problem is to locate sufficient conditions on R, F, G so that a result like Theorem 1.1 may be proved for the discrete time case.

3. CONCLUSION

In both parts of this paper we attempted to find conditions which would allow us to determine how parameter changes would affect stopping regions and values of multidimensional optical stopping problems. For diffusion processes we generalized the results of [1] and showed that if the value function is increasing, increases in mean will increase value and expand the continuation region while if the value function is convex, increases in variance will have the same effect. However, these results were of quite limited use since we have not been able to say much about when and where the value function is convex or increasing.

We took a different approach to discrete time processes. There we located conditions on the parameters of the stopping problem itself which allowed us to determine a class of parameter changes which would increase value and make the continuation region larger. The conditions which we imposed were very stringent; they are much stronger than the ones we imposed in the diffusion process case. However, they did allow us to get results which can actually be used and verified in particular cases.

One could imagine exending the results of section 2 to the d dimensional case by defining "nondecreasing" and "convexity" for the matrix function $G(\cdot):R^{d+1} \to R^{d\times d}$ in such a way that steps (2.18)-(2.20) and steps (2.21)-(2.23) remain valid. For $\{\varepsilon_n\}_{n=1}^{\infty}$ i.i.d. The ordering $\leq^*$ on matrices defined by

$$A \leq^* B \quad \text{iff} \quad E\, V\,(A\varepsilon) \leq E\, V\,(B\varepsilon)$$

for all convex maps $V:R^d \to R$ will "work". Given an ordering on matrices define "nondecreasing" and "convexity" of G in the natural way: For all $\alpha \in [0,1]$, $X_1, X_2 \in R^d$ $X_1 \leq X_2 \Rightarrow G(X_1) \leq^* G(X_2)$ and

$$G(\alpha X_1 + (1 - \alpha)X_2) \leq^* \alpha\, G(X_1) + (1 - \alpha)G(X_2)$$

respectively.

But we have not characterized $\leq^*$. Locating and characterizing a useful ordering on matrices that will enable us to extend the section 2 results to multi-dimensions is an open problem.

[1] We thank J. Conlisk, W.D. Dechert, D. Gilat, and H. Weinberger for stimulating comments on this work as well as catching errors. Special thanks go to H. Weinberger for editorial aid and error catching. We also thank the NSF for research support. None of the above are responsible for errors or opinion contained in this article.

REFERENCES

1. Brock, William A., Michael Rothschild and Joseph E. Stiglitz: "Stochastic Capital Theory", Social Systems Research Institute Paper No. 8303.

2. Chow, Y.S., H. Robbins and D. Siegmund: Great Expectations: The Theory of Optimal Stopping (Boston: Houghton Mifflin, 1971).

3. Krylov, N.V., Controlled Diffusion Processes (New York: Springer-Verlag, 1980).

4. Miroshnichenko, T.P., "Optimal Stopping of the Integral of a Wiener Process". Theory of Probability and its Applications (1975), 20: 387-391.

THE COURNOT PROBLEM WITH BOUNDED MEMORY STRATEGIES

Yieh-Hei Wan
Department of Mathematics
State University of New York at Buffalo
Buffalo, New York 14214

1. COURNOT PROBLEM

In [1] Smale considered a repeated game with bounded memory. In this model, the players only kept some kind of average of the past outcomes in their memory, and decisions were based on this memory. Here, we aim to examine the classical Cournot problem from this viewpoint.

Consider two firms producing a homogeneous good. Denote by $q_i \in A_i = [0,L]$, the level of output of the ith firm, $i = 1,2$. Assume the price $p = \max\{0, a-(q_1 + q_2)\}$. The profit of the ith firm is given by $\pi_i = q_i p - cq_i$. Here, for simplicity, we take the constants c, a, L so that $0 < c < a \leq L$. Now, the total profit $\Pi = \pi_1 + \pi_2$ is a function of the total output $Q = q_1 + q_2$, given by

$$\Pi = Q(p - c) = \begin{cases} Q(a - c - Q) & \text{for } Q \leq a \\ -Qc & \phantom{\text{for }} Q > a \end{cases}.$$

This function has the following graph:

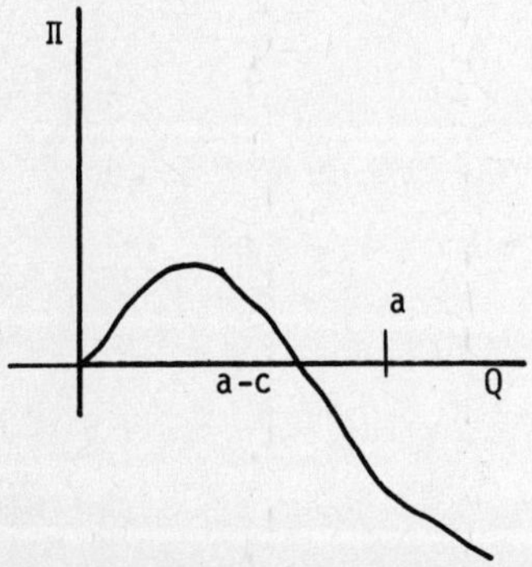

Figure 1

Π attains its maximum value Π_{max} at $Q = \frac{a - c}{2}$, and its minimum value Π_{min} at $Q = 2L$.

To gain better understanding of this problem, we take a game theoretical approach and we describe the map $\pi = (\pi_1, \pi_2): A \to X$ geometrically as Fig. 2 with $A = A_1 \times A_2 = [0,L] \times [0,L]$ and X = convex hull of $\pi(A)$.

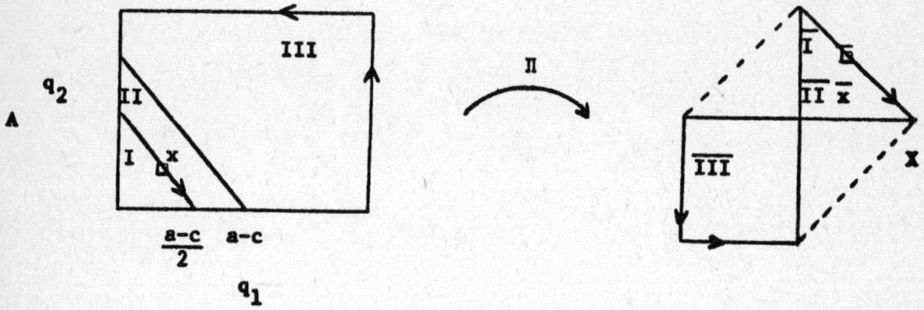

Figure 2

π is a fold map along $Q = \frac{a - c}{2}$, and $\pi(I) = \overline{I}$, $\pi(II) = \overline{II}$, $\pi(III) = \overline{III}$, $\pi(\square) = \overline{\square}$. Here, $x = \left(\frac{a - c}{3}, \frac{a - c}{3} \right)$ stands for the <u>Cournot output</u>, and $\square = \left(\frac{Q^*}{2}, \frac{Q^*}{2} \right)$, $Q^* = \frac{a - c}{2}$, the <u>collusion output</u>. The collusion output can be obtained when the two firms agree to act cooperatively. They maximize the total profit and share it evenly.

In this article, we aim to explain <u>why the collusion solution is likely to happen, when two competitive firms play the above game repeatedly</u>.

Following Smale [1], we adapt the bounded rationality to resolve this problem. Each firm chooses a "good" strategy. While competing with each other the best they can, a collusion solution will be reached asymptotically.

Section 2 is devoted to basic definitions and a precise statement of the main result. Section 3 contains a description of a class of good strategies and a proof of the main result. An extension of the main result to N firms $(N > 3)$ is given in the last Section.

2. BOUNDED MEMORY, DYNAMICS

To fix the idea, we use the following averaging procedure: given the average $\hat{x}_T$ over period 1 to period T, and the outcome X_{T+1} at period T + 1, the average $\hat{x}_{T+1}$ from period 1 to period T + 1 is given by $\hat{x}_{T+1} = \frac{\hat{x}_T + x_{T+1}}{2}$.

A continuous map $s_i : X \to A_i$ in which the ith firm takes the action $s_i(\hat{x}_T)$ for period T + 1 based on the average outcome $\hat{x}_T$ from period 1 to period T is called a <u>bounded memory strategy</u> for the ith firm. Once the bounded strategies $s = (s_1, s_2)$ are chosen, $\hat{x}_{T+1} = \frac{\hat{x}_T + \pi o x(\hat{x}_T)}{2}$ and one gets a <u>discrete autonomous system</u> on X (i.e. $\hat{x}_1, \hat{x}_2, \ldots$) generated by $x \to \frac{x + \pi o s(x)}{2}$. (s,x) is a (stationary) <u>solution</u> iff $x = \frac{x + \phi_s(x)}{2}$ or $x = \phi_s(x)$, where $\phi_s(x) = \pi o s(x)$. The solution (s,x) is <u>globally stable</u> if for every path $x_1, x_2, \ldots \to x$ as $n \to \infty$. The solution (s,x) is called a <u>Nash solution</u> iff, to each i, $x_i \geq x_i'$, for any solution (s',x') such that $s_j' = s_j$ with $j \neq i$. It has been proved in [1] that the Nash solutions defined above are also Nash equilibria considered as an extended solution for the associated supergame.

Clearly, what we have just defined (in this section) make sense for an N person game in normal form.

<u>Proposition</u> 1. (i.e. Proposition 1 in Wan [2]) (s,x) is a Nash solution iff to each i, $s_i(x)$ maximizes $\pi_i(a)$ subject to $s_j \circ \pi(a) = a_j$ for all $j \neq i$ with the maximum value x_i.

Proof: It suffices to observe: the possible outcomes for the ith firm by varying his strategy $s_i = \{\pi_i(a) | s_j \circ \pi(a) = a_j,$ for all $j \neq i\}$.

<u>Example</u>. (cf. [1]) The classical Nash solution is (i) a Nash solution, and (ii) globally stable.

Notice that $(\frac{\Pi_{max}}{2}, \frac{\Pi_{max}}{2})$ dominates all possible fair asymptotic solutions.

In the next section we define a class of strategies called good strategies and show that such strategies always exist. Our main result is the following:

Theorem D. If s_1 and s_2 are good strategies, $s = (s_1, s_2)$ and $x^* = \left(\frac{\pi_{max}}{2}, \frac{\pi_{max}}{2}\right)$,

(i) then (s, x^*) is a Nash solution, and

(ii) x^* is a globally stable solution of the system generated by $x \to \frac{x + \pi \circ s(x)}{2}$.

The assertion (i) means the two firms are competitive, and they yield the collusion solution x^*. The assertion (ii) shows that our resolution is rather robust.

3. GOOD STRATEGIES

We seek good strategies in the form: $s_i = s_i(\Pi)$, $\Pi_{min} \leq \Pi \leq \Pi_{max}$, $i = 1,2$, where $\Pi = \pi_1 + \pi_2$. Denote by $Q = Q(\Pi)$ the monotone decreasing inverse of $\Pi = \Pi(Q) = Q(p - c)$ $(Q(\Pi) \geq Q^*)$.

Definition 1. A bounded strategy $s_1 = s_1(\Pi)$ is said to be good if

(i) $s_1(\Pi_{max}) = Q^*/2$.

(ii) $Q^*/2 \leq s_1(\Pi) < Q(\Pi)/2$, for $\Pi < \Pi_{max}$

(iii) $\pi_2(s_1(\Pi), Q(\Pi) - s_1(\Pi)) < \Pi_{max}/2$, for $0 \leq \Pi < \Pi_{max}$

If each firm chooses the strategy $s_i = Q^*/2$, then, we obtain a globally stable collusion solution, which cannot be Nash. Conditions (i), (ii) indicate that our good strategy is a modification of the strategy $s_1 = Q^*/2$. Suppose the condition (iii) fails for some Π, $0 \leq \Pi < \Pi_{max}$, and the 2nd firm chooses $s_2 = Q(\Pi) - s_1(\Pi)$. Then the first firm can only get less than half of that total profit Π, and it is not acceptable for the first firm.

The strategy $s_1 = s_1(\Pi)$, s_1 is good iff the associated curve $\Pi \to (s_1(\Pi), Q(\Pi) - s_1(\Pi))$, $\Pi < \Pi_{max}$ lies in the triangle region $\{(q_1,q_2) | \frac{Q^*}{2} \leq q_1 < q_2, q_1 + q_2 \leq 2L\}$ minus the shaded region $\{(q_1,q_2) | \pi_2 \geq \frac{\Pi_{max}}{2}\}$ as described by Figure 3.

Combining steps (α) and (β), the proof of our Theorem D is completed.

4. EXTENSION TO N FIRMS ($N \geq 3$).

Now, consider N firms producing a homogeneous good, with the same linear cost function cq_i, and capacity, $0 \leq q_i \leq L$. The profit of the ith firm is given by $\pi_i = q_i p - cq_i$, with price $p = \max\{0, a - Q\}$, $Q = \sum q_i$ the total output. Again, for simplicity, we assume $0 < c < a \leq L$. As before, the toal profit $\Pi = \sum \pi_i$ is a function of the total output $Q = \sum q_i$, with graph given by Fig. 1. Denote by $Q = Q(\Pi)$ its monotone decreasing inverse with $Q(\Pi) \geq Q^* = \frac{a - c}{2}$.

By simple computations, we obtain the Cournot-Nash output $(\frac{a - c}{N + 1}, \ldots, \frac{a - c}{N + 1})$. and the collusion output $(\frac{Q^*}{N}, \ldots, \frac{Q^*}{N})$, with $Q^* = \frac{a - c}{2}$. The collusion solution $x^* = (\frac{\Pi_{max}}{N}, \ldots, \frac{\Pi_{max}}{N})$ dominates all the fair asymptotic solutions.

Our main result and its proof can be generalized to N firms as well.

Definition 2. A bounded strategy $s_1 = s_1(\Pi)$ is to be good if

(i) $s_1(\Pi_{max}) = Q^*/N$

(ii) $Q^*/N \leq s_1(\Pi) < Q(\Pi)/N$ for $\Pi < \Pi_{max}$

(iii) $\Pi_1'(s_1(\Pi), Q(\Pi) - s_1(\Pi)) < \frac{N - 1}{N} \Pi_{max} - \frac{N - 2}{N - 1} (\Pi_{max} - \Pi)$, for $0 \leq \Pi < \Pi_{max}$,

where $\Pi_1' = \pi_2 + \ldots + \pi_N = Q_1(p - c)$ is a function of q_1 and $Q_1 = q_2 + \ldots + q_N$.

If condition (iii) fails for some Π, and the aggregate output Q_1 for the firms other than the first becomes $Q(\pi) - s_1(\Pi)$, then the first firm can only obtain profit less than $\frac{\Pi}{N}$, with Π the total profit.

The strategy $s_1 = s_1(\Pi)$ is good iff the curve $(s_1(\Pi), Q(\Pi) - s_1(\Pi))$, $\Pi < \Pi_{max}$, lies in the region

$$\{(q_1, Q_1) | \frac{Q^*}{N} \leq q_1 < \frac{N - 1}{N} Q_1,\ q_1 + Q_1 \leq NL\}$$

$$\{(q_1, Q_1) | \Pi_1'(q_1, Q_1) \geq \frac{N - 1}{N} \Pi_{max} - \frac{N - 2}{N - 1} (\Pi_{max} - \Pi),\ \Pi \geq 0\}.$$

Since $\frac{N - 1}{N} \Pi_{max} - \frac{N - 2}{N - 1} (\Pi_{max} - \Pi) > \frac{N - 1}{N}$ II for $0 \leq \Pi < \Pi_{max}$, the region

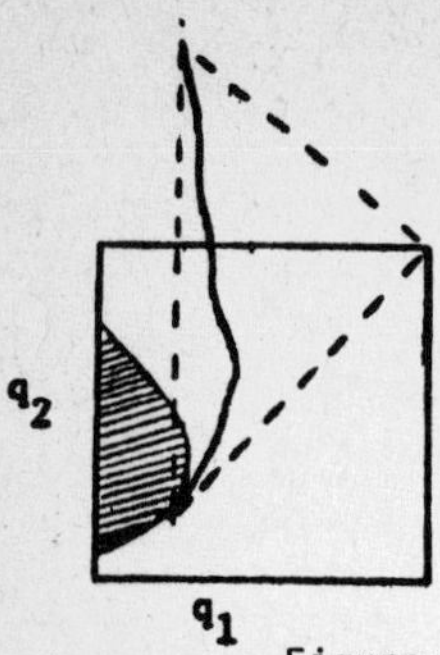

Figure 3

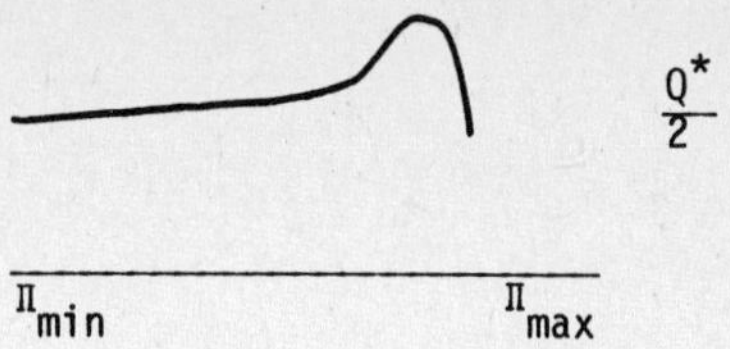

Figure 4

The shaded region has a smooth boundary $\pi_2 = \frac{\Pi_{max}}{2}$ and intersects the region $\{(q_1,q_2)|q_1 > q_2\}$ only at $\square = (\frac{Q^*}{2}, \frac{Q^*}{2})$. Therefore, one obtains the existence of good strategies as defined before. A possible graph of a good strategy is given by Figure 4.

Now, we present the proof of our Theorem D.

(α) It is not hard to establish that if s_2 is a good strategy,

$$\{(q_1,q_2)|s_2 \circ \pi(q) = q_2\} \subseteq \{(q_1,q_2)|q_1 < q_2\} \cup \{(Q(\Pi) - s_2(\Pi), s_2(\Pi))\}$$

(When $q_1 + q_2 < Q^*$, (q_1,q_2) is in the first set by (i) and (ii). When $q_1 + q_2 > Q^*$, $Q(\pi_1(q) + \pi_2(q)) = q_1 + q_2$, so (q_1,q_2) is in the second set.) Since $\pi_1(q_1,q_2) < \Pi_{max}/2$, on $q_1 < q_2$, and $\pi_1(Q(\Pi) - s_2(\Pi),s_2(\Pi)) < \Pi_{max}/2$, by (iii) of definition 1), one concludes that π_1 has a maximum at $(\frac{Q^*}{2},\frac{Q^*}{2})$ on the feasible set $\{(q_1,q_2)|S_2 \circ \pi(q) = q_2\}$. Similarly, π_2 has a maximum at $(\frac{Q^*}{2},\frac{Q^*}{2})$ on the feasible set $\{(q_1,q_2)|s_1 \circ \pi(q) = q_1\}$. Hence, (s,x^*) is a Nash solution by Proposition 1.

(β) Define $\Phi:[\Pi_{min},\Pi_{max}] \to [\Pi_{min},\Pi_{max}]$ by $\Phi(\Pi) = \pi_1 \circ s(\Pi) + \pi_2 \circ s(\Pi)$. From (ii) of definition 1 of good strategies, $Q^* < s_1(\Pi) + s_2(\Pi) < Q(\Pi)$. Since $Q(\Pi)$ is strictly decreasing, $\Phi(\Pi) > \Pi$ for $\Pi < \Pi_{max}$. Let $\Pi_T = \sum \hat{x}_T$ the total average profit at period T. For $\Pi_{T+1} = \frac{\Pi_T + \Phi(\Pi_T)}{2}$, $\Pi_T \nearrow \Pi_{max}$ as $T \to \infty$. Hence,

$$a_T = s(\Pi_T) \to s(\Pi_{max}) = (\frac{Q^*}{2},\frac{Q^*}{2}).$$

$$x_T = \pi(a_T) \to \pi(\frac{Q^*}{2},\frac{Q^*}{2}) = (\frac{\Pi_{max}}{2}, \frac{\Pi_{max}}{2}),$$

and $\hat{x}_T \to (\frac{\Pi_{max}}{2}, \frac{\Pi_{max}}{2})$ as $T \to \infty$.

$\{(q_1,Q_1)|\Pi_1' \geq \frac{N-1}{N}\Pi_{max} - \frac{N-2}{N-1}(\Pi_{max} - \Pi), \Pi \geq 0\}$ has a smooth boundary

$\Pi_1' = \frac{N-1}{N}\Pi_{max} - \frac{N-2}{N-1}(\Pi_{max} - \Pi)$, $\Pi \geq 0$, and meets the region $\{(q_1,Q_1)|(N-1)q_1 \geq Q_1\}$ only at $(\frac{Q^*}{N}, \frac{N-1}{N}Q^*)$. (cf. Fig. 5).

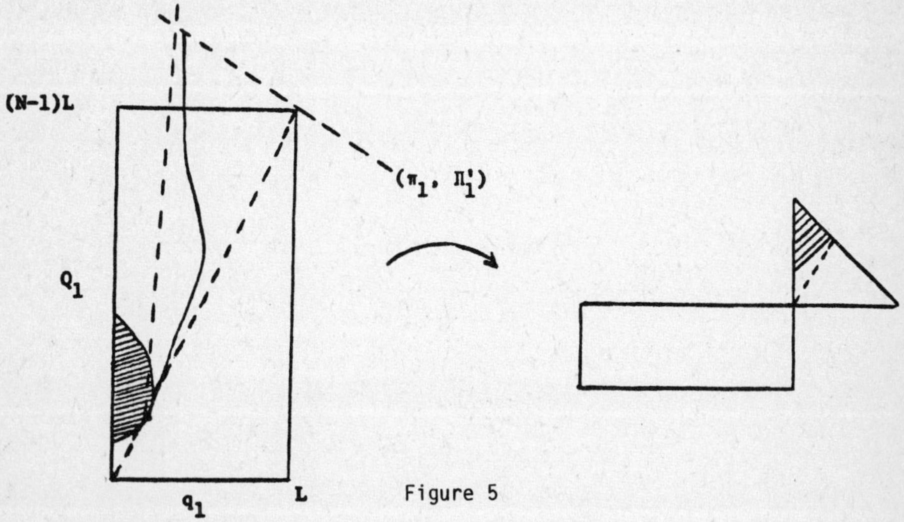

Figure 5

Hence, good strategies introduced in Definition 2 do <u>exist</u>, and their graphs look like those in Fig. 4.

<u>Lemma 1</u>. Set $S_1 = s_2 + \ldots + s_N$, $s_2,\ldots,s_N$ good strategies. Then

(i) $S_1(\Pi_{max}) = \frac{N-1}{N}Q^*$

(ii) $\frac{N-1}{N}Q^* \leq S_1(\Pi) < \frac{N-1}{N}Q(\Pi)$, for $\Pi < \Pi_{max}$

(iii) $\pi_1(Q(\Pi) - S_1(\Pi), S_1(\Pi)) < \frac{\Pi_{max}}{N}$, for $0 \leq \Pi < \Pi_{max}$

To see (iii), note that

$$(Q - s_2)(p - c) < \frac{N-1}{N}\Pi_{max} - \frac{N-2}{N-1}(\Pi_{max} - \Pi)$$
$$\vdots$$
$$(Q - s_N)(p - c) < \frac{N-1}{N}\Pi_{max} - \frac{N-2}{N-1}(\Pi_{max} - \Pi)$$

imply

$$[(N-1)Q - S_1](p - c) < \frac{(N-1)^2}{N}\Pi_{max} - (N-2)(\Pi_{max} - \Pi).$$

For $Q(p - c) = \Pi$, the above inequality becomes

$$(Q - S_1)(p - c) + (N - 2)\Pi < \frac{\Pi_{max}}{N} + (N - 2)\Pi \quad \text{or}$$

$$\pi_1(Q - S_1, S_1) = (Q - S_1)(p - c) < \frac{\Pi_{max}}{N}.$$

Theorem 0. If $s_1, s_2, \ldots, s_N$ are good strategies and $x^* = (\frac{\Pi_{max}}{N}, \ldots, \frac{\Pi_{max}}{N})$, then

(i) (s, x^*) is a Nash solution, and

(ii) x^* is a globally stable solution of $x \to \frac{x + \pi \circ s(x)}{2}$.

We present the proof of Theorem 0 in two steps.

(α) $\pi_1 = q_1(p - c)$ can be regarded as a function of q_1 and Q_1.

$$\{(q_1, Q_1) | s_j \circ \pi(q) = q_j, j \neq 1\} \subseteq \{(q_1, Q_1) | S_1(\Pi(Q)) = Q_1\}$$

$$\subseteq \{(q_1, Q_1) | (N - 1)q_1 < Q_1\} \cup \{(Q(\Pi) - S_1(\Pi), S_1(\Pi))\}$$

(by Lemma 1, (i), (ii)).

Since, $\pi_1 < \frac{\Pi_{max}}{N}$ on $\{(q_1, Q_1) | (N - 1)q_1 < Q_1\}$ and on $\{Q(\Pi) - S_1(\Pi), S_1(\Pi))\}$ (by Lemma 1, (iii)) π_1 has a maximum at $(\frac{Q^*}{N}, \frac{N - 1}{N} Q^*)$ on the feasible set $\{(q_1, Q_1) | s_j \circ \Pi(q) = q_j, j \neq 1\}$. By symmetry considerations, to each i, π_i has a maximum at $(\frac{Q^*}{N}, \ldots, \frac{Q^*}{N})$ on the set $\{(q_1, \ldots, q_N) | s_j \circ \pi(q) = q_j$, for all $j \neq i\}$. By Proposition 1, we conclude that (s, x^*) is a Nash solution.

(β) Define $\Phi: [\Pi_{min}, \Pi_{max}] \to [\Pi_{min}, \Pi_{max}]$ by $\Phi(\Pi) = \sum_i \pi_i(s, \Pi))$. From (ii) of definition 2, $Q^* < \sum_i s_i(\Pi) < Q(\Pi)$, and thus $\Phi(\Pi) > \Pi$ for $\Pi < \Pi_{max}$. Let $\Pi_T = \sum_i \hat{x}_T$. Then $\Pi_T \nearrow \Pi_{max}$ as $T \to \infty$. Hence, $a_T = s(\Pi_T) \to (\frac{Q^*}{N}, \ldots, \frac{Q^*}{N})$, $x_T \to x^*$, and $\hat{x}_T \to x^*$ as $T \to \infty$. This means that (s, x^*) is globally stable. Consequently, we finish the proof of Theorem 0.

Let us end this article by raising two questions.

Problem A. Establish similar results for Cournot problem with convexity hypotheses or unequal cost functions.

Problem B. Find suitable conditions on the payoff functions, so that one can generalize the main result in this report.

References

[1] S. Smale, The Prisoner's Dilemma and Dynamical Systems Associated to Non-Cooperative Games, Econometrica, 1981.

[2] Y.H. Wan, Nash solutions for games with bounded memory. Mathematical Modelling, Vol. 2, p. 1-18, 1981.

QUANTITY ADJUSTMENT IN AN ARROW-DEBREU-MCKENZIE TYPE MODEL*

William Novshek, California Institute of Technology
and Economics Department,
Stanford University, Stanford, California 94305

Hugo Sonnenschein, Economics Department,
Princeton University, Princeton, New Jersey 08540

1. Introduction

Our purpose is to examine long run entry/exit dynamics in a limit economy with infinitesimal firms and in Cournot economies (where firms recognize their influence on price) which are "close" to the limit economy. In the short run certain factors are immobile, and short run equilibrium prices reflect only the relative scarcity of factors that are instantaneously variable. The returns to immobile factors are not necessarily equalized. In the long run all factors are free to vary, and the factors that are immobile in the short run "flow towards that branch of production" in which there are profits to be realized. We formalize this in a long run entry/exit dynamics for a limit economy with infinitesimal firms. We also examine the long run dynamics in Cournot economies, with non-infinitesimal firms, because we view perfect competition as an idealization which should be interpreted as a limit of imperfect competition. With this view, the properties of the dynamics (and the equilibria) of the Cournot economies are the true objects of interest, and the dynamics (and the equilibria) of the limit economy are of interest only insofar as they represent limits of the results for a sequence of Cournot economies which converge to the limit economy. See Novshek and Sonnenschein [1983] for an extensive discussion of this point of view and the basic framework of the analysis. Here we amplify and extend the discussion of dynamics in that paper by explicitly treating decreasing returns to scale in the aggregate and also discussing the dynamics in the Cournot economies. Since we are interested in elucidating the ideas involved we make no effort to provide the most general results possible. Instead we intensively explore a

---

* We gratefully acknowledge the support of the National Science Foundation and our universities.

partial equilibrium example and briefly discuss the reasoning necessary to prove the general equilibrium results. Section 2 introduces the dynamics in a "perfectly competitive", partial equilibrium example. Section 3 extends the example to discuss the dynamics in Cournot markets which are "close" to the limit example of Section 2. Section 4 discusses the reasons behind the general equilibrium result that if the consumer sector acts as a single agent then there exists a unique perfectly competitive equilibrium and it is globally stable for the long run entry/exit dynamics. The results show that when the consumer sector acts as a single agent the dynamics and equilibria of the limit economy provide a good idealization of the results for a "close" Cournot economy with small (relative to the economy) but non-infinitesimal firms.

2. Dynamics in a "Perfectly Competitive" Partial Equilibrium Market: An Example

Consider a market for a single homogeneous good with inverse demand function $P(Y) = 3 + 2 \ln 2 - Y$ and a continuum of infinitesimal firms $\beta \in [0,\infty)$. The cost to firm β of producing output y is $c(y,0,\beta) = (1+\beta)/2 + y + y^2(1+\beta)/2$. Since the firm is infinitesimal it cannot affect aggregate output or market price. It must act as a price taker. In the short run the firm must pay the fixed cost $(1+\beta)/2$ whether or not it produces output. In the long run the firm can shut down completely and produce no output at cost zero. The firm's short run supply at price p is the output y which maximizes $py - c(y,0,\beta)$. This is $(p-1)/(1+\beta)$ if $p \geq 1$ and zero otherwise. In the long run the firm has the option of exiting and avoiding the fixed cost, so short run maximizers which lead to negative profit are not long run maximizers. The long run supply is $(p-1)/(1+\beta)$ if $p > 2 + \beta$, and zero if $p < 2 + \beta$. At $p = 2 + \beta$ the firm is indifferent between shutting down completely and producing output one.

In the short run the set of active firms is fixed. Suppose $\beta \in [0,b]$ are active. Then the short run equilibrium is an aggregate output $Y^*(b)$, and a price $P(Y^*(b))$, such that the integral of the active firms' optimal responses to price $P(Y^*(b))$ is $Y^*(b)$: that is, $Y^*(b) = \int_0^b \{[P(Y^*(b)) - 1]/(1+\beta)\}\, d\beta$. This is a well defined function of b. Similarly, the long run equilibrium is an output Y^* and price $P(Y^*)$ such that $Y^* = \int_{\{\beta | P(Y^*) \geq 2+\beta\}} \{[P(Y^*) - 1]/(1 + \beta)\} d\beta$, where the set of active firms is endogenously determined ($\beta \leq P(Y^*) - 2$). Given our functional form for P, $Y^* = 2 \ln 2$, $P(Y^*) = 3$, and $\beta^* = 1$ is the marginal firm, that is, the least efficient active firm.

Before discussing the long run, entry/exit dynamics it is natural to discuss the short run dynamics. We consider three stages of dynamics, and assume each stage is "instantaneous" relative to the next stage. In the first stage, given any aggregate output Y, price adjusts to P(Y). This is the usual tatonnement price dynamics (price changes in proportion to $P^{-1}(p) - Y$) and it is stable since inverse demand is downward sloping. The second stage is quantity adjustment among the active firms ($\beta \in [0,b]$) till the short run equilibrium is attained. We assume firms are myopic in their adjustment: If Y(t) is the aggregate output at time t then the corresponding price is P(Y(t)) and firm β's desired output is $[P(Y(t)) - 1]/(1 + \beta)$ (assuming $Y(t) \leq 2 + 2 \ln 2$). If its current output is $y(\beta,t)$ we assume the firm changes its output in proportion to the difference between its desired output at the current price and its actual output:

$\dot{y}(\beta,t) = [P(Y(t)) - 1]/(1 + \beta) - y(\beta,t)$. The rate of change of aggregate output is

$$\dot{Y}(t) = \int_0^b \{[P(Y(t)) - 1]/(1 + \beta) - y(\beta,t)\} d\beta$$

$$= [P(Y(t)) - 1] \int_0^b (1/(1 + \beta)) d\beta - Y(t).$$

It is easy to see that this is stable. If $Y(t) > Y^*(b)$ then $P(Y(t)) < P(Y^*(b))$ and $\dot{Y}(t) < [P(Y^*(b)) - 1] \int_0^b (1/(1 + \beta)) d\beta - Y^*(b) = 0$. Similarly, $Y(t) < Y^*(b)$ implies $\dot{Y}(t) > 0$. Stability follows from the fact that the inverse demand curve cuts the short run supply from above. We assume this short run adjustment is instantaneous relative to the long run entry/exit adjustment.

The third stage consists of the entry/exit dynamics. We assume that firms with the greatest incentive act first. Since firms' efficiencies are ordered by

β, if in the short run equilibrium with active firms $\beta \in [0,b]$, firm b receives strictly positive (strictly negative) profit then firms with β just above (just below) b enter (exit). We assume the rate of entry is proportional to the profit "on the margin":

$$\dot{b}(\tau) = P(Y^*(b(\tau)))\ [P(Y^*(b(\tau))) - 1]/(1 + b(\tau)) - c([P(Y^*(b(\tau))) - 1]/(1 + b(\tau)),\ 0,\ b(\tau)).$$

This is also stable since $b(\tau) \lesseqgtr 1$ implies the profit of firm $b(\tau) \gtreqless 0$. This follows from the fact that inverse demand cuts the long run supply curve from above.

3. Dynamics in a Cournot Partial Equilibrium Market: The Example Continued

For each $\alpha > 0$ consider a market $M(\alpha)$ with inverse demand as in Section 2 but a countable infinity of firms $j \in \{1,2,3,\dots\}$. In $M(\alpha)$ the cost to firm j of producing output y is $c(y,\alpha,j\alpha) = \alpha(1 + j\alpha)/2 + y + y^2(1 + j\alpha)/2\alpha$. Firms are not infinitesimal so aggregates are found by summation.

In what sense does $M(\alpha)$ converge to the market in Section 2 as α converges to zero? First notice that the average cost for firm j to produce y in market $M(\alpha)$ is

$$\begin{aligned} c(y,\alpha,j\alpha)/y &= \alpha(1 + j\alpha)/2y + 1 + y(1 + j\alpha)/2\alpha \\ &= c(y/\alpha,0,j\alpha)/(y/\alpha) \end{aligned}$$

which is the average cost for β to produce y/α in the limit market. Thus the average cost curves in $M(\alpha)$ are just rescalings of corresponding average cost curves in the limit market. Second, note that the social cost function for aggregate output in $M(\alpha)$, $C(Y,\alpha) = \min\ \{\sum_{j=1}^{\infty} c(y_j,\alpha,j\alpha)\ |\ \sum_{j=1}^{\infty} y_j = Y\}$, converges to the social cost function for aggregate output in the limit market,

$$C(Y) = \min\ \{\int_0^{\infty} c(y(\beta),0,\beta)d\beta\ \Big|\ \int_0^{\infty} y(\beta)d\beta = Y\}.$$

Thus the markets $M(\alpha)$ converge to the limit market both in terms of the distribution of firm types and the aggregate production possibilities.

The equilibrium concept in $M(\alpha)$ is Cournot equilibrium (Nash equilibrium in quantities). In the short run, if firms $j \in \{1,2,\ldots,J\}$ are active in $M(\alpha)$, $\{y_1,\ldots,y_J\}$ is a short run equilibrium if for all $j \in \{1,2,\ldots,J\}$, for all $y \geq 0$ $P(\sum_{i=1}^{J} y_i)y_j - c(y_j,\alpha,j\alpha) \geq P(\sum_{i=1}^{J} y_i - y_j + y)y - c(y,\alpha,j\alpha)$. In the long run firms are free to enter and leave so $\{y_1, y_2,\ldots\}$ is an equilibrium if for all $j \in \{1,2,\ldots\}$, for all $y \geq 0$,

$$P(\sum_{i=1}^{\infty} y_i)y_j - c(y_j,\alpha,j\alpha) \geq P(\sum_{i=1}^{\infty} y_i - y_j + y)y - c(y,\alpha,j\alpha)$$

and $P(\sum_{i=1}^{\infty} y_i)y_j - c(y_j,\alpha,j\alpha) \geq 0$.

It is easy to show that for any α and J there is a unique short run equilibrium. It is also possible to show that the difference between the aggregate output in the short equilibrium for $M(\alpha)$ with (the greatest integer less than or equal to) b/α firms and the aggregate short run equilibrium output in the limit market with firms $\beta \in [0,b]$ is on the order of α.

It is possible to show that for all α a long run equilibrium exists, though it is not always unique. However, the difference between the aggregate output in any long run equilibrium for $M(\alpha)$ and the aggregate output in the long run equilibrium for the limit market is on the order of α. Thus, in terms of short and long run equilibria, the limit market provides a good idealization of the results for Cournot markets $M(\alpha)$ with α small.

We now turn to the dynamics in $M(\alpha)$. The first stage dynamics, the tatonnement, are identical to those in the limit market since they do not depend at all on firms. The second stage adjustment to the short run equilibrium is analogous to the second stage in the limit market, but firms' desired outputs are determined as Cournot "best responses" rather than price taking best responses. If $\{y_1(t),\ldots,y_J(t)\}$ are the current outputs of firms then firm j's desired production level is $r(\sum_{i\neq j} y_i(t),\alpha,j\alpha) := \alpha(2 + 2\ln 2 - \sum_{i\neq j} y_i(t))/(1 + 2\alpha + j\alpha)$ which is the optimal output for firm j if the aggregate output of other firms is fixed at $\sum_{i\neq j} y_i(t)$. Firms are myopic and change their output in proportion to the difference between current desired output and current actual output, $\dot{y}_j(t) = r(\sum_{i\neq j} y_i(t),\alpha,j\alpha) - y_j(t)$. This short run dynamic adjustment process is stable. The properties of the adjustment process are quite similar to the properties for stage 2 in the limit market. This is most easily seen by assuming all firm's outputs are bounded by $K\alpha$ for some finite K. Then the difference between $r(\sum_{i \neq j} y_i(t), \alpha, j\alpha)$ and $s(P(\sum_{i=1}^{J} y_i(t)), \alpha, j\alpha)$ (where $s(P(\sum_{i=1}^{J} y_i(t)), \alpha, j\alpha) := \alpha(P(\sum_{i=1}^{J} y_i(t)) - 1)/(1 + j\alpha)$ is the optimal response of a price taking firm with cost function $c(y, \alpha, j\alpha)$ facing price $P(\sum_{i=1}^{J} y_i(t)))$ is on the order of α^2, and the adjustment process for a Cournot competitor is approximately the same as for a price taking firm.

In the long run, additional firms enter if they see profit opportunities at the current short run equilibrium. As in the limit market, we assume that firms with the greatest incentive act first. Firms are myopic when making their entry decisions, recognizing their own effect on price but believing that the output of other firms will not change after entry. This process is also stable in the sense that it will converge to some long run equilibrium from any starting point. Recall that all long run equilibria are approximately the same--differences in aggregate output are on the order of α and each aggregate output differs from 2 ln 2 by a term on the order of α. There exists a K such that if the set of active firms is $\{1,2,\ldots,J(\alpha)\}$ and $J(\alpha)/\alpha$ differs from 1 by more than $K\alpha$ then the entry/exit decision of the "marginal" Cournot firm is the same as the entry/exit decision of a price taking firm with the same cost function facing the current short run equilibrium price.

4. General Equilibrium

We now turn to the dynamics in general equilibrium. We will only sketch the framework. The reader is referred to Novshek and Sonnenschein [1983] and the references therein for details. Production sets rather than cost functions are used to define production possibilities for each firm. It is now possible for different firms to operate in different "industries" producing different outputs or using different inputs. The feedback effects of profits must be taken into account when determining prices which clear markets, and in general, the general equilibrium inverse demand function P (which depends on a vector of outputs of different commodities) may need to be a selection from an inverse demand correspondence. The consumer sector is defined in terms of a set of consumers each with preferences, an initial endowment of goods, and ownership shares of firms. In the limit economy each "industry" is made up of a continuum of infinitesimal firms, and decreasing returns to scale in the aggregate are allowed (that is, firms within an "industry" may differ in their productive efficiencies). The Cournot economy $E(\alpha)$ is defined in a manner analogous to the definition of $M(\alpha)$ in Section 3, and Cournot economies converge to the limit economy as α converges to zero. The three stages of dynamics in general equilibrium are analogous to the three stages in partial equilibrium. The relationship between the dynamics and equilibria of $E(\alpha)$ and the dynamics and equilibria of the limit economy are analogous to the relationships in the partial equilibrium example[1] so for simplicity we will only discuss the dynamics in the limit economy. Our purpose is to explain the reasoning behind the following result.

<u>Theorem</u>: If the consumer sector acts as a single agent with a differentiable demand function then there exists a unique equilibrium and it is globally stable for the long run entry/exit dynamics.

When the consumer sector acts as a single consumer it is well known that there is a unique equilibrium. The equilibrium allocation is the unique bundle which maximizes the single consumer's preference level subject to the production possibilities available in the aggregate. The equilibrium prices are the unique supporting prices for the consumer's choice of the equilibrium bundle. It is also

---

1 However, additional complications may arise for long run equilibrium. A long run equilibrium may not exist for some arbitrarily small α. Even for those α though, when the consumer sector acts as a single consumer the long run entry/exit dynamics in $E(\alpha)$ will "converge" to the long run equilibrium of the limit economy in the following sense. For any $\varepsilon > 0$, for α sufficiently small, starting from any point the dynamics in $E(\alpha)$ will lead to aggregate outputs which eventually all lie in an ε neighborhood of the long run equilibrium of the limit economy.

well known that with a single consumer, for any aggregate production vector Y there is a unique vector of supporting prices, so the general equilibrium inverse demand function P(Y) is well defined.

Before discussing the entry/exit dynamics it is natural to examine the first and second stage dynamics. With a single consumer it is well known that the first stage tatonnement is globally stable: for any Y, prices converge to P(Y). For a fixed set of active firms the short run equilibrium allocation is the unique bundle which maximizes the consumer's preference level subject to the production possiblities available in the aggregate with this fixed set of active firms. The stability of the short run adjustment process follows from the observation that any change in a firm's output moving in the direction of higher profit for the firm at the current prices must move aggregate output in a direction that increases the consumers preference level. (Since the current prices are supporting prices for the consumer's choice of the current bundle, the consumer's indifference surface--the set of equally preferred bundles--through the current bundle is tangent to the set of aggregate outputs with profit equal to the current aggregate profit at the current prices.) The short run adjustment process continues until the consumer's preference level cannot be increased given the production possibilities available to the fixed set of active firms. Thus this process converges to the short run equilibrium.

In the long run, entry (exit) in any "industry" takes place in proportion to the current profit received by the firm on the margin (the least efficient active firm) in that industry in the current short run equilibrium. Proof of the stability of this process follows from the observation that entry or exit takes place if and only if the new short run aggregate production set increases the preference level available to the single consumer in short run equilibrium. The reasoning as exactly as for the second stage short run dynamics. The long run entry/exit adjustment continues until the preference level of the consumer cannot be increased. This occurs at the unique long run equilibrium. Note that the relative speeds of adjustment in the different industries played no role in the argument.

5. Conclusion

We have sketched the quantity adjustment dynamics for an Arrow-Debreu-McKenzie type general equilibrium model and shown that when the consumer sector acts as a single agent the dynamics are globally stable. What happens when the consumer sector does not act as a single agent? In Novshek and Sonnenschein [1983] we present a simple, nonpathological, general equilibrium example with two consumers, two commodities, and identical firms. This economy has a unique long run equilibrium which is independent of the fraction of each firm owned by the first consumer (since profit is zero in long run equilibrium). However, the stability of long run entry/exit dynamics depends on the fraction of each firm owned by the first consumer. In general, the stability properties of the second and third stage dynamics depend on the local properties of the Walras correspondence, P(Y), which have not yet been fully characterized.

References

Novshek, William and Hugo Sonnenschein, [1983], "General Equilibrium with Free Entry: A Synthetic Approach to the Theory of Perfect Competition", California Institute of Technology, Social Science Working Paper 497.

CONVERGENCE OF MYOPIC FIRMS TO LONG-RUN EQUILIBRIUM VIA THE METHOD OF CHARACTERISTICS

Philippe Artzner

Institut de Recherche
Mathematique Avancee
Universite Louis Pasteur, Strasbourg

Carl P. Simon

Institute for Mathematics and its Applications
University of Minnesota
Minneapolis, Minnesota 55455
and
Departments of Economics and Mathematics
University of Michigan
Ann Arbor, MI 48109

Hugo Sonnenschein

Department of Economics
Princeton University
Princeton, New Jersey 08544

Sonnenschein (1981, 1982) models the evolution of firms from short run to long run equilibrium. The short run equilibrium is based on Rosen's (1974) model of an economy with a continuum of differentiated products and a continuum of consumers. The economy contains a standard commodity, the numeraire, amounts of which are denoted by y, and a one-dimensional continuum of differentiated products, which are parametrized by a type index x that lies on the circle. Each consumer demands one unit of one type of the differentiated commodity, and each firm produces exactly one type of commodity at each point in time. Given an initial distribution of firms, the initial equilibrium price function for commodities is defined by the condition that supply equals demand for all commodities. As time evolves, firms adjust the commodity they produce. They perform this adjustment in a myopic way by maximizing the rate of change in profit subject to a quadratic cost of adjustment. This has them move in the direction of higher profit at a velocity which is proportional to the rate of change of profit and defines a vector field. The specification of the differentiated product and the availiability of a continuum of firms provides a natural setting in which one can make precise the idea that firms are myopic. As firms move, the density of firms changes and prices are assumed to adjust continually so that at each instant the economy is in short run equilibrium. As prices change, the gradient of profit changes, which leads to further changes in the distribution of firms, and so on. The process comes to a halt only when profits are everywhere the same.

The above model is used to study the possibility of convergence over time to the unique equal-profit equilibrium. Such convergence might not be expected since firms know only the prices charged by their closest neighbors and no future prices. Since the distribution of firms which occurs at the long run equilibrium is the only distribution consistent with Pareto optimality, the analysis helps us to understand when it is the case that short run profits of nearby firms provide adequate signals for guiding an economy effectively toward an efficient allocation of resources.

Sonnenschein gave an explicit description of the evolution of the distribution of firms for only a very special example. An important assumption in his presentation was that the demand behavior of the consumer sector is of the class generated by a single consumer. Let us call such demand behavior "single consumer demand". Sonnenschein argued that convergence should hold for a rather general class of economies with single consumer demand by showing that, as the firms myopically adjusted their product, single consumer utility increased and thus was a Lyapunov function for the process. Nothing general was established about the specific form of the evolution of the distribution of firms, the evolution of the profile of profits, the movement of individual firms, etc.

The purpose of this paper is to provide a finer and more rigorous analysis of the problem of convergence to long run equilibrium in a setting with a continuum of commodities and myopic firms. Since Novshek and Sonnenschein (1983) provide an example of a simple economy with <u>two</u> consumers in which such convergence does not occur, we assume that there is but one consumer in the economy. However, the formal analysis also covers the case of a continuum of consumers who generate "single consumer demand" in the aggregate.[1] In addition, we place the product types on the real line, a setting which seems more natural than the circle. Although we restrict attention in this paper to the very simple technologies considered in Sonnenschein's special example, we allow fairly general preferences for the consumer sector. Using the method of characteristics from the theory of partial differential equations, we are able to say quite a lot about the form of convergence to equilibrium. In particular, we are able to show that the movement of individual firms is monotonic, i.e., a firm which adjusts its production to a product that is "more to the right" will continue to do so until equilibrium is reached. In addition, the profit obtained from producing a particular commodity type will either rise forever or fall forever, as long as it continues to be produced. Product types which yield highest or lowest profits will continue to do so as the distribution evolves; the difference between the maximum and minimum levels of profit will decrease monotonically to zero.

Novshek and Sonnenschein (1984) also study entry/exit dynamics as the economy moves from a short run equilibrium to a long-run one. Our approach differs from theirs most significantly with respect to the assumption here that firms use only local information about prices in determining their adjustment of product choice over time. This comes about naturally because firms are assumed to pay a cost of adjustment which is significant relative to their profits. With only local price information used, one expects that it is less likely for the distribution of firms to converge to the long-run distribution. However, there appears to be enough system-wide information in the short-run equilibrium prices to force convergence, at least with "single consumer demand". In the cases considered here, the convergence is monotone in every essential dimension.

This paper is organized as follows. In Section 1, we define and characterize the short run equilibrium with the distribution of firms fixed. In Section 2, we explain how firms change the choice of product they produce, analyze the resulting dynamics, establish convergence to long-run equilibrium, and study the nature of this convergence.

1. Short Run Equilibrium

We consider a one-consumer (private-ownership) economy with a numeraire commodity, called leisure, and a continuum of other commodities, called food types. There is a continuum of competitive firms and a continuum of (identical) simple technologies for producing food from leisure. The consumer chooses an amount of leisure and a measure on the food types. These measures are called menus. Given prices for foods, the consumer is constrained to pick an amount of leisure and a menu such that the value of his choice does not exceed his income. In the short run the distribution of firms is fixed and demand must equal supply for each of the food types and for leisure.

We begin the formalism by defining the commodity space and prices.

We denote amounts of leisure by non-negative quantities: y, $\bar{y}$, y', etc.

We index food types by real numbers x, x', etc., which form a compact interval $X = [a,b]$ on the real line.

Menus are positive measures on X, the set of food types, which have cumulative distribution functions (c.d.f.) that are piecewise continuously differentiable. The set of menus is denoted by $\mathcal{M}$.

Price systems are Lebesgue measurable, real-valued functions on X.

A consumption plan or leisure-menu bundle is an element of $R_+ \times \mathcal{M}$, i.e., an amount of leisure and a menu.

The firm side of the economy is modeled as follows. There is a unit mass of firms, each of which is to be considered infinitesimal and each of which produces a single food type. A firm that produces the food of type x does so by converting one (infinitesimal) unit of leisure into an (infinitesimal) unit of food x. The initial distribution of firms will be specified by a measure μ_0 of mass one on the interior of X. In the short run, firms are forced to stay in the market; because of the special form of the technology, they must demand one infinitesimal unit of labor and supply one infinitesimal unit of food, independent of prices. These choices by the firms are profit maximizing, since they have no alternative. Note that at the price system $p(x)$, the profit of a firm producing food of type x is $p(x) - 1$. If there are no firms in a subinterval of X, then there is no production of food or demand for labor in that interval. Because of the special form of the technologies, the amount of food supplied of type no-greater than x is also the amount of labor demanded by the firms producing those foods, for all x.

Formally, μ_0 is the initial distribution of firms. We assume that μ_0 has all the properties that menus in $\mathcal{M}$ have. In addition, $\mu_0(X) = 1$. The amount of food supplied of type no greater than x is $\mu_0((-\infty,x]) = F_{\mu_0}(x)$, where F_{μ_0} is the cumulative distribution function (c.d.f.) of μ_0.

We next specify preferences and define short-run equilibrium. The consumer starts with an initial endowment of leisure; he takes prices as given and picks the most preferred leisure-menu bundle that he can afford. In short-run equilibrium, supply equals demand given the initial distribution of firms.

Formally, $U:R_+ \times \mathcal{M} \to R$ is a utility function; and $\bar{y}$ in R_+ is the initial endowment of leisure.

A short-run Walrasian price system for the economy $\mathcal{E} = (U,\bar{y},\mu_0)$ is a price system $p(x)$ such that

$$(1) \qquad y' + \int_X p(x)d\mu'(x) > (\bar{y} - 1) + \int_X p(x)d\mu_0(x)$$

whenever $U(y',\mu') > U(\bar{y} - 1,\mu_0)$.

To understand (1), note that the income of the consumer depends on the price system p and is equal to his initial holding of numeraire plus the integral of the profit-maximizing actions of the firms. Since, in total, firms must demand one unit of leisure as input and produce the measure μ_0 of food, the sum of the value of the consumer's $\bar{y}$ units of leisure plus his dividends from the firms is

$$I(p) = \bar{y} + \int_X (p(x) - 1)d\mu_0(x) .$$

This is equal to the right hand side of the first inequality in (1). Thus, when (1) is satisfied, the consumer maximizes utility on the budget set defined by $(p,I(p))$ by choosing the bundle $(\bar{y} - 1,\mu_0)$. In equilibrium, the supply of leisure is $\bar{y}$; it is matched by the consumer's demand for leisure $(\bar{y} - 1)$ plus the firms' demands for leisure

$$\int_X d\mu_0(x) = 1.$$

Similarly, the demand for foods (μ_0) is equal to the supply. Finally, because firms have a trivial technology, profits are maximized when the supply is μ_0, independent of prices.

For concreteness, we will work with utility functions of the form:

(2) $$U(y,\mu) = y + \int_X W(x,G_\mu(x))d\mu(x) \;, \quad \mu \in \mathcal{M},$$

where W is a continuously differentiable (C^1) non-negative function and G_μ is the c.d.f. associated with μ. In many situations the consumer may have a preferred distribution G_λ of characteristics arising from a probability measure λ. For example, (2) might have the form

(3) $$\begin{aligned} U(y,\mu) &= y + \int_X [k - \psi(G_\lambda(x),G_\mu(x))]d\mu(x) \\ &= y + k\mu(X) - \int_X \psi(G_\lambda(x), G_\mu(x))d\mu(x) \;, \end{aligned}$$

where ψ is a C^1 distance-like function[2] on R^+ and k is a positive constant, chosen large enough so that $k - \psi$ is positive over the relevant range. Note the trade-off in the last two terms in (3); the consumer is rewarded for menus of larger mass but penalized for menus which deviate from his preferred menu λ. One can write (3) more generally as

(4) $$U(y,\mu) = y + k\mu(X) - \int_X Z(x,G_\mu(x))G_\mu'(x)dx$$

where $Z(x,z)$ is a non-negative C^1 function which for each x has a unique local minimum at a point $z = G_\lambda(x)$.

Sonnenschein (1982) works with Lebesgue measure on $[0,1]$ as the preferred λ and with $\psi(x,z) = (x - z)^2$. In our context, the utility function in his paper[3] would be

(5) $$U(y,\mu) = y + \mu(X) - \int_X (x - G_\mu(x))^2 d\mu(x) \;.$$

PROPOSITION 1. <u>Suppose that the utility function</u> U <u>has the form</u> (2) <u>where</u> W <u>is a</u> C^1 <u>positive function</u>. <u>If</u> p <u>is a differentiable equilibrium price for the economy</u> $\mathcal{E} = (U,\bar{y},\mu_0)$, <u>then</u>

(6) $$p'(x) = \frac{\partial W}{\partial x}(x,G_{\mu_0}(x)) \quad \text{for all } x \text{ in } X \text{ and}$$

(7) $$p(b) = W(b,1) \;.$$

<u>Proof</u>: In equilibrium the consumer must

(8) $$\begin{aligned} &\text{maximize } U(y,\mu) \text{ on the constraint set} \\ &y + \int_X p(x)d\mu(x) \le (\bar{y} - 1) + \int_X p(x)d\mu_0(x). \end{aligned}$$

Since U is increasing in y, all income is spent at the maximizer and the constraint becomes an equality constraint. Substituting from the constraint into (2) yields:

$$\tilde{U}(\mu) = \{(\bar{y} - 1) + \int_X p(x)d\mu_0(x)\} - \int_X[p(x) - W(x,G_\mu(x))]G_\mu'(x)dx .$$

By the usual necessary conditions in the Calculus of Variations[4], the G_μ which maximizes $\tilde{U}$ subject to the constraint $G_\mu(a) = 0$ must satisfy Euler's equation

$$(9) \qquad p'(x) = \frac{\partial W}{\partial x}(x,G_\mu(x))$$

and the free boundary condition

$$(10) \qquad p(b) = W(b,G_\mu(b)) .$$

Because the economy is in equilibrium, μ must equal μ_0 in (9) and (10) and $G_\mu(b) = \mu(X) = \mu_0(X) = 1$ in (10). □

In the next section we will prove that, under some mild hypotheses, such economies converge over time to a long run equilibrium in which all firms are realizing the same profit. By (7) and the condition that W is positive, the long run equilibrium price will be positive. If we further require that $W > 1$, then long run profits will also be positive. Firms may be willing to experience some negative profits along the path toward a long-run positive-profit equilibrium. One can also add further assumptions to the utility function in (2) or (4) which would guarantee positive profits along the whole time path.

Equation (9) can be considered as an inverse demand function. The function G_μ which satisfies (9):

$$(11) \qquad G_\mu(x) = \Phi(x,p'(x))$$

can be considered as an infinitesimal demand function which indicates how much of each food type will be chosen when the price system is $p(x)$. For the utility function (5) in Sonnenschein (1982), (9) and (11) become

$$(12) \qquad p'(x) = 2[G_\mu(x) - x] \qquad G_\mu(x) = x + \frac{1}{2}p'(x) .$$

Of course, in order for (9) to be a true inverse demand relation, we need to know that (9) and (10) are sufficient, not just necessary, to determine a solution of (8). Because (2) is linear in G'_μ, most of the usual second order sufficiency conditions of the Calculus of Variations do not apply. Basically, we need $U(y,\mu)$ to be concave or at least quasi-concave in μ.

PROPOSITION 2. If U is concave in (y,μ), then any positive C^1 function which satisfies (6) and (7) is an equilibrium price system for $\mathcal{E} = (\overline{U},y,\mu_0)$.

Proof: This is just the general theorem that first order conditions are also sufficient for concave functions. See, for example, Kamien and Schwartz (1981, p. 41).

Remark. The equilibrium menus will always have mass one because the distribution of firms is given by a measure of mass one and there is no free disposal. Negative prices may be required in order to bribe the consumer to take more of some commodities and thus move further from his ideal distribution. If the utility function (3) is such that a consumer, facing problem (8), will always choose a menu of mass one, then one can say a bit more. [For example, assume that the consumer needs a unit mass of food to survive but is shot for gluttony if he takes more than one unit.] In this case, note that we can always add a constant to any $p(x)$ which satisfies the constraint in (8) and still satisfy this constraint. By this means, we can keep prices positive and, if desired, greater than one in order to keep profits positive for all firms at all times. The free boundary condition (10) in the calculus of variations problem of Proposition 1 is, in this case, replaced by the boundary condition: $G_\mu(b) = 1$. Since (10) is no longer a necessary condition, W need not be positive in order for long run equilibrium prices to be positive, and consequently the constant k in (3), (4), and (5) can be chosen as zero.

In this case, it is easy to see that a generalization of the utility function (5), namely

$$U(y,\mu) = y - \int_X \Psi(x - G_\mu(x))d\mu(x) , \tag{13}$$

where Ψ is a convex function, is concave in μ. For, let $P(z)$ be an antiderivative of $\Psi(z)$. Since

$$\frac{d}{dx} P(x - G_\mu(x)) = \Psi(x - G_\mu(x))\,(1 - G'_\mu(x)) ,$$

(13) can be written as

$$(14)\qquad \begin{aligned} U(y,\mu) &= y - \int_X \Psi(x - G_\mu(x))dx + P(x - G_\mu(x))\Big|_{x=a}^{x=b} \\ &= y - \int_X \Psi(x - G_\mu(x))dx + [P(b - 1) - P(a)] . \end{aligned}$$

Since the last term is independent of μ and Ψ is convex, U is a concave function of (y,μ).

It is worthwhile to note that for the case where μ lies in $\mathcal{M}_1$, the convex subset of $\mathcal{M}$ consisting of the measures of total mass 1, and U is of the form (13), a direct calculation shows that the first order condition (6) is also sufficient for equilibrium.

PROPOSITION 2'. *If* U *has the form* (13) *where* $\Psi(z)$ *is a* C^1 *convex function, if menus are restricted to probability measures, if* G_{μ_0} *is a given c.d.f., and if* $p(x)$ *satisfies* (6):

$$(15)\qquad p'(x) = \Psi'(x - G_{\mu_0}(x)) ,$$

then p *is an equilibrium price system for the economy* $\mathcal{E} = (U,\bar{y},\mu_0)$.

Proof: Let (y',ν) be another leisure-menu bundle in $R_+ \times \mathcal{M}_1$. Suppose $U(y',\nu) > U(y,\mu_0)$. Then

$$\begin{aligned} 0 &< U(y',\nu) - U(y,\mu_0) \\ &= (y' - y) + \int_X [\Psi(x - G_{\mu_0}(x)) - \Psi(x - G_\nu(x))]dx && \text{by (14)} \\ &< (y' - y) + \int_X \Psi'(x - G_{\mu_0}(x))(G_\nu(x) - G_{\mu_0}(x))dx && \text{by concavity} \\ &= (y' - y) + \int_X p'(x)\,(G_{\mu_0}(x) - G_\nu(x))dx && \text{by (15)} \\ &= (y' - y) + \int_X p(x)(G'_\nu(x) - G'_{\mu_0}(x))dx && \text{by integration by parts} \end{aligned}$$

Therefore,

$$y + \int_X p(x)\, G'_{\mu_0}(x)dx < y' + \int p(x)\, G'_\nu(x)\, dx$$

at price system $p(x)$. Any bundle which gives more utilty than (y,μ_0) costs more at price system $p(x)$. ⊢

2. Dynamics to Long Run Equilibrium

A. Definition of the Decentralized Dynamics

Section 1 describes a short run equilibrium at a fixed moment of time. This section will describe the time evolution of the distribution of firms, as the firms move guided by a decision rule based on the profits of nearby firms. We will show that this distribution, which at each time is also the current distribution of the differentiated commodities, converges toward a limiting distribution at which all firms are making the same profit. If the consumer has a preferred menu, his chosen menus will converge to it as $t \to \infty$.

The mathematics used is the study of the characteristic curves of a quasi-linear partial differential equation. This equation arises from the continuity equation for the distribution of mass with the velocity field derived from profit considerations, i.e., firms will move in the direction of greatest increase of profit, modulo a cost of adjustment.

We assume that, at each fixed moment of time, the economy is in the short-run equilibrium described in Section 1. At time t each firm makes a decision about whether or not to change the type of commodity it produces and, if so, at what rate. This change occurs smoothly and at some cost to the firm. In particular, we assume:

<u>a firm producing type</u> $x(t)$ <u>at time</u> t <u>incurs a flow of readjustment costs</u> $c(w(x,t))$ <u>where</u> $w(x,t) = \frac{d}{dt} x(t)$.

We assume that the behavior of firms is myopic with respect to time and commodity type. The firm producing characteristic x at time t foresees a rate of change of flow of profit equal to

$$\frac{\partial \pi}{\partial x} \cdot \frac{dx}{dt} = \frac{\partial p}{\partial x} \cdot w(x,t) ,$$

when it moves at velocity $w(x,t)$. Following Sonnenschein (1982), we assume that each firm chooses $w(x,t)$ in order to maximize the rate of change of its flow of profit less the costs of adjustment, i.e., to maximize

$$\frac{\partial p}{\partial x} \cdot w - c(w) ,$$

and that the cost of readjustment is the quadratic[5]

$$c(w) = \frac{1}{2} w^2 .$$

This leads to the simple expression for the velocity field:

$$(16) \qquad w(x,t) = \frac{\partial}{\partial x} p(x,t) \quad \text{or} \quad w = \text{grad } p.$$

The study in Section 1 leads us to

$$(17) \qquad w(x,t) = \frac{\partial W}{\partial x} (x,F(x,t)) ,$$

by (6), (16), and the equilibrium condition $F(x,t) = G_\mu(x,t)$ for all (x,t). Note that the total mass of firms to the left of x is involved in determining the velocity of the firms at x. We emphasize this by writing the actual velocity as $v(x,F(x,t))$.

B. The Continuity Equation

Since the total mass from $-\infty$ to x determines the time evolution of the distribution of firms, we take as the primary object of study the integral form of the continuity equation:

$$(18) \qquad \frac{\partial}{\partial t} F(x,t) + v(x,F) \frac{\partial F}{\partial x} = 0 ,$$

which describes the evolution of the cumulative distribution function F of a measure μ_t of finite total mass (possibly varying in time).

One can obtain equation (18) directly by noting that if the firm which is producing x at time t is producing $x(t + \tau)$ at time $t + \tau$, then (for continuous W) all the firms to the left of x at t are precisely the firms to the left of $x(t + \tau)$ at time $t + \tau$. Therefore,

$$F(x(t + \tau),t + \tau) = F(x,t) .$$

Differentiate this equation with respect to τ to obtain (18).

In the Appendix, we show how, with some assumptions on the velocity function v, we can recover (18) from the more common[6] (and weaker) form of the continuity equation which describes the evolution of the densities of the distribution:

(19) $$\frac{\partial f}{\partial t} + \frac{\partial}{\partial x}\left[v\left(x,\int_{-\infty}^{x} f(z,t)dz\right) \cdot f(x,t)\right] = 0.$$

Because of the special dependence of v on f via the c.d.f. of f, one can use the theory of a single partial differential equation only with (18).

C. Statements of the Main Results

In the rest of this Section, we address the following problems:

(20) the existence and uniqueness of a solution $F(x,t)$ to (18) such that $F(\cdot,0)$ is a given initial cumulative distribution function F_0,

(21) qualitative properties of the solution $F(x,t)$ and the convergence of $F(\cdot,t)$ to a limiting c.d.f. as t tends to $+\infty$.

We will need to make the following assumptions on the data of these problems. We will provide some justification for these assumptions below:

(22) $v(x,z)$ is a C^1 function with $\frac{\partial v}{\partial z} > 0$;

(23) the zero set of v in $X \times [0,1]$ is the graph of some continuous increasing function L defined on some bounded interval $[\alpha,\beta]$ with $L(\alpha) = 0$ and $L(\beta) = 1$:

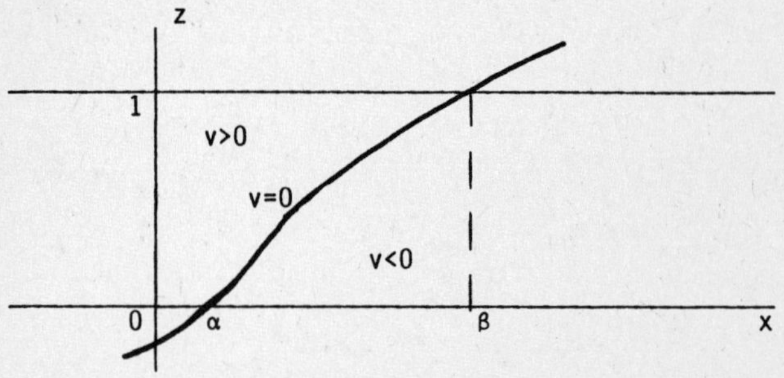

Figure 1: $\{v = 0\}$ in $X \times [0,1]$

(24) <u>the initial c.d.f.</u> F_0 <u>is</u> C^1

As illustrated in Figure 1, Assumptions (22) and (23) imply that in the strip $X \times [0,1]$, v is positive above and to the left of $v^{-1}(0)$ and negative below and to the right of $v^{-1}(0)$. If, as in (3), (4), or (5), the consumer has a preferred distribution G_λ with $G'_\lambda > 0$ on Supp λ,

$$W(x,z) = k - \psi(G_\lambda(x),z)$$

where ψ is a C^2 distance function. By (9),

$$v(x,z) = \frac{\partial W}{\partial x}(x,z) = -\frac{\partial \psi}{\partial x}(G_\lambda(x),z)\, G'_\lambda(x). \tag{25}$$

Since ψ is a distance function, the zero set of $v(x,z)$ is exactly the graph of G_λ: $z = G_\lambda(x)$, and v satisfies (23). Furthermore, it is reasonable to expect a regular distance function $\psi(x,z)$ to satisfy $\frac{\partial^2 \psi}{\partial z \partial x} < 0$ since $\frac{\partial \psi}{\partial x}$ is zero on the diagonal D in xz-space, positive above and to the left of D, and negative below and to the right of D, i.e., $\frac{\partial \psi}{\partial x}$ is a decreasing function of z near D. For such a ψ, e.g., $\psi(x,z) = (x - z)^2$ as in Sonnenschein (1982), the v defined by (25) will satisfy (22) too.

Assumptions (22) and (23) will ensure the convergence of $F(\cdot,t)$ toward the limiting distribution L on $[\alpha,\beta]$, with $F(x,t)$ tending toward 0 for $x \in (-\infty,\alpha]$ and $F(x,t)$ tending toward 1 for x in $[\beta,+\infty)$, as the Figures below suggest. In Figure 2, $L(x) > F_0(x)$ and $v(x,F_0(x)) < 0$; mass flows from the right to the left through x. In Figure 3, $L(x) < F_0(x)$ and $v(x,F_0(x)) > 0$; mass flows from left to the right through x.

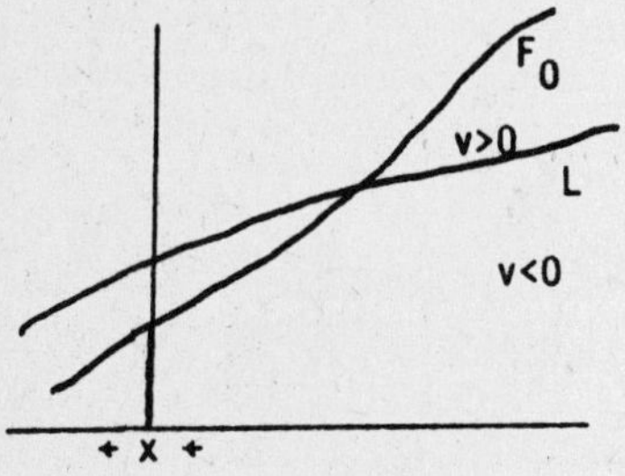

Figure 2. $L(x) > F_0(x)$

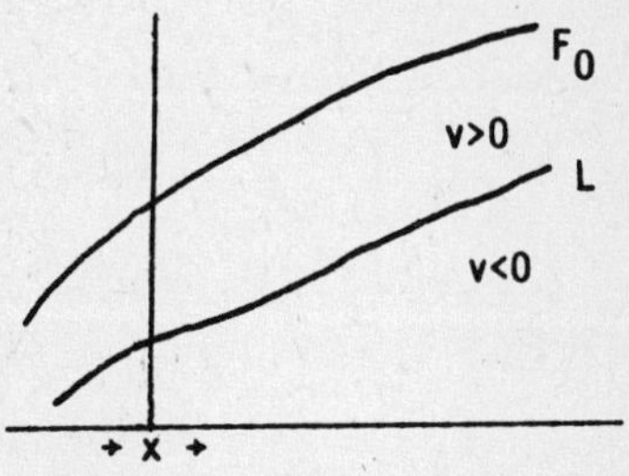

Figure 3. $L(x) < F_0(x)$

We shall prove:

PROPOSITION 3. <u>Under assumptions</u> (22), (23), <u>and</u> (24) <u>on</u> v <u>and</u> F_0, <u>equation</u> (18) <u>has a unique solution</u> $F(x,t)$ <u>for all</u> $t \geq 0$ <u>which satisfies</u> $F(x,0) = F_0(x)$ <u>for all</u> x <u>in</u> X.

PROPOSITION 4. <u>Under assumptions</u> (22), (23), (24), <u>the solution</u> $F(\cdot,t)$ <u>above is a cumulative distribution with compact support</u>. <u>The endpoints of this support</u>, a_t <u>and</u> b_t, <u>converge monotonically to</u> α <u>and</u> β <u>respectively as</u> $t \to +\infty$.

PROPOSITION 5. <u>Under assumptions</u> (22), (23), (24), <u>as</u> t <u>tends to</u> $+\infty$, <u>the solution</u> $F(\cdot,t)$ <u>of</u> (18) <u>converges uniformly on</u> X <u>to the function</u> $\bar{L}$ <u>defined by</u>:

$$\bar{L}(x) = \begin{cases} 0 & \text{for } x \in [a,\alpha), \\ L(x) & \text{for } x \in [\alpha,\beta], \\ 1 & \text{for } x \in (\beta,b]. \end{cases}$$

<u>The convergence is monotone for each</u> x.

D. <u>Study of the Characteristic Curves of (18)</u>.

To study the partial differential equation (18), we employ the technique of characteristics, which uses the fact that any solution $F(x,t)$ of the quasi-linear homogeneous PDE

$$\frac{\partial F}{\partial t} + v(x,F)\,\frac{\partial F}{\partial x} = 0 \tag{18}$$

is constant on a solution curve ("characteristic curve") of the ordinary differential equation

$$\frac{dx}{dt} = v(x,F_0(\xi)) \quad , \; x(0) = \xi. \qquad (F_0(x) = F(x,0)) \tag{26}$$

Then, to show that (18) has a solution and to study the behavior of these solutions, one shows that the solution curves of (26) fill up the space and do not cross in xt-space. By the remark above, these solution curves (i.e., characteristics) will then be the level curves of the solution $F(x,t)$ of (18) with the values of F on these level curves determined by the values of

$F(x,0) = F_0(x)$.

Let

$$x = \phi(t,\xi)$$

denote the solution of the initial value problem (26) with $\phi(0,\xi) = \xi$. Since v and F_0 are piecewise continuously differentiable, so is ϕ. (See for example, Hale (1980, p. 21).) Let C_ξ denote the corresponding characteristic curve

$$C_\xi = \{(x,t) \mid x = \phi(t,\xi), t \geq 0\}$$

through $(\xi,0)$ in the xt-half-plane $(t \geq 0)$.

Lemma 1. *Under hypotheses (22) and (23), the initial value problem (26) has a unique solution $\phi(t,\xi)$ which is defined for all $t \geq 0$.*

Proof. For fixed ξ in X, equation (26) defines a vector field on the line $z = F_0(\xi)$ in xz-space, as drawn in Figure 4. Let $z = L(x)$ parametrize the zero set of v as in Assumption (23) with $L(\alpha) = 0$ and $L(\beta) = 1$. By (23), our vector field has a unique zero at

$$Q(\xi) = (L^{-1}(F_0(\xi)),(F_0(\xi))).$$

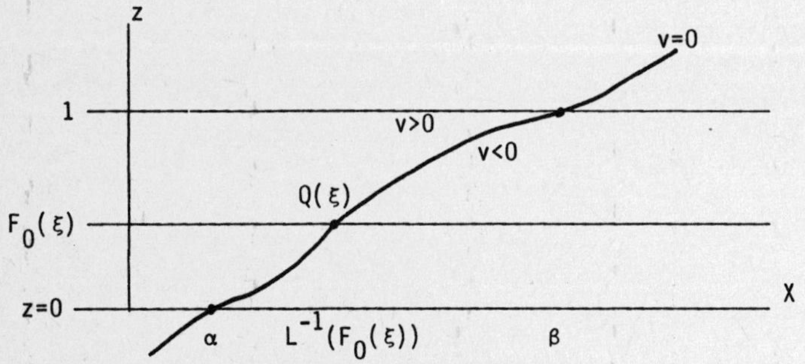

Figure 4. Phase Portrait of (26)

By (21) (see Figure 1), the vector field points toward $Q(\xi)$ on both sides of $Q(\xi)$, i.e., $\phi(t,\xi)$ tends toward $L^{-1}(F_0(\xi))$. Since no solution runs off to infinity as t increases, all solutions are defined for all time. □

Lemma 2 describes in more detail the behavior of the flow $\phi(t,x)$.

Lemma 2 Assume (22) and (23); let α, β, and L be as in Assumption (23).

i) If $F_0(\xi) = L(\xi)$, then $\phi(t,\xi) = \xi$ for all t and C_ξ is the vertical half-line $\{\xi\} \times R_+$.

ii) If $\xi < L^{-1}(F_0(\xi))$, then $\phi(t,\xi)$ tends to $L^{-1}(F_0(\xi))$ in a monotonically increasing manner; C_ξ has a vertical asymptote.

iii) If $\xi > L^{-1}(F_0(\xi))$, then $\phi(t,\xi)$ tends to $L^{-1}(F_0(\xi))$ in a monotonically decreasing manner; C_ξ has a vertical asymptote.

iv) In particular, if $F_0(\xi) = 0$, then $\phi(t,\xi)$ tends monotonically to α; if $F_0(\xi) = 1$, then $\phi(t,\xi)$ tends monotonically to $\beta = L^{-1}(1)$.

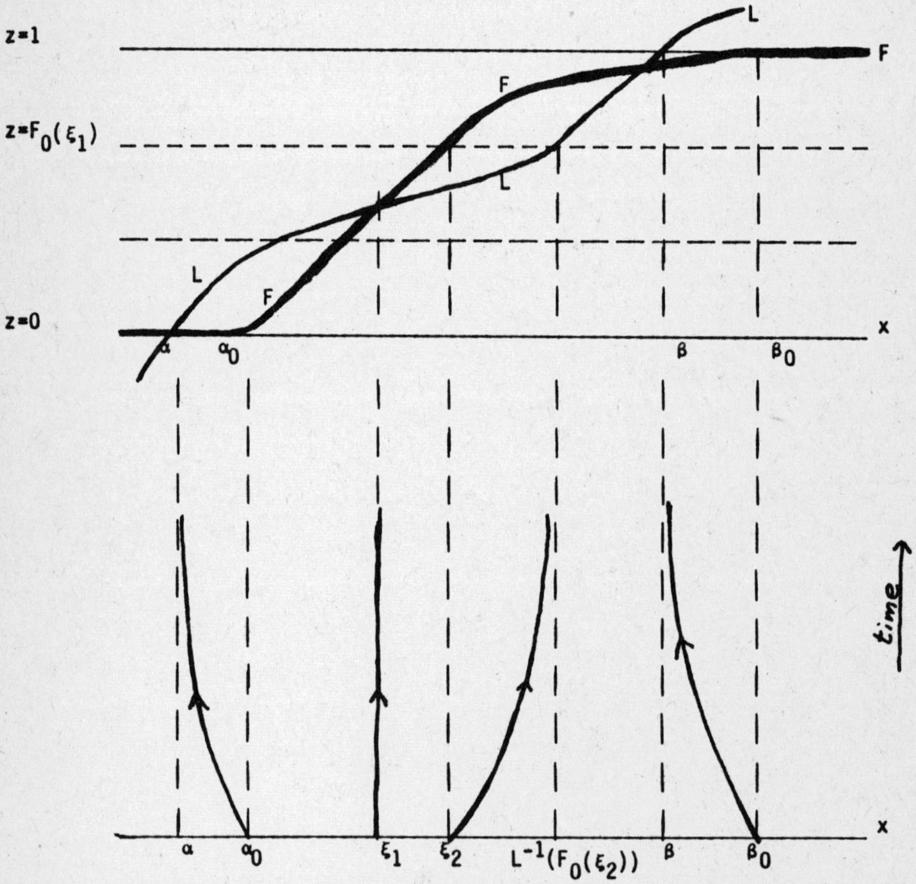

Figure 5. Phase Portrait in xz-space and the corresponding characteristic curves in xt-space.

Proof: The proof of Lemma 2 is the same as that of Lemma 1, with a little more attention paid to directions of convergence. Figure 5 summarizes the statement and proof of Lemma 2. The top half of Figure 5 is Figure 4 with the graph of F_0 added; the bottom half describes the corresponding characteristic curves. At a point like ξ_1 where the graphs of F_0 and L cross, $v(\xi_1,F_0(\xi_1)) = v(\xi_1,L(\xi_1)) = 0$; so $\phi(t,\xi_1) = \xi_1$ for all t and C_{ξ_1} is vertical. At a point like ξ_2, $L(\xi_2) < F(\xi_2)$, i.e., $\xi_2 < L^{-1}(F(\xi_2))$. In this case, $(\xi_2,F_0(\xi_2))$ lies to the left of $Q(\xi_2) = (L^{-1}(F_0(\xi_2)),F_0(\xi_2))$, in the region where $v > 0$. So the flow ϕ increases monotonically toward $L^{-1}(F_0(\xi_2))$, and C_{ξ_2} has the vertical asymptote $x = L^{-1}(F(\xi_2))$. This illustrates Case ii). The point $\xi = \alpha_0$ illustrates Cases iii) and iv). Here, $F(\alpha_0) = 0$ and we are working with the ODE $\dot{x} = v(x,0)$; all solutions of this ODE tend asymptotically and monotonically to $\alpha = L^{-1}(0)$.

Lemma 3. *Let $\phi(t,\xi)$ still denote the solution of (26) under assumptions (22) and (23). If $\xi < \xi'$, then $\phi(t,\xi) < \phi(t,\xi')$ for all $t > 0$. Consequently, characteristics C_ξ and $C_{\xi'}$ will never cross.*

Proof: As described in Hale (1980, p. 21), $x = \phi(t,\xi)$ is C^1 in both variables and $\frac{\partial x}{\partial \xi}$ satisfies the linear "variational equation":

$$(27) \qquad \frac{d}{dt}\left(\frac{\partial x}{\partial \xi}\right) = \frac{\partial v}{\partial x}(\phi(t,\xi),F_0(\xi))\frac{\partial x}{\partial \xi} + \frac{\partial v}{\partial z}(\phi(t,\xi),F_0(\xi))\frac{\partial F_0}{\partial \xi}(\xi),$$

with the initial condition $\frac{\partial x}{\partial \xi}(0) = 1$, since $x(0,\xi) = \xi$ for all ξ. Equation (27) is a first order linear non-homogeneous ODE in $\frac{\partial x}{\partial \xi}$ (where one takes $\phi(t,\xi)$ as known). Hence, we can write its explicit solution:

$$(28) \qquad \frac{\partial x}{\partial \xi} = \left[1 + \int_0^t h(s)\exp\left(-\int_0^s \frac{\partial v}{\partial x}(\phi(\tau,\xi),F_0(\xi))d\tau\right)ds\right] \cdot \exp\left(\int_0^t \frac{\partial v}{\partial x}(\phi(\tau,\xi),F_0(\xi))d\tau\right),$$

where the "1" in (28) follows from $\frac{\partial x}{\partial \xi}(0) = 1$ and

$$h(s) \equiv \frac{\partial v}{\partial z}(\phi(s,\xi),F_0(\xi))\frac{\partial F_0}{\partial \xi}(\xi),$$

the last term in (27). Since $\frac{\partial v}{\partial z} \geq 0$ by (21) and since $\frac{\partial F_0}{\partial \xi}$ is a non-negative density when F_0 is a c.d.f., $h(s) \geq 0$. Consequently, (28) implies that $\frac{\partial x}{\partial \xi}(t,\xi) > 0$ for all t,ξ. Since for each fixed t, the function $\xi \to \phi(t,\xi)$ is monotone increasing, characteristics do not cross for any t. □

Finally, we show that if we extend v from $X \times [0,1]$ to $R \times [0,1]$ in a natural way, characteristics of (18) fill up the whole positive xt-half-plane.

Lemma 4. *Assume that v, L, and F_0 satisfy assumptions (22), (23) and (24). Extend $v: X \times [0,1] \to R$ to $\overline{v}: R \times [0,1] \to R$ so that $\frac{\partial \overline{v}}{\partial x}$ is bounded away from $-\infty$ on $R \times [0,1]$. Then, for each (x,t) with $t > 0$, there is a unique $\xi = \xi(x,t)$ such that $x = \phi(t,\xi(x,t))$, i.e., characteristic curves fill up the whole xt-half plane.*

Proof. Since $\phi(t,\xi)$ is defined and C^1 for all (t,ξ) by Lemma 1, we need only show that for each $t_1 > 0$ the image of

$$\xi \to \phi(t_1,\xi) \tag{29}$$

maps R *onto* R, i.e., that for each $t_1 > 0$ the image of (29) is not bounded away from $+\infty$ or $-\infty$.

Suppose that $\frac{\partial \overline{v}}{\partial x} > -c > -\infty$ on $R \times [0,1]$. Then

$$\exp\left(\int_0^t \frac{\partial \overline{v}}{\partial x}(\phi(\tau,\xi),F_0(\xi))d\tau\right) > \exp\left(\int_0^t(-c)dt\right) = e^{-ct} .$$

Since the expression in square brackets in (28) is ≥ 1,

$$0 < e^{-ct} < \frac{\partial x}{\partial \xi}(t,x)$$

i.e., $\frac{\partial x}{\partial \xi}$ is bounded away from zero by an expression which is independent of ξ. This implies that the map (29) sends R *onto* R.

The uniqueness in the statement of Lemma 4 follows from Lemma 3. □

We next use these four lemmata to prove Propositions 3, 4, and 5.

E. Proof of Proposition 3: Existence and Uniqueness of Solutions

Extend v to $\overline{v}$ as in Lemma 4. Under Assumptions (22) through (24), Lemmas 1 through 4 tell us that $x = \phi(t,\xi)$ and $\xi = \xi(x,t)$ are C^1-diffeomorphisms (inverse to each other) between $R \times \{0\}$ and $R \times \{t\}$, which depend smoothly on t. Define

$$F(x,t) = F_0(\xi(x,t)).$$

Then, F is C^1 and constant on each characteristic curve C_ξ.

$$0 = \frac{d}{dt} F(\phi(t,\xi),t) = \frac{\partial F}{\partial t} + \frac{\partial F}{\partial x}\frac{d\phi}{dt}$$

$$= \frac{\partial F}{\partial t} + v(x,F)\frac{\partial F}{\partial x} \quad \text{at} \quad (x,t).$$

Clearly, F equals F_0 on $R \times \{0\}$.

By Lemma 2, as diagrammed in Figure 5, all characteristic curves to the left of $\alpha = L^{-1}(0)$ tend monotonically and asymptotically to $x = \alpha$ from the left and all characteristic curves to the right of $\beta = L^{-1}(1)$ tend monotonically and asymptotically to $x = \beta$ from the right. In particular, if $x < a$, the characteristic curve through (x,t) tends to α as $t \to +\infty$ and to a point to the left of $(x,0)$ as $t \to 0$; if $x > b$, the characteristic curve through (x,t) tends to β as $t \to +\infty$ and to a point to the right of $(x,0)$ as $t \to 0$. Consequently, $F(x,t) = 0$ for all $x < a$ and all $t \geq 0$ and $F(x,t) = 1$ for all $x > b$ and all $t \geq 0$. This behavior is independent of the extension $\overline{v}$ of v.

If G is any other solution of Problem (20), G will be zero outside $X \times R_+$, G will be constant on characteristics of Equation (18), and the value of G on any characteristic will be determined by its value on $R \times \{0\}$ where $G(x,0) = F_0(x)$. Consequently, G must equal F on the whole half-plane.

Note that this proof of the existence and uniqueness of a solution to Problem (20) does not require that one work on a compact subset of R, provided we make an additional assumption on $v(x,t)$ to guarantee that the characteristics fill up the whole upper half-plane. The above proof worked under the hypothesis that

$\frac{\partial v}{\partial x}$ is bounded away from $-\infty$. Alternatively, one could assume that the integral of $\frac{1}{v(x,0)}$ diverges for $x = -\infty$ and the integral of $\frac{1}{v(x,1)}$ diverges for $x = +\infty$.

F. Proof of Proposition 4: F_t is a c.d.f. and its endpoints converge.

By construction and by Lemma 3, each $F(\cdot,t)$ is zero on $(-\infty,\alpha_t]$, where $\alpha_t = \phi(t,\alpha_0)$ and is one on $[\beta_t,+\infty)$, where $\beta_t = \phi(t,\beta_0)$; on (α_τ,β_t), $F(\cdot,t)$ is monotone since F_0 is monotone on

$$(\alpha_0,\beta_0) = \xi((\alpha_t,\beta_t),t) \ .$$

By part iv) of Lemma 2, $\alpha_t = \phi(t,\alpha_0)$ converges monotonically to α and β_t converges monotonically to $\beta = L^{-1}(1)$.

G. Proof of Proposition 5: Convergence of F_t to Γ.

The proof of Proposition 5 basically follows from Lemma 2, using the intuition from Figure 5. For $\xi = \alpha_0$, the left end-point of the support of the initial distribution F_0, $\phi(t,\xi)$ converges monotonically to α, the left end-point of the support of the distribution L. The characteristic curve C_{α_0} in the xt-half-plane has $\{\alpha\} \times R_+$ as vertical asymptote. If $x < \alpha$, C_{α_0} is eventually to the right of $\{x\} \times R_+$, i.e., there is a T such that $x < \phi(t,\alpha_0)$ for all $t > T$. By Lemma 3, for $t > T$, $\xi(x,t) < \alpha_0$ and

$$0 < F(x,t) = F_0(\xi(x,t)) < F_0(\alpha_0) = 0 \ ;$$

i.e., $x < \alpha$ implies $F(x,t) = 0$ for t large enough. The same method shows that $F(x,t) = 1$ for $x > \beta$ and t sufficiently large.

We can asssume now that $\alpha < x < \beta$. If $L(x) = F_0(x)$, $\xi(x,t) = x$ for all t by part i) of Lemma 2 and

$$F(x,t) = F_0(\xi(x,t)) = L(x) \quad \text{for all } t.$$

If $L(x) < F_0(x)$, let x_0 be the supremum of the set $F_0^{-1}(L(x))$. Since $F_0(x_0) = L(x)$, $\phi(t,x_0) \to x$ as $t \to +\infty$ and the characteristic curve C_{x_0} has $\{x\} \times R_+$ as a vertical asymptote and it lies to the left of this asymptote by part ii) of Lemma 2. (See Figure 6.) All characteristics C_z for $x_0 < z \leq x$ have their asymptote to the right of $\{x\} \times R_+$ since $L < F_0$ on $(x_0,x]$.

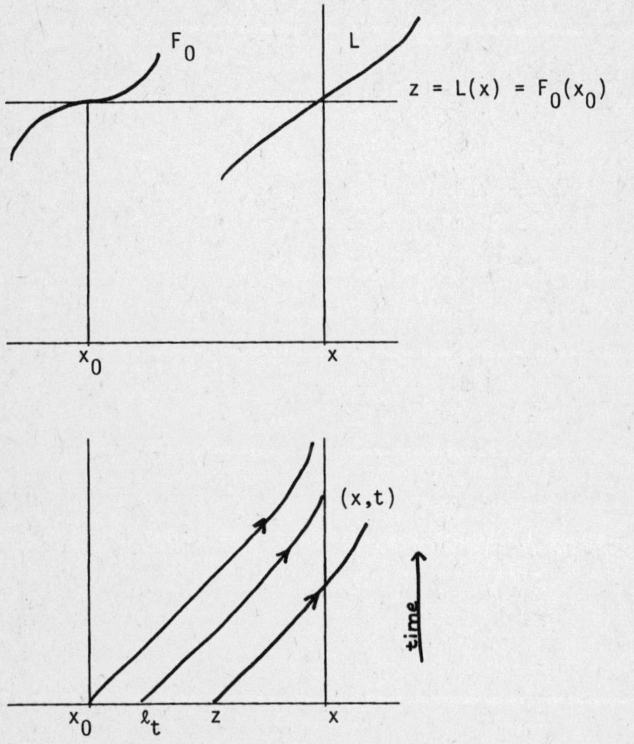

Figure 6. The graphs of L and F_0 near x_0 in xz-space and the characteristics C_{x_0} in xt-space.

For fixed t, the characteristic through (x,t) meets the x-axis at some point $\ell_t > x_0$, as in Figure 6. As t increases to $+\infty$, ℓ_t decreases but stays to the right of x_0. Let $\ell \geq x_0$ be the limit of ℓ_t as $t \to \infty$. Since $(x,t) = C_{\ell_t} \quad \{x\} \times R_+$ and C_ℓ lies to the left of each C_{ℓ_t}, the asymptote of C_ℓ cannot lie to the right of $\{x\} \times R_+$. Since $x_0 \leq \ell$, C_ℓ cannot lie to the left of $\{x\} \times R_+$. Since C_{x_0} is the last characteristic curve with asymptote $\{x\} \times R_+$, ℓ must equal x_0. Since $F(x,t) = F_0(\xi(x,t))$, $F(x,t)$ converges monotonically to $F_0(\ell) = F_0(x_0) = L(x)$. The proof for the case $L(x) > F(x)$ is similar.

Since all the supports of the distributions $F(\cdot,t)$ are contained in the same compact set $X = [a,b]$, the convergence is uniform. □

H. Economic Interpretation

To summarize Propositions 3, 4, 5: under some natural assumptions on the velocity field $v(x,F)$, the initial value problem

$$\frac{\partial}{\partial t} F(x,t) + v(x,F) \frac{\partial F}{\partial x} = 0 , \quad F(x,0) = F_0(x) \tag{18}$$

has a unique solution $F(x,t)$ which is defined and smooth for all t, each $F(\cdot,t)$ is a cumulative distribution with compact support, and $F(\cdot,t)$ tends uniformly to the c.d.f. L, whose graph is the zero set of v in $X \times [0,1]$. Given the reasonable utility function (3) where ψ is a distance function and G_λ is a c.d.f. which expresses the consumer's desired distribution or his needs for various amounts of the differentiated product, then $F(\cdot,t)$, which at each t must equal the short run optimally-chosen distribution G_μ, will tend uniformly to G_λ on $X \times [0,1]$ as $t \to +\infty$.

Furthermore, by (16) the short-run equilibrium profit function $\pi(x,t)$ and price function $p(x,t)$ satisfy

$$\frac{\partial \pi}{\partial x} (x,t) = \frac{\partial p}{\partial x} (x,t) = w(x,t) = v(x,F(x,t)) . \tag{31}$$

Since $v(x,F(x,t))$ tends to 0, so do $\frac{\partial \pi}{\partial x}$ and $\frac{\partial p}{\partial x}$, i.e., <u>the economy tends to an equal-profit long-run equilibrium</u>. As discussed just below Proposition 1, if W in (2) is ≥ 1, then these long run profits will be non-negative.

We can even say some things about how profits and prices evolve as time increases. For example, by the proof of Proposition 5, if $F_0(x) = L(x)$, then $F(x,t) = L(x)$ for all t. If ξ_1 and ξ_2 are adjacent characteristics where $F_0(\xi_i) = L(\xi_i)$, then the sets of needs[7] between ξ_1 and ξ_2 will be satisfied at each time by the set of goods between ξ_1 and ξ_2 (i.e., $[\xi_1,\xi_2]$ is an invariant interval for $F(\cdot,t)$). Since $v = 0$ when $F_0(\xi) = L(\xi)$, $\frac{\partial p}{\partial x}(t,\xi) = 0$

for all t and ξ will remain a critical point of π and p for all t, e.g., always a local min or always a local max. If ξ_1 and ξ_2 are adjacent characteristics where $L(\xi_i) = F_0(\xi_i)$ as above so that ξ_1 and ξ_2 are adjacent critical points of p, say ξ_1 is a local max and ξ_2 a local min of $p(x,t)$, then

$$p(\xi_1,t) - p(\xi_2,t) = \int_{\xi_1}^{\xi_2} w(x,t)dx = \int_{\xi_1}^{\xi_2} v(x,F(x,t))dx$$

will be a positive but decreasing function of t since each $v(x,F(x,t)) \to 0$ as $t \to \infty$. The gap between an adjacent max and min of p tends monotonically to zero.

Furthermore, just as in Sonnenschein (1982), one can show that utility increases monotonically as $F(x,t) \to L(x)$, i.e., as the economy evolves toward long-run equi-profit equilibrium.

Finally, note that our analysis with a general $v(x,F)$ in (18) and (31) allows us to study more general cost of adjustment functions than the quadratic $c(w) = \frac{1}{2}w^2$ used in this paper and in Sonnenschein (1982). In fact, let $C(w)$ be any C^2 function from $R_+ \to R_+$ such that

i) $C'(0) = 0$,

ii) $C'' > 0$ on $R_+ - \{0\}$.

Let $h: R_+ \to R_+$ be the inverse of C': $h(0) = 0$ and $h' > 0$ by i) and ii). Each firm chooses a speed of adjustment $w(x,t)$ to maximize

$$\frac{\partial p}{\partial x} \cdot w - C(w) \quad \text{, i.e.,}$$

$$\frac{\partial p}{\partial x} = C'(w) \quad \text{or} \quad w = h\left(\frac{\partial p}{\partial x}\right) .$$

By (9) and (31), we now have

$$v(x,F(x,t)) = w(x,t) = h\left(\frac{\partial W}{\partial x}(x,F(x,t))\right).$$

If the consumer has a preferred distribution G_λ as in (3), then v still equals zero only on the graph of G_λ, i.e., v satisfies (23). Since $h' > 0$, this v should still satisfy (22). Consequently, all the convergence results in this paper hold for these more general cost of adjustment functions.

Appendix 1.

In this appendix, we study the relationship between the differential and integral forms of the continuity equations on the whole real line. More precisely, we show that under mild assumptions on v, the system

$$\text{(32)}\qquad \begin{aligned} &\frac{\partial f}{\partial t} + \frac{\partial}{\partial x}[v(x,F)\cdot f] = 0 \\ &F(t,x) = \int_{-\infty}^{x} f(z,t)dz \\ &F(0,x) = F_0(x) \end{aligned}$$

implies the system

$$\text{(33)}\qquad \begin{aligned} &\frac{\partial F}{\partial t} + v(x,F)\frac{\partial F}{\partial x} = 0 \\ &f(t,x) = \frac{\partial F}{\partial x}(x,t) \\ &F(0,x) = F_0(x). \end{aligned}$$

When we work with the whole real line which is not compact, we need an assumption on v which will ensure that the characteristic curves of (33) fill up the positive xt-half-plane; e.g.,

$$\text{(34)}\qquad \begin{aligned} &\int_{-\infty} \frac{dx}{v(x,0)} \quad \text{diverges, or} \\ &\frac{\partial v}{\partial x} \quad \text{bounded away from } -\infty \text{ and } \frac{\partial v}{\partial z} > 0. \end{aligned}$$

Write $f = \frac{\partial F}{\partial x}$ in the first equation of (32) to find

$$\text{(35)}\qquad \begin{aligned} &\frac{\partial}{\partial x}\left[\frac{\partial F}{\partial t} + v(x,F)\frac{\partial F}{\partial x}\right] = 0 \quad \text{or} \\ &\frac{\partial F}{\partial t} + v(x,F)\frac{\partial F}{\partial x} = k(t) \end{aligned}$$

for some function $k(t)$. We will show that

$$K(t) \equiv \int_0^t k(s)ds \ , \qquad t \geq 0$$

is identically zero.

On the characteristic curve C_ξ of (35) through $(\xi,0)$, one has

$$\frac{dx}{dt} = v(x,F_0(\xi)) \quad \text{and} \quad F(x,t) = F_0(\xi) + K(t).$$

The middle equation of (32) implies that for each t, $\lim_{x \to -\infty} F(x,t) = 0$. Hypothesis (34) implies that $\phi(t,\xi) \to -\infty$ as $\xi \to -\infty$, as shown in the proof of Lemma 4. Therefore, the image of $(-\infty,\alpha_0) = F_0^{-1}(0)$ by the map (29) will be a connected infinite internal $(-\infty,\alpha_{t_1})$. On the latter

$$F(x,t_1) = F_0(\xi(x,t_1)) + K(t_1) = K(t_1),$$

but $F(x,t_1)$ tends to 0 as $x \to -\infty$, i.e., $K(t_1) = 0$. □

Appendix 2.

Sonnenschein (1982) uses the special utility function (5). By (9), (12), (31), equation (18) becomes in this situation

$$\frac{\partial F}{\partial t} + 2[F(x) - x] \frac{\partial F}{\partial x} = 0.$$

Its characteristic curves satisfy

$$\frac{dx}{dt} = 2[F_0(\xi) - x] \qquad x(0) = \xi.$$

This simple linear ODE can easily be solved explicitly:

$$x(t) = e^{-2t} \xi_0 + (1 - e^{-2t})F_0(\xi_0) = \phi(t,\xi_0) \ . \tag{36}$$

Note that $\phi(t,\xi_0)$ is a convex combination of $\xi_0(= L(\xi_0))$ and $F_0(\xi_0))$ and tends monotonically to $F_0(\xi_0)$. One easily checks from (36) that $\phi(t,\xi_0)$ is invertible and that $\phi(t,\xi_0) \to \pm\infty$ as $\xi_0 \to \pm\infty$ for each t. Let $\xi(t,x)$ be the inverse of $x \to \phi(t,x)$ for each t, i.e., $F(x,t) = F_0(\xi(t,x))$. To see that $F(x,t)$ converges uniformly to x, note that

$$F(x,t) - x = F_0(\xi(t,x)) - x$$
$$= -e^{-2t}[\xi(t,x) - F_0(\xi(t,x))] \quad \text{by (36).}$$

Therefore, $|F(x,t) - x| \leq \kappa e^{-2t}$ where $\kappa = \sup|F_0(\xi) - \xi|$ for ξ in the convex hull of $[0,1]$ and $[\alpha_0,\beta_0]$.

ENDNOTES

1. Novshek and Sonnenschein's model is different. It is not completely clear that their example can be adjusted to establish lack of convergence in the present context.

2. By distance-like, we mean $\psi(x,x) = 0$ and for $x \neq z$: $\psi(x,z) > 0$, $(z - x)\frac{\partial\psi}{\partial z} > 0$, and $(z - x)\frac{\partial\psi}{\partial x} < 0$.

3. Recall that Sonnenschein (1982) worked with a continuum of consumers instead of a single consumer and therefore had no need for the $\mu(X)$-term in (5).
4. See, for example, Kamien and Schwartz (1981).

5. We will show in Section 2.H that one can work with more general cost of readjustment functions.
6. See, for example, Sonnenschein (1982), Garabedian (1964, p. 501).
7. Here we consider the consumer's desired c.d.f. G_λ as describing his "needs".

Acknowledgements

This research was partially supported by grants from NATO and NSF. Parts of it were completed during extended visits by Simon and Sonnenschein at the University of Strasbourg, Artzner at the University of Michigan, and Artzner and Simon at the Institute for Mathematics and its Applications (IMA) at the University of Minnesota. We would especially like to thank Hans Weinberger, director of IMA for many fruitful discussions about partial differential equations, and Larry Blume.

References

1. Garabedian, P.R., 1964: Partial Differential Equations, New York: Wiley.

2. Hale, J., 1980. Ordinary Differential Equations. Huntington, N.Y.: R.E. Krieger Pub. Co.

3. Kamien, M.I. and N. Schwartz. 1981. Dynamic Optimization: The Calculus of Variations and Optimal Control in Economics and Management. New York: North Holland.

4. Novshek, W. and H. Sonnenschein, 1983. "General Equilibrium with Free Entry: A Synthetic Approach to the Theory of Perfect Competition." California Institute of Technology, Social Science Working Paper 467.

5. Novshek, W. and H. Sonnenschein, 1984. "Quantity Adjustment in an Arrow-Debreu-McKenzie Type Model." This volume.

6. Rosen, S., 1974. "Hedonic Prices and Implicit Markets: Product Differentiation". American Economic Review 65, 567-585.

7. Sonnenschein, H., 1981. "Price Dynamics and the Disappearance of Short Run Profits: An Example". Journal of Mathematical Economics 8, 201-204.

8. Sonnenschein, H., 1982. "Price Dynamics Based on the Adjustment of Firms". American Economic Review 72, 1088-1096.

SPECIAL PROBLEMS ARISING IN THE STUDY OF ECONOMIES WITH INFINITELY MANY COMMODITIES

Larry E. Jones

School of Management
Northwestern University
Evanston, Illinois 60201

1. Introduction

In recent years, researchers in economics and related fields have become increasingly interested in social structures in which the natural choice sets for individual agents are infinite dimensional. Examples include:

(i) The use of L_∞ and ℓ_∞ to model economies with continuous time with either finite and infinite horizon, infinite horizon discrete time, and uncertainty with an infinite state space (see Bewley [8] and Brown and Lewis [11]).

(ii) The use of ca(T) where T is a compact metric space to model economies in which goods with a continuum of characteristics or qualities are available (see Mas-Colell [35] and Jones [29] and [30]).

(iii) The use of L_2 and Martingale theory to model certain economies with financial instruments under uncertainty (see Harrison and Kreps [27] and Duffie and Huang [21]).

The infinite dimensional character of these economies creates several technical problems not met in the standard finite dimensional treatments with which economists are familiar (see Debreu [18]). The purpose of this paper is to discuss the effects of these problems on the classical results of economic theory. Although attention will be restricted to problems arising in a price-taking context, it is to be expected that similar problems will arise in more general settings for similar reasons (e.g., the interplay between compactness and continuity in the choice of topology).

We will adopt Debreu [18] as our standard for the results of economic theory. Accordingly, the results we will be interested in are:

(a) The existence and continuity of supply.

(b) The existence and continuity of demand.

(c) The existence of competitive equililbrium.

(d) The existence of Pareto optimal allocations.

(e) The Pareto optimality of competitive equilbria.

(f) The fact that Pareto optimal allocations can be supported as competitive equilibria after suitable redistribution of the ownership of initial resources and firms.

The strategy that we will adopt in this paper is to present and analyze a series of examples. The nature of each of the examples is that it provides a counterexample to one or more of the most direct translations of the above results from the finite dimensional to the infinite dimensional setting. The point of this exercise is not to say that these problems are unsolvable. Indeed, an active area of current research is in showing just how these problems can be solved. Rather, the point is to show that the extent to which these problems can be solved is limited. Hopefully, the examples will help us understand exactly what these limitations are. (Note that many of the problems can be solved for the examples presented here through a clever choice of the consumption and/or price space. This does not seem like a useful observation, however, since these are usually regarded as primitives in the mathematical statements that the desired results always boil down to.)

There are, of course, many results from mathematical economics other than those listed above which one would like to extend to an infinite dimensional setting but which will not be discussed here. These include the representation of preference orderings by utility functions, the continuity of the equilibrium correspondence, the existence of equilibrium with infinitely many consumers, the relationship between Nash equilibria of games with many players and competitive equilibria, the equivalence of the core of an economy and its competitive equilibria with infinitely many consumers, and the genericity of the local uniqueness of competitive equilibria. Some of the literature concerning these issues is briefly mentioned in section 3.

The remainder of this paper is organized as follows. In section 2, our notation and few key mathematical preliminaries are introduced along with the collection of examples. In section 3 a brief summary of the existing literature and results for infinite dimensional economies is presented.

2. Notation and Examples

2.1 Notation and Mathematical Preliminaries

We will follow the notation of Debreu [18] as much as is possible.

Throughout, L is a locally convex topological vector space with topology τ. It will always be assumed that τ is Hausdorff. (See Dunford and Schwartz [23] or Schaefer [41] for details on topological vector spaces.)

Consumers will be indexed by i when necessary and producers will be indexed by j.

Consumption sets will be denoted by X_i and production sets will be denoted by Y_j. Typical elements will be denoted by x and y, respectively. Subscripts will be dropped when they are not needed.

Following Debreu [16], prices will be assumed by lie in the topological dual of L, $L' = (L,\tau)'$ and will be denoted by p. Note that there are typically many topologies consistent with L' being the dual of L. Further, given L, many different choices of L' are possible (τ must be adjusted accordingly). Of course, these alternative choices give rise to different collections of compact subsets, continuous preference orderings and closed production sets. Thus, the choice of both L' and the topology for L will be an important consideration in what follows.

In all of the examples we will consider, L will have a natural order structure. To preserve the similarity between the results in Debreu [18] and the examples to be considered here, attention will be restricted to the case where $X_i = L_+$, the nonnegative elements of L. Similarly, L'_+ will denote the nonnegative elements of L'. Finally, $L'_{++} = \{p \in L'_+ | x \in L_+, x \neq 0 \Rightarrow px > 0\}$.

As is usual, $\succsim_i \subset L_+ \times L_+$ will denote the agent's preferences. Throughout, we will assume that the $\succsim_i$ are complete, transitive, reflexive, convex, and weakly monotone. Agents' endowments will be denoted by ω_i. We will always assume that $\omega_i \in X_i$ for all i.

If L is a topological vector space and L' is a vector space of linear functionals on L, $\sigma(L,L')$ is the weakest topology on L such that each element of L' is continuous. Note that $\sigma(L,L')$ is Hausdorff as long as L' separates the points of L.

Following Hildenbrand [28], recall that a correspondence ϕ from the topological space S to the topological space T is <u>upper hemicontinuous</u> (u.h.c.) if for every open set $G \subset T$, $\{s \in S | \phi(s) \subset G\}$ is an open subset of S. (Equivalently, for every closed set $F \subset T$, $\{s \in S | \phi(s) \cap F \neq \emptyset\}$ is closed in S.)

In many of the examples considered below the space and the topology will be such that (L,τ) is not metrizeable. Normally, this situation requires the use of generalized sequences or nets (see Kelly [33] for definitions and a discussion) for a discussion of topological properties rather than just sequences. For example, in a general topological space, it does not follow that a set is closed if it contains the limit point of all its convergent sequences. That is, this property is a necessary but not sufficient one for the set under consideration to be closed. It does follow, however, that to conclude that a set is not closed it is sufficient to produce a sequence in that set which converges to a point outside of it. Since we are solely concerned with the construction of counterexamples, this will be an extremely useful fact in what follows.

To economize on notation, unless explicitly stated otherwise, L_p will always mean $L_p([0,1],\underline{F},\lambda)$ where $\underline{F}$ is the Borel subsets of $[0,1]$ and λ is Lebesgue measure on $[0,1]$.

We now turn to the examples. To simplify the presentation, we will deviate somewhat from the order listed in section 1.

2.2 Properties of Demand

There are two properties of demand that are of interest here. These are nonemptiness and continuity.

For $(p,\omega) \in L'_+ \times L_+$ define $\gamma_i(p,\omega)$ by $\gamma_i(p,\omega) = \{x \in L_+ | p \cdot x = p \cdot \omega$ and $x' \in L_+$ and $x' \succ_i x \Rightarrow p \cdot x' > p \cdot x\}$. When $L = R^k$ for some k, one can show (Debreu [18], 4.10, (10)):

(A) If $\succsim_i$ is continuous, γ_i is nonempty valued and upper hemi-continuous at $(p,\omega) \in L'_{++} \times L_+$.

First, we consider the nonempty valuedness of γ. It is straightforward to show that if $\succsim$ is τ-upper semicontinuous ($\{x' \in L_+ | x' \succsim x\}$ is τ-closed for all x) and the budget set is τ-compact, then γ is nonempty. The compactness of the budget set is quite difficult to obtain even in what seems to be very reasonable circumstances. This can be seen in Example 1.

Example 1. Let $L = L_\infty$, $L' = L_1$, $\tau = \sigma(L_\infty, L_1)$. Suppose $\omega = x(t)$ where $x(t) \equiv 1$. Two examples of preferences both given by utility functions will be considered:

$$U_1(x) = \int_0^1 t x(t) dt$$

and

$$U_2(x) = \int_0^1 u\left(\int_t^1 x(s) ds\right) dt$$

where u is continuous, strictly increasing, strictly concave, and $u(0) = 0$.

It can be shown that both U_1 and U_2 are τ continuous. Each of the two utility functions has relative advantages. The first is linear in x which will make the point more transparent, but it is only weakly convex. The second is slightly more complex but has the advantage that it gives rise to strictly convex preferences.

Let $p(t) \equiv 1$. Then, $p \in L'_{++}$, but it is easy to see that both $\gamma_1(p,\omega)$ and $\gamma_2(p,\omega)$ are empty. This is because both sets of preferences prefer having consumption "piled up" at 1 when prices are constant across goods. In essence, demand for both of these agents is δ_1, where δ_t is the Dirac measure at t, when $p(t) \equiv 1$. Unfortunately, this possibility has been ruled out by the choice of L_∞ as the consumption set.

However, note that this consideration need not cause problems with the existence of equilibrium. In fact, economies with preferences such as these are covered by the existence result in Bewley [8]. Thus, there are equilibria with price systems in L_1 (in fact, in $C[0,1]$) for the one consumer exchange economies with the preferences and endowments given above. Essentially, prices adjust away from $p(t) \equiv 1$ so that demand does lie in L_+. Thus, the existence of equilibrium does not require that demand be nonempty for all prices. Rather it need only be true that prices exist such that both demand exists and markets are cleared.

Next is a discussion of the continuity properties of demand. This is a more difficult problem than the existence of demand since the topologies for both L and L' will have to be selected. One of the most fundamental problems that must be faced is that the map $\bullet: L' \times L \to \mathbb{R}: (p,x) \to p \cdot x$ is not jointly continuous for some choices of the topologies τ and τ' on L and L'.

In the examples we will consider, ω will be held fixed.

Let $ca(T)$ and $C(T)$ be the countably additive measures on T and the continuous real valued functions on the topological space T.

Example 2. Let $L = ca[0,1]$ and let τ be the variation norm topology on L (this is essentially setwise convergence of measures). Let L' be the norm dual of L. Note that although no useful characterization of L' exists, it follows that $C[0,1] \subset L'$.

For $x \in L_+$, define $U(x) = \int 1dx = x[0,1]$. Let

$$p^n(t) = \begin{cases} 2 - \dfrac{2n}{n-2}t & \text{for } 0 < t < 1/2 - 1/n, \\ 2 - \dfrac{2n}{n+2} + \dfrac{2n}{n+2}t & 1/2 - 1/n < t < 1. \end{cases}$$

See Figure 1.

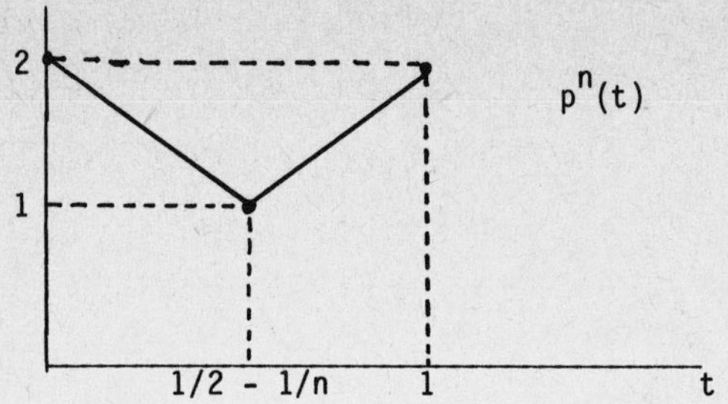

Figure 1

Then, $\|p^n - p\| \to 0$ where

$$p(t) = \begin{cases} 2 - 2t & \text{for } 0 \leq t < 1/2, \\ 2t & \text{for } 1/2 \leq t \leq 1. \end{cases}$$

Furthermore, when $\omega = \delta_0$, $p^n \cdot \omega = p \cdot \omega = 2$ for all n. Yet $\gamma(p^n,\omega) = 2\delta_{1/2 - 1/n}$ and $\gamma(p,\omega) = 2\delta_{1/2}$. Thus, $\|\gamma(p^n,\omega) - \gamma(p,\omega)\| \not\to 0$ so that γ is not norm to norm continuous. Note that γ: $L'_{++} \to L_+$ is $\sigma(L,L') \times \|\cdot\|$ to $\sigma(L,L')$ continuous, however.

At first sight one might think that the problem is that one is asking too much by putting the norm topology on L in this example. In fact, γ is not even nonempty for all $p \in L'_{++}$ (e.g., $p(t) = t + 1$ for $t > 0$, $p(0) = 2$). Indeed, as noted above, if one sets $\tau = \sigma(L,C[0,1])$ and $L' = C[0,1]$, τ' = the norm topology on $C[0,1]$, γ is nonempty and upper hemicontinuous on L'_{++}. It is important that the topology on L' be the norm topology, however, as the next example shows.

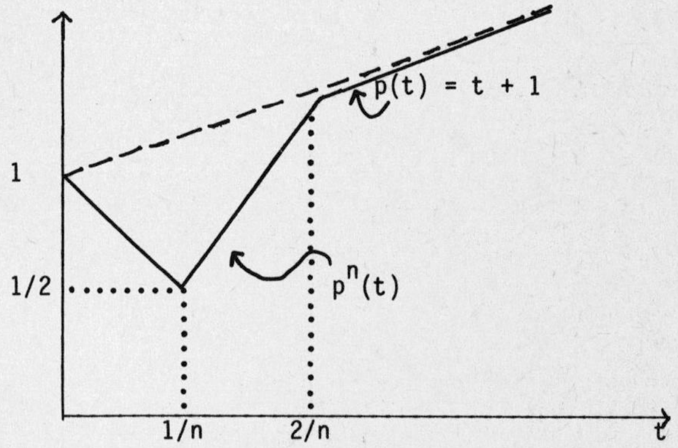

Figure 2

Example 3. Let $L = ca[0,1]$, $L' = C[0,1]$, $\tau = \sigma(L,L')$ and $\tau' = \sigma(L',L)$. As in Example 2, the utility function is given by $U(x) = x([0,1])$ and the endowment is $\omega = \delta_0$. Consider the sequence p^n, p as given in Figure 2, above. Then, using IV.6.4 of Dunford and Schwarz [23], it follows that $p^n \to p$ $\sigma(L',L)$. Further, $p^n \cdot \omega = p \cdot \omega = 1$ for all n. Yet $\gamma(p^n,\omega) = 2\delta_{1/n}$ and $\gamma(p,\omega) = \delta_0$ whence $\gamma(p^n,\omega) \not\to \gamma(p,\omega)$ in the $\sigma(L,L')$ topology.

Thus, the problem of discontinuities of demand do not revolve solely around the choice of topology for L. Given this, a natural question to ask is whether there always exists a choice of topologies for L and L' such that γ is continuous. To see that this is not true in general, it is sufficient to given an example in which τ' is the strongest topology on L' consistent with (L',L) and τ is the weakest topology on L consistent with (L,L').

Define χ_A to be the characteristic function of the set A, $\chi_A(t) = 1$ if $t \in A$, 0 otherwise.

Example 4. Let $L = L' = L_2$, τ' = the L_2 norm topology, and $\tau = \sigma(L_2,L_2)$. As above, let the utility function be given by $U(x) = \int_0^1 x(t)dt$ for $x \in L_+$ and let $\omega = 2\chi_{[1/2,1]}$.

Define p^n and p by

$$p^n(t) = 1/2\chi_{[0,1/n)} + \chi_{[1/n,1]}$$

$$p(t) = \chi_{[0,1]}\ .$$

Then, $p^n \cdot \omega = p \cdot \omega = 1$ for all $n \geq 2$ and $\|p^n - p\|_2 \to 0$. Yet, $x^n \cdot \chi_{[0,1]} = 2$ for all $x^n \in \gamma(p^n,\omega)$ and $x \cdot \chi_{[0,1]} = 1$ for all $x \in \gamma(p,\omega)$. Thus, γ is not τ' to τ upper hemicontinuous since $\{x \in L_+ | 0 < x \cdot \chi_{[0,1]} < 1\frac{1}{2}\}$ is a τ-open subset of L_+ containing $\gamma(p,\omega)$ but having null intersection with $\gamma(p^n,\omega)$ for all n.

Note that this example uses the unboundedness of the budget set in a very important way. In fact, this is crucial since it can be shown that the truncated demand correspondence (obtained by truncating the budget set) is norm to $\sigma(L,L')$ continuous in general. This fact is not of much use as far as proving existence is concerned, however, since the natural set of prices is not norm compact.

2.3 Properties of Supply

Next is a discussion of the supply correspondence.

For $p \in L'_+$ define $\eta(p) = \{y \in Y | p \cdot y \geq p \cdot y' \text{ for all } y' \in Y\}$.

When $L = \mathbb{R}^k$, one can show (Debreu [18], 3.5, (3)):

(B) If Y is compact, $\eta(p)$ is nonempty and upper hemicontinuous on L'_+.

It is straightforward to show that if Y is compact in any topology compatible with (L,L'), $\eta(p)$ is nonempty for all $p \in L'_+$. However, notice that the compactness of Y is quite strong here. That is, in the finite dimensional case, for most economies of interest, $(Y + \{\omega\}) \cap L_+$ is bounded and hence even if Y itself is not compact, it can, under relatively weak conditions, be replaced by another production set $\hat{Y}$ such that the equilibria are not altered and Y is compact. This fact does not hold in general when L is infinite dimensional as the following example demonstrates.

Example 5. Let $L = L_\infty \times R$, $L' = L_1 \times R$ and $\tau = \sigma(L_\infty, L_1) \times d)$ where d is the usual Euclidean topology on R. Let

$$Y = \{(y_1, y_2) \in L_\infty \times \mathbb{R} | y_2 \leq 0 \quad \text{and} \quad \int_0^1 y_1(t)dt + y_2 \leq 0\}.$$

Suppose that there is one consumer who has an endowment given by $\omega = (0,r)$ where $r > 0$. Then, it follows that $x^n = (nr\chi_{[0,1/n]}, 0) \in (Y + \{\omega\}) \cap L_+$ for all n and yet $\|x^n\|_\infty \to \infty$.

One can replace this production set by one which is norm bounded as a partial solution to this problem, but note that there are situations in which this will change the economic substance of the problem (see the example in section 2.5, below).

Next the continuity properties of $\eta(\cdot)$ will be considered. We will be brief since the examples closely parallel the discussion of continuity of demand given in section 2.2.

Example 6. As in Example 3, let $L = ca[0,1]$, $L' = C[0,1]$, $\tau = \sigma(L,L')$ and $\tau' = \sigma(L',L)$. Consider the production set

$$Y = \{y \in L | y\{1\} \geq 0 \text{ , } B \subset [0,1/2] \Rightarrow y(B) \leq 0 \text{ ,}$$
$$y\{1\} \leq -3y[0,1/2] \text{ and } \|y\| \leq 4\} \text{ .}$$

Then 1 is the only output of the firm and all commodities between 0 and 1/2 (inclusive) are inputs. Consider the sequence of prices as defined in Example 3 (Figure 2). It is easy to see that Y is τ-compact and that for n finite, the unique profit maximizing decision is given by

$$y^n = \delta_1 - 3\delta_{1/n} \text{ .}$$

However, the unique profit maximizing decision when prices are p is zero. Thus, η is not τ' to τ continuous.

As in the case of demand, it can be shown that if Y is $\sigma(L,L')$ compact and L is the Banach space dual of L', η is norm to $\sigma(L,L')$ continuous. Again, it should be emphasized that this is not a useful fact for the proof of existence of equilibrium since the natural price space is not in general norm compact.

2.4 Pareto Optimality of Equilibrium

There is little to be said on this topic. As has been shown by Debreu [16] in his classic paper on economies with infinitely many commodities, competitive equilibria are Pareto optimal under very general circumstances. In fact, Debreu shows that this result holds in our framework as long as preferences are non-satiated.

It follows from this fact that if the economy has no equilibria it has no optima and vice versa. This observation is an important one as far as the construction of examples is concerned. It will be used repeatedly below.

Notice, however, that Debreu's result depends critically upon the assumption of finitely many agents. A natural extension of the Arrow-Debreu model which becomes possible when infinitely many commodities are allowed is to include infinitely many atomic (in the measure theoretic sense) consumers as well. Equilibria need not be optimal in this setting as Samuelson [40] has shown in the context of the overlapping generations model.

2.5 Existence of Pareto Optima

In this section we will consider the failure of the existence of Pareto optima. In this regard, it can be shown (given the assumptions that $X_i = L_+$ and $\omega_i \in X_i$) (Debreu [18], 6.2, (1)):

(C) If $L = \mathbb{R}^k$ for some k, Y is closed and convex, $Y \cap L_+ = \{0\}$, and the $\succsim_i$ are continuous, a Pareto optimum exists.

Since (C) is institution independent (i.e., there are no markets) it should not be surprising that, roughly speaking, the only types of failures possible are due to a lack of compactness of the set of attainable states for the economy. Two examples will be considered. The first has one consumer with production and the second has two consumers with no production.

Example 7. In this example, we will combine the preferences given in Example 1 with the production set given in Example 5. Let $L = L_\infty \times R$ and let $\tau = \sigma(L_\infty, L_1) \times d$. Define Y by

$$Y = \{(y(t),y) \in L \mid y(t) \geq 0,\ y \leq 0 \text{ and } \textstyle\int_0^1 y(t)dt \leq -y\}.$$

Consider a one-consumer world with endowment given by $\omega = (x(t),1)$ where $x(t) \equiv 0$ and preferences are given by

$$V_1(x(t),x) = \int_0^1 tx(t)dt + x/2$$

or

$$V_2(x(t),x) = \int_0^1 u(\int_t x(s)ds)dt + v(x)$$

where u and v are strictly increasing, strictly concave and continuously differentiable with $u'(0) > v'(1)$.

It is easy to see that some production should take place in this economy, yet that given any allowable production plan the consumer's welfare can be improved by leaving the input level the same but increasing the index of the output.

The problem here is that $(Y + \{\omega\}) \cap L_+$ is not bounded and hence it is not compact. This problem can be solved by replacing Y by

$$\hat{Y} = \{y \in Y \mid \|y(t)\|_\infty + |y| \leq K\}.$$

However, note that this significantly changes the feasible allocations and that the constraint, $\|y(t)\|_\infty + |y| \leq K$, will be binding at the optimum.

Example 8. Let $L = C[0,1]$, $L' = ca[0,1]$ and $\tau = \sigma(L,L')$.

Consider two consumers with preferences given by

$$U_1(x) = \int_0^1 tx(t)dt$$

and

$$U_2(x) = \int_0^1 (1 - t)x(t)dt .$$

Suppose that initial endowments are given by $\omega_1 = \omega_2 = 1/2\chi_{[0,1]} \in L$. It is easy to see that no nontrivial optima exist (i.e., optima in which neither consumer gets 0) for this economy. This follows because consumer 1 should get all commodities to the right and consumer 2 should get all commodities to the left but there is no decomposition of the aggregate endowment as the sum of two continuous functions with these properties. This example will be used again below.

2.6 Supportability of Optima by Price System

This section deals with the problem of decentralizing a given Pareto optimal allocation through the use of a price system. For this section, the disucssion will be limited to the exchange case. For this case, the following result holds (Debreu [18], 6.4., (1)).

(D) If $L = \mathbb{R}^k$, k finite, the $\succsim_i$ are continuous and convex, and x_i^* is an optimum such that $\succsim_i$ is nonsatiated at x_i^* for some i, there is a $p^* \neq 0$ supporting x_i^*.

Two examples will be examined -- one with one consumer and one with two consumers. The first example shows how the fact that L_+ has an empty interior in many examples can cause problems. The second arises essentially due to a noncompactness problem in the price space.

Example 9. Let $L = L' = \ell_2$, the square summable sequences, and $\tau = \sigma(\ell_2,\ell_2)$. Define U by

$$U(x) = \sum_{i=1}^{\infty} u(x(i);i)$$

where

$$u(s;i) = i^{-2}(1 - e^{-i^2 x}) \text{ , for } i = 1,2,\ldots$$

See Figure 3.

Finally, define ω by $\omega(i) = 1/i^2$. It can be shown that U is τ-continuous. However, there is clearly no price system in ℓ_2 for this economy. That is, the only prices which clear the market are those where $p(i) = u'(\omega(i);i) = e^{-1}$ for all i. However, this sequence clearly is not square summable.

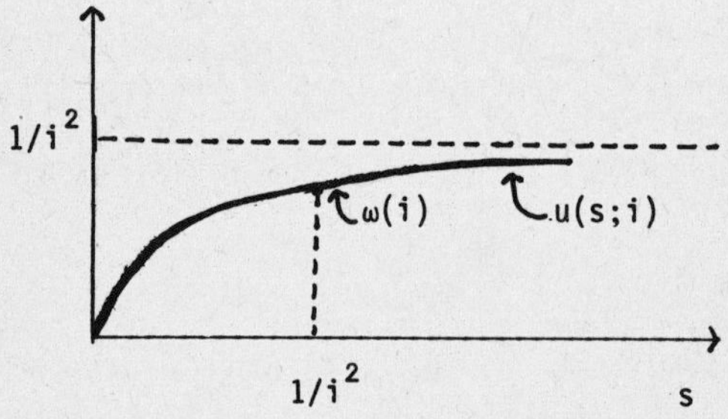

Figure 3

Note that this example is basically the same as both Example 1 in Jones [30] and the example of section IV in Mas-Colell [35]. The basic intuition behind all three of these examples is that prices are measures of relative marginal values and that continuity assumptions on preferences do not, in and of themselves, place sufficiently strong restrictions on the sequence of marginal utilities to guarantee that it lies in the dual of the commodity space.

Next, a two-person example is considered.

Example 10. Let $L = L_\infty$, $L' = C^1(0,1)$, the continuous functions on (0,1) which have continuous and bounded derivatives, $\tau = \sigma(L,L')$. Following Example 8, consider the two-person economy with preferences given by

$$U_1(x(t)) = \int_0^1 tx(t)dt$$

$$U_2(x(t)) = \int_0^1 (1 - t)x(t)dt \ .$$

These preferences are clearly continuous (since they are linear).

Let $\omega = \chi_{(0,1)}$.

It is easy to see that $x_1 = \chi_{(0,1/2)}$ and $x_2 = \omega - x_1$ is an optimal distribution of ω. Yet, there is no price system in L' which supports this allocation. However, there is a price system with continuous prices. This is given by $p(t) = \max(t, 1 - t)$.

Notice that the failure in this example is of a fundamentally different nature than that of the previous one. In Example 9, the problem is that prices cannot be found in L' to support an individual's allocation. This does not cause a problem here. For example, for any $x \in L_+$, the price $p(t) = t$ lies in L'_+ and supports x for consumer 1. Simiarly $p(t) = 1 - t$ supports any allocation in L_+ for consumer 2. The problem in this example lies in the process through which individual prices are aggregated into social prices.

2.7 Existence of Competitive Equilibrium

This section will be brief since most of the examples have already been presented in the previous sections. We will simply note that these examples give rise to problems with the existence of equilibrium.

For completeness, one statement of existence is given for the finite dimensional case (Debreu [18], 5.7, (1)). Let $Y = \Sigma Y_j$.

(E) If $L = \mathbb{R}^k$ for some finite k, the $\succsim_i$ are nonsatiated, continuous and convex, $0 \in Y_j$ for all j, Y is closed and convex, $Y \cap -Y = \{0\}$, $-\mathbb{R}^k_+ \subset Y$ and $\omega_i >> 0$ for all i, a competitive equilibrium exists.

In the present context, there is some ambiguity as to how to translate the statement "$\omega_i >> 0$ for all i". There seem to be two possibilities. The first is that ω_i is in the τ interior of L_+. The problem with this version is that it rules out almost all of the interesting economies from the start since they have positive cones with empty interiors (e.g., the L_p spaces $1 < p < \infty$). For this reason, the following translation is used which is equivalent to the statement above that if $L = \mathbb{R}^k$: for all i, $\omega_i \cdot p > 0$ for all $p \in L'_+$ such that $p \neq 0$.

As far as counterexamples to (E) are concerned, note that Example 7 gives two counterexamples in the case with one consumer and production. As was pointed out, the problem arises due to the lack of compactness of $(Y + \{\omega\}) \cap L_+$. There are two potential remedies in this case. The first is to bound Y. If this is done, it is straightforward to check that the resulting economies satisfy the assumptions in Bewley [8]. Again, it should be emphasized that this constraint will be binding in equilibrium. The second remedy is to reinterpret L as $L = ca[0,1] \times R$. (Note that both utility functions are well defined in this case.) Then, letting $L' = C[0,1] \times R$ and $\tau = \sigma(L,L')$, it is easy to check that the resulting economies satisfy the assumptions in Jones [30] with $T = [0,1] \cup \{2\}$ (i.e., $(Y + \{\omega\}) \cap L_+$ is a bounded collection of measures), and hence, equilibria exist with prices in $C[0,1] \times R$.

Example 8 also gives rise to an example in which equilibria do not exist. In this case, letting $Y = -L_+$, we see that although $(Y + \{\omega\}) \cap L_+$ is closed and bounded, it is not compact. This suggests that it might be enought to guarantee somehow that $(Y + \{\omega\}) \cap L_+$ is compact. This cannot work in general, however, as this example shows. Letting $Y = \{0\}$, we see that $(Y + \{\omega\}) \cap L_+ = \{\omega\}$ which is indeed compact, yet still no equilibrium exists. Again, the problem can be easily resolved for the example by reinterpreting L as either L_∞ or $ca[0,1]$ and appealing to the results in Bewley [8] or Jones [30].

Example 9 shows yet another way in which (E) can fail and illustrates one of the main distinctions between finite and infinite dimensional economies. This lies in the difference between the assumptions of separation theorems for convex sets in the two cases. In finite dimensions, the relevant result is Minkowski's theorem while in infinite dimensions, the relevant result is some version of the Hahn-Banach theorem. The primary difference between these two results is that the Hahn-Banach theorem requires that the separated set have a nonempty interior.

This will not be satisfied in general since the upper contour sets of preference orderings are subsets of L_+ which has an empty interior in most examples of interest in economics. Note that this example cannot be adjusted in a simple way so that it fits in the framework of either Bewley [8] (since ω is not bounded away from 0) or Jones [30]. As of yet, no technique has been developed to resolve the type of problem suggested by this example other than to rule it out by considering only economies in which preferences are such that situations such as this do not arise (this is the solution adopted by both Jones [30] and Mas-Colell [36]).

As a final point concerning this example, one might think that a solution to this problem can always be found by expanding the price space. That is, if we made L' large enough, we could get a topology on L which is strong enough so that L_+ has a nonempty interior. The example shows that this cannot work in general since in this case the supporting prices do not even lie in the algebraic dual of L (i.e., $p \cdot x$ is not finite for all $x \in L_+$).

This is, I think, a very important point and as such should be emphasized further. Although we have restricted our attention to the topological dual in our search for equilibrium prices, there is nothing intrinsically topological about the notion of equilibrium. This suggests that the algebraic dual might be the correct place to look for prices. As Example 9 shows, this cannot be a successful endeavor in complete generality.

Example 10 shows yet another way that (E) can fail when L is infinite dimensional. In this case it seems that the chosen price space is not rich enough to allow for the aggregation of individual marginal rates of substitution that is required in equilibrium theory.

Finally, it should be pointed out that in all of the examples that have been considered in this section, the preferences that have been used are $\sigma(L,L')$ continuous. Araujo [2] has shown, by an example, that this assumption is necessary for existence to hold in Bewley's framework. That is, the example given in Araujo shows that if preferences are norm continuous but not $\sigma(L,L')$ upper semicontinuous, Pareto optima need not exist. It follows from this that equilibria need not exist as well.

3. Summary of Existing Results

The purpose of this section is to provide the reader with an outline of the existing results in the field of infinite dimensional economies. I have tried to be as complete and current as possible, but I do not doubt that I have neglected some. Further, for reasons of space, I have given only the barest clues as to the contents of the cited papers. Despite these shortcomings, I hope that the outline will offer some guidance to the reader who is interested in pursuing a particular topic further.

(1) Supportability of Optima by Prices. The first result in this regard is that of Debreu in [16]. In that paper, he shows that if either the production set or the consumption set has nonempty interior, optima can be supported as equilibria. More recently, there are two papers dealing with this subject. First is the paper by Back [4], who treats the problem when $L = L_\infty$. Second is the paper by Mas-Colell [37] who shows that optima can be supported when preferences are derived from utility functions defined on an open set including L_+.

(2) Existence of Equilibrium with Finitely Many Consumers. There is now a wide literature on this subject. The first example is that of Bewley [8] for L_∞. His arguments have been generalized and improved upon by Bojan [10], el Barkuki [6], Brown and Lewis [11], Magill [34], Toussaint [42] and [43], and Florenzano [25].

The case of $L = ca(T)$ where T is a compact metric space is covered in Jones [30]. Mas-Colell [36] gives an existence result for the exchange case when L is a Banach Lattice with predual. This result has been recently generalized by Yannelis and Zame [46] to the case of unordered preferences.

For the case of Banach Lattices with order continuous norm, Brown [13] contains an existence proof based on Kuhn-Tucker techniques. This is a generalization of an argument intiated in Debreu and Hildenbrand [20].

Aliprantis and Brown [1] contains a theorem for the case where L is a Riesz space using demand functions as primitives.

Chichilnisky and Heal [15] establish an existence result for Hilbert spaces assuming that agents have utility functions defined over the whole space.

Finally, two recent results have extended Bewley's proof to Banach spaces with preduals. These are Duffie [22] and Jones [31]. In both cases, it is assumed that the production set has a nonempty interior (Duffie's condition is slightly weaker than this). In addition, in [31], it is shown that Mas-Colell's Banach Lattice result for the exchange case [36], can be obtained as a special case of the result for an economy with a constant returns to scale production set with nonempty interior.

(3) Existence of Continuous Utility Functions. The classic results on this topic are Debreu [17] and Eilenberg [24]. In fact, these results do cover some infinite dimensional economies of interest. More recently, such a theorem has been proven by Mas-Colell [36] for bounded (order) subsets of a Banach Lattice.

(4) Continuity of the Equilibrium Correspondence. For the finite dimensional case, Hildenbrand [28] contains a very general result. To my knowledge, the only result treating this problem for the infinite dimensional case is that reported in Jones [30] where L is the countably additive measures on a compact metric space.

(5) Existence of Equilibrium with Infinitely Many Consumers and Infinitely Many Commodities. The list of references on this topic has also grown considerably in recent years. The first example of this is a result for ℓ_∞ by Bewley [7] for the case of bounded consumption sets. A similar result for hyperfinite exchange economies appears to Brown and Lewis [12].

For the case $L = ca(T)$, where T is a compact metric space, two results have appeared. The first is that of Mas-Colell [35] with bounded consumption sets featuring indivisibilities. The second is that in Jones [29] which treats the model of [35] without bounding consumptions sets or introducing indivisibilities.

A recent result by Ostroy [38] contains a result which covers, for example, the L_p spaces and is based in Vind's [44] approach to modeling consumers.

Finally, there is the literature on the existence of equilibrium in overlapping generations models including the papers by Balasko, Cass, and Shell [5] and Wilson [45].

(6) The Equivalence of the Core and Competitive Equilibria. The classic theorem in this regard for the finite dimensional case is, of course, the result of Aumann [3].

There are several infinite dimensional versions of this result in the literature. The first is due to Gabszewicz [26] and covers the case where $L = C(S)$ the continuous real valued functions on a compact metric space. In addition, Bewley [9] has provided a similar result for the L_∞ case and Mas-Colell [35] contains an equivalence result when $L = ca(T)$ and consumption sets have indivisibilities.

Finally, there is the recent very general result by Ostroy [39].

(7) Local Determinateness of Equilibria. The classic result for the finite dimensional model is due to Debreu [19] and has been extended in many ways. To my knowledge there have been only two results of this type for the infinite dimensional case. These are in the papers by Brown and Genakoplos [14] and Kehoe and Levine [32] and both deal with the overlapping generations model.

There are many other topics in economic theory which are relevant to modeling infinite dimensional economies but which we have neglected here. Most notable is the entire field of capital theory, which almost always deals with infinite horizon models. This is a literature which is sufficiently distinct in aim that the omission seemed appropriate.

References

[1] Aliprantis, C. and D. Brown, "Equilibria in Markets with a Riesz Space of Commodities", Journal of Mathematical Economics, 11 (1983), 189-208.

[2] Araujo, A., "Lack of Equilibria in Economies with Infinitely Many Commodities: The Need of Impatience", Informes de Matematica, 009-82, IMPA, Rio de Janiero.

[3] Aumann, R., "Existence of Competitive Equilibria in Markets with a Continuum of Traders", Econometrica, 34 (1966), 1-17.

[4] Back, K., "On Price Systems in Economies with Infinitely Many Commodities", Northwestern University Discussion Paper, 1984.

[5] Balasko, Y., D. Cass and K. Shell, "Existence of Competitive Equilibrium in a General Overlapping Generations Model", Journal of Economic Theory, 23 (1980), 306-322.

[6] El'Barkuki, R.A., "The Existence of an Equilibrium in Economic Structures with a Banach Space of Commodities", Akademiia Nauk Azerbaidzan, SSR Dokl (1977), 8-12.

[7] Bewley, T., "Equilbrium Theory with an Infinite Dimensional Commodity Space", unpublished Ph.D. dissertation, University of California, Berkeley, 1970.

[8] Bewley, T., "Existence of Equilibria in Economies with Infinitely Many Commodities", Journal of Economic Theory, 4 (1972), 514-540.

[9] Bewley, T., "The Equality of the Core and the Set of Equilibria in Economies with Infinitely Many Commodities and a Continuum of Agents", International Economic Review, 14 (1973), 383-394.

[10] Bojan, P., "A Generalization of Theorems on the Existence of Competitive Economic Equilibrium to the Case of Infinitely Many Commodities", Mathematica Balkanika, 490 91974), 491-494.

[11] Brown, D. and L. Lewis, "Myopic Economic Agents", Econometrica, 49 (1981), 359-368.

[12] Brown, D. and L. Lewis, "Existence of Equilibrium in a Hyperfinite Exchange Economy: I and II", Cowles Foundation Discussion Paper No. 581, 1981.

[13] Brown, D., "Existence of Equilibria in a Banach Lattice with Order Continuous Norm", Cowles Foundation Discussion Paper, 1983.

[14] Brown, D. and J. Genakoplos, "Understanding Overlapping Generations Models as a Lack of Market Clearing at Infinity", Cowles Foundation Discussion Paper, 1984.

[15] Chichilnisky, G. and G.M. Heal, "Existence of Equilibrium in Hilbert Spaces", Columbia University Working Paper, 1983.

[16] Debreu, G. "Valuation Equilibrium and Pareto Optimum", Proceedings of the National Academy of Sciences, 40 (1954), 588-592.

[17] Debreu, G., "Representation of a Preference Ordering by a Numerical Function", in Decision Processes, R. Thrall, C. Coombs and R. Davis (eds.), New York, John Wiley, 1954.

[18] Debreu, G., Theory of Value, New Haven: Cowles Foundation, 1959.

[19] Debreu, G., "Economies with a Finite Set of Equilibria", Econometrica, 38 (1970), 387-392.

[20] Debreu, G. and W. Hildenbrand, "Equilibrium Under Uncertainty", personal notes, 1973.

[21] Dufie, D. and C. Huang, "Implementing Arrow-Debreu Equilibria by Continuous Trading of a Few Long-Lived Securities", Stanford University Discussion Paper, 1983.

[22] Duffie, D., "Competitive Equilibria in General Choice Spaces", Stanford University Discussion Paper, 1984.

[23] Dunford, N. and J. Schwartz, Linear Operations, Part I, New York: Interscience, 1957.

[24] Eilenberg, S., "Ordered Topological Spaces", American Journal of Mathematics, 63 (1941), 39-45.

[25] Florenzano, M., "On the Existence of Equilibria in Economies with an Infinite Dimensional Commotidy Space", University of California, Berkeley, Discussion Paper, 1982.

[26] Gabszewicz, J., Couers et Allocations Concurrentielles dans des Economies d'Echange avec un Continu de Biens, Louvain: Librairie Universitaire, 1968.

[27] Harrison, M. and D. Kreps, "Martingales and Arbitrage in Multiperiod Securities Markets", Journal of Economic Theory, 20 (1979), 381-408.

[28] Hilbenbrand, W., Core and Equilibria of a Large Economy, Princeton: Princeton University Press, 1974.

[29] Jones, L., "Existence of Equilibria with Infinitely Many Consumers and Infinitely Many Commodities: A Theorem Based on Models of Commodity Differentiation", Journal of Mathematical Economics, 12 (1983), 119-138.

[30] Jones, L., "A Competitive Model of Commodity Differentiation", Econometrica, 52 (1984), 507-530.

[31] Jones, L., "A Note on the Price Equilibrium Existence Problem Banach Lattices", Northwestern University Working Paper, 1984.

[32] Kehoe, T., and D. Levine, "Regularity in Overlapping Generations Exchange Economies", Massachusetts Institute of Technology Working Paper, 1982.

[33] Kelley, J., General Topology, New York: Springer-Verlag, 1955.

[34] Magill, M., "An Equilibrium Existence Theorem", Journal of Mathematical Analysis and Applications, 84 (1981), 162-169.

[35] Mas-Colell, A., "A Model of Equilibrium with Differentiated Commodities", Journal of Mathematical Economics, 2 (1975), 263-295.

[36] Mas-Colell, A., "The Price Equilibrium Existence Problem in Banach Lattices", Harvard University Discussion Paper, 1983.

[37] Mas-Colell, A., "Notes on Pareto Optima in Linear Space", Harvard University Working Paper, 1984.

[38] Ostroy, J., "The Existence of Walrasian Equilibrium in Large-Square Economies", Journal of Mathematical Economics, forthcoming.

[39] Ostroy, J., "Thick and Thin Market Nonatomic Exchange Economies", University of California, Los Angeles, Discussion Paper, 1983.

[40] Samuelson, P., "An Exact Consumption-Loan Model With or Without the Social Contrivance of Money", Journal of Political Economy, 66 (1958), 467-482.

[41] Schaefer, H., Topological Vector Spaces, New York: Springer-Verlag, 1971.

[42] Toussaint, S., "On the Existence of Equilibrium in Economies with Infinitely Many Commodities", University of Mannheim Discussion Paper, 1981.

[43] Toussaint, S., "On the Existence of Equilibria in Economies with Infinitely Many Commodities and Without Ordered Preferences", University of Mannheim Discussion Paper, 1982.

[44] Vind, K., "Edgeworth Allocations in an Exchange Economy with Many Traders", International Economic Review, 5 (164), 165-177.

[45] Wilson, C., "Equilibrium in Dynamic Models with an Infinity of Agents", Journal of Economic Theory, 24 (1981), 95-111.

[46] Yanellis, N. and W. Zame, "Equilibria in Banach Lattices without Ordered Preferences", University of Minnesota Discussion Paper, 1984.

Introduction to Expectations Equilibrium

Lawrence Blume†

Department of Economics
University of Michigan
Ann Arbor, MI 48109

and

James Jordan†

Department of Economics
University of Minnesota
Minneapolis, MN 55455

1. Introduction

In markets for commodities, such as financial assets, whose future worth or utility is unknown, market clearing prices reflect information and beliefs about returns to commodity ownership. Should the distribution of information be differential—should traders come to market with different information—we can expect traders to make further inferences about the worth of the commodity by trying to infer other traders' information from the equilibrium price. This additional statistical role for prices poses significant problems for the study of market equilibrium that are not present when the distribution of information is uniform or when there is no uncertainty. Rational expectations equilibria (REE's) in market models are equilibria that take account of this additional function for market prices.

An excellent survey of the literature on rational expectations equilibrium is given by Radner [1982], and a symposium of more recent papers is contained in vol. 26, no. 2 of the **Journal of Economic Theory**. Rather than attempt another survey, we will devote the present paper to a highly simplified example in which many of the principal issues are analytically transparent.

2. The example

All of the difficult problems in rational expectations equilibrium theory arise from the interaction of the statistical role of market prices with their traditional market clearing role. However, the particular mechanism by which market-clearing prices are determined is not itself important. Indeed, the relation between traders' expectations and market-clearing prices is highly sensitive to traders' endowments and preferences (state-dependent utility functions), so that few restrictions on this relation can be imposed at any acceptable level of generality. For this reason, we can abstract from the market setting, and replace market prices with an arbitrary endogenously determined statistic.

Suppose that the set of possible states of the world is $\{a, b\}$, and denote by q, $0 < q < 1$, the probability that nature chooses state a. (In other words, q is the prior probability that the decisionmaker assigns to state a.) Our example has only one decisionmaker. This decisionmaker must choose a decision from the the unit interval $D = [0, 1]$. He has a utility function which depends upon the state, $u : D \times \{a, b\} \to R$, with $u(\cdot, a)$ and $u(\cdot, b)$ strictly concave. The decisionmaker observes a statistic $p : D \times \{a, b\} \to R$ from which he makes inferences about the state of the world. We call the statistic p to hint that in market models it is price that serves this purpose. The difference between drawing inferences from observations on p and the standard inference problems of statistics is that p is not given exogenously, but is in part determined by the action taken by the decisionmaker.

3. Rational expectations equilibria

In the context of the model presented in section 2 the idea of REE's can be formulated. A *Rational Expectations Equilibrium (REE)* is a 4-tuple (p_a, p_b, d_a, d_b) satisfying:

$$d_a \quad \textit{maximizes} \quad E\{u(d, \cdot)|\, p_a\} \quad \textit{in} \quad D,$$

$$d_b \quad \textit{maximizes} \quad E\{u(d, \cdot)|\, p_b\} \quad \textit{in} \quad D,$$

---

† Support from the National Science Foundation is gratefully acknowledged.

$$p_a = p(d_a, a),$$
$$p_b = p(d_b, b).$$

REE's which reveal the state of the world, that is, with $p_a \neq p_b$, are called *fully revealing*. In solving the decision problem, the decisionmaker neglects the effects of his action on the determination of the observation he sees. This assumption is artificial in a one decisionmaker model, but it is motivated by recalling that, in a market model, this statistic is the market clearing price vector, and that in a competitive environment each trader assumes he has no effect on equilibrium price determination. The informational requirements for solving this decision problem are simple. The decisionmaker must know p_a, p_b and q.

To illustrate the existence conundrum, we make our example more specific. Let $u(d,a) = -d^2$, $u(d,b) = -(d-r)^2$, $p(d,a) = d$ and $p(d,b) = 1 - 2d$.

First we find fully revealing equilibria. Were the decisionmaker to know the state he would choose $d(a) = 0$ and $d(b) = r$. Then $p_a = 0$ and $p_b = 1 - 2r$. These prices reveal the true state of the world—and thus describe a fully revealing REE—so long as $r \neq 1/2$.

To find non-revealing REE's, observe that were the decisionmaker not to know which state of the world obtained, he would choose $d_a = d_b = (1-q)r$. Should he so choose, the equilibrium statistics would be $p_a = (1-q)r$ and $p_b = 1 - 2(1-q)r$. In equilibrium it must be the case that $p_a = p_b$, and so $(1-q)r = 1/3$. (Note that there are many (q, r) pairs that support both revealing and non-revealing REE's.)

Non-existence of REE's also occurs in the context of this example. If $r = 1/2$ an equilibrium cannot be revealing because in this case $p_a = p_b$. If $(1-q)r \neq 1/3$, the equilibrium cannot be non-revealing, for in this case $p_a \neq p_b$. Thus there is no REE if $r = 1/2$ and $q \neq 1/3$.

The pattern of equilibrium exhibited in this figure is representative of the outcomes in REE market models with a finite number of states. Equilibrium exists for an open and dense set of parameter values, but there is a lower dimensional set of parameter values for which equilibrium does not exist. Furthermore, except for a lower dimensional set of parameter values, equilibrium is fully revealing.

Our demonstration of existence is typical of the way in which existence proofs proceed in the finite state case (see Radner [1979]). Assume the equilibrium is fully revealing, and jiggle the excess demand function to ensure that the equilibrium prices are all different. This establishes density of the set of economies for which REE's exist, and openness is not hard to show. This proof technique is responsible for the coarseness of the equilibrium analysis. The proof assumes the property of the equilibrium it wants to find, and fiddles with excess demand to make it happen, but there is no way to ensure that perfectly competitive traders will act so as to reveal this information in equilibrium. For example, if, at the equilibrium prices, the information observed only by trader i is not payoff relevant to him, there is no reason to assume it will be revealed in equilibrium even though it may be relevant to someone else. These equilibrium prices clear markets, but they are not implementable in any reasonable way. These flaws in the equilibrium analysis have motivated research into alternative equilibrium concepts.

4. Dynamic equilibria in forecasting rules

A different approach to informational equilibria is taken in Blume and Easley [1982] and Bray [1982]. In the static REE models, each trader has a "forecasting rule" which relates prices to distributions of states of the world. The equilibrium idea is that the forecasting rule used by each trader is correct. This approach supposes that there is some dynamic mechanism for learning by which each trader singles out the correct forecasting rule. Another approach is to study such mechanisms directly and identify as equilibria the signals realized by the limit of the dynamic process—whatever that limit may be.

This dynamic approach to the learning problem can be described in the simple model of section 2. A *forecasting rule* is a function $q : R \mapsto [0,1]$, where $q(p)$ is the probability of state a inferred from the observation of signal p in R. Given $q(\cdot)$, define $d : R \mapsto D$ by:

$$d(p) \quad \textit{maximizes} \quad q(p)u(d,a) + (1 - q(p))u(d,b) \quad \textit{in} \quad D.$$

Let

$$p_a = p(d(p_a), a),$$
$$p_b = p(d(p_b), b).$$

Assume that solutions to these equations exist and are unique. Solutions to these equations are *temporary equilibrium prices*. Forecasting rule revision is based on the ex post observation of the state of the world and the temporary equilibrium prices.

Let Q be a class of forecasting rules (e.g. continuous, or linear). Fix q_0, let nature generate a or b, compute p_{a1} or p_{b1} as required, and then inform the decisionmaker about the realized state of the world. The decisionmaker has a rule for revising the model given the data available to him—ex post knowledge about the state of the world, and the prices that obtained in the temporary equilibrium. For example, the decisionmaker may be a Bayesian statistician, or he may run a regression. Using this rule, he revises q_0 to q_1, and the process repeats. The problem is to characterize the limit behavior of the sequence (p_{at}, p_{bt}). Does it converge? If so, does it converge to an REE pair?

The results from this research program are mixed. Bray [1982] demonstrated convergence to REE's in a linear economy with normally distributed states of nature, where Q contains only linear forecasting rules. Traders in the Bray economy revise their beliefs by running least squares regressions and forecasting with the estimated regression coefficients. Blume and Easley [1982] study non-linear economies with finite numbers of states of nature and an arbitrary, but finite, set of continuous fofecasting rules. Traders are Bayesian. Models consistent with REE behavior are locally stable, but so may be models not consistent with REE's, and limit behavior is in general dependent upon the particular sample paths of the state of nature process.

The conclusion to be drawn from this disparate set of results is that the convergence properties of these learning models depends crucially on the set of models Q to be selected from. The difficulty is the following. In the Bray model, the Blume-Easley model and our simple model, the limit behavior of the economy is i.i.d. Given a forecasting rule which relates current prices only to current states of the world, i.i.d. states of the world imply that the signal (price) process must be i.i.d. So in selecting a forecasting rule, each decisionmaker is implicitly assuming an i.i.d. price-state process. But so long as decisionmakers are revising their forecasting rules from the entire history of prices and states of the world, the true price-state process is not i.i.d. The likelihood functions of the decisionmakers are misspecified, and the true stochastic process of prices is not contained in the space of forecasting rules. In the Blume-Easley model, learning comes down to determining which i.i.d. process in the set Q assigns highest probability to sample paths "close" to the actual sample path of the economy, and the answer to this question depends in a rather arbitrary way upon the specification of Q.

This equilibrium is further complicated by existence questions. Temporary equilibrium may not exist if the forecasting rules in Q are not continuous. But the REE equilibrium correspondence (relating states of the world to prices) may have no continuous selections. If this is the case, and if forecasting rules consistent with REE's are in Q, and if some kind of Bayesian updating is used by the decisionmaker to revise his forecasting rule, it is possible that at some point in the learning process a discontinuity may appear at a crucial point, and so temporary equilibrium may fail to exist. (This phenomenon could be illustrated in our simple model if the state space and the signal space were expanded appropriately.) Because of this non-existence problem, the arbitrary nature of limit behavior and the non-robustness of results, the dynamic forecasting rule models do not provide a satisfactory alternative to REE's.

5. Recursive dynamics and informational equilibrium

Yet another dynamic approach to informational equilibrium is offered in Kobayashi [1977], Jordan [1982] and Blume and Easley [1983]. The previous analyses of information foundered on the simultaneous determination of actions, signals and expectations. It seems natural to unwind this simultaneity by undertaking statistical inference only with previously determined endogenous data. (This assumption is not easily defendable on conceptual grounds, but nonetheless is conventional in the macroeconomics expectations literature.) In simple market models this assumption gives the economy a recursive structure that removes the troublesome discontinuities discussed in the previous sections. Furthermore, it is automatic in the analyses of these models that only the payoff-relevant information of any trader is revealed in the equilibrium analysis.

Two streams of thought have led to the study of dynamic equilibria in recursive dynamical systems. On the one hand, the abstract study of mechanisms led to a search for means of implementing informational equilibrium. Reiter [1976] was particularly influential in this regard. To this way of thinking, the dynamics being studied are not "real dynamics", but "virtual dynamics", and the dynamical system really models an informational tatonnement process for converging to an equilibrium. On the other hand, some work on these models was motivated by the search for a real time informational dynamic. Perhaps the first work in this direction was Kobayashi [1977]. In this interpretation the problem of capital gains and other non-informational intertemporal links becomes important, and so we shall take this up at the end of the section.

Consider again the model of section 2. We let the decision problem evolve in the following way: At stage 0 nature chooses state a or b, with q denoting the probability that a is chosen. This choice is fixed through the remainder of the sequence. The decisionmaker chooses d_0 to maximize

$$qu(d,a) + (1-q)u(d,b).$$

The decisionmaker observes the appropriate p_{a1} or p_{b1} where

$$p_{a1} = p(d_0, a),$$

$$p_{b1} = p(d_0, b).$$

At stage 1 the decisionmaker chooses $d_1(p)$ to maximize

$$E\{u(d,\cdot)|\, p_1\}.$$

The process continues, with the decision at each iteration being chosen to maximize expected utility given the entire past sequence of signals.

To see how this dynamic model works, consider the example of section 3. Take $u(d,a) = -d^2$ and $u(d,b) = -(d-r)^2$. At the first stage, the decisionmaker is uninformed, and so he will act to maximize $qu(d,a) + (1-q)u(d,b)$. Thus $d_0 = (1-q)r$. Then

$$p_{a1} = (1-q)r,$$
$$p_{b1} = 1 - 2(1-q)r.$$

Two things can happen. If $(1-q)r \neq 1/3$, the signal reveals the state. Henceforth, if nature had originally chosen a, d_t will be 0. Had nature chosen b, d_t would be r. Subsequently, then,

$$p_{at} = 0,$$
$$p_{bt} = 1 - 2r,$$

so that this iterative process converges in two steps. Observe that if $r = 1/2$, $p_{at} = p_{bt}$. Nonetheless, since the decisionmaker does not forget information, he remains informed and this is an equilibrium.

Should $(1-q)r = 1/3$, no information is revealed by the signal. Thus the maximization problem remains unchanged in the next stage, and indeed in all subsequent stages. The signal remains the same in all periods, and the decisionmaker remains uninformed. Again, only two steps are required.

The results in our decision model are similar to those found in trading models. Equilibrium always exists. Typically, with finite numbers of states, it is ultimately revealing. Finally, with finite numbers of states, convergence occurs after a finite number of iterations. This last result does not hold when the state space is not finite, but nonetheless the sequence of signals does converge in the limit. Moreover, there is no revelation of payoff irrelevant information.

It is interesting to compare equilibrium behavior in the static model and in the recursive model. On the line $(1-q)r = 1/3$ both revealing and non-revealing static equilibria exist (except when $r = 1/2$), but only non-revealing dynamic equilibria exist. When $r = 1/2$, no equilibria exist in the static model (except when $q \neq 1/3$), but revealing equilibria exist in the dynamic model.

As a learning model, however, the dynamic model is unappealing because of the knowledge it requires the decisionmaker to possess. To compute d_0 and d_1, the decisionmaker needs to know q and the signal function p. In the general equilibrium setting which our example is intended to mimic, knowledge of p requires substantial knowledge of the private characteristics of the other decisionmakers in the economy, knowledge which is incompatible with the decentralized nature of market equilibrium. As in section 4 above, we are faced with the question of whether there are learning rules or estimation procedures which will produce the required knowledge. However, as a result of the recursive nature of the dynamic model, the answer in this case is much more encouraging. Under some additional smoothness assumptions on the payoff and signal functions, we can adapt to the present example a learning procedure described by Jordan [1982a] for exchange economies.

Suppose that the state is distributed independently and identically over time according to the probability q, and that each drawing of the state is followed by the two-stage iterative process described above. The decisionmaker does not know q or the signal function p. We envision the following sequence of events. In sample period t, nature draws the state $s_t \in \{a, b\}$, which is not observed by the decisionmaker. Based on an estimate $\hat{q}_t$ of q, the decisionmaker then chooses d_{0t}, and observes the signal $p_t = p(d_{0t}, s_t)$. Based on an estimated conditional probability $\hat{q}_t(a \mid p_t)$, the decisionmaker then chooses d_{1t}. Finally the decisionmaker observes s_t and collects his payoff $u(d_{1t}, s_t)$.

The estimation of q is straightforward. Simply let $\hat{q}_t$ be the frequency with which state a has been observed in previous periods. The estimation of the conditional probability $\hat{q}_t(a|p_t)$ is not so simple. The decision d_{0t} is a continuous variable, so if $\hat{q}_t$ differs from previous estimates of q, d_{0t} may differ from previous choices of d_0, resulting in a signal $p_t = p(d_{0t}, s_t)$ which has never previously been observed. Moreover, since $\hat{q}_t$ fluctuates in a nonstationary fashion, the joint distribution of (p_t, s_t), which determines the true conditional probability of the state given p_t, is nonstationary. However, we will construct a type of conditional frequency estimate that behaves asymptotically like a conditional frequency drawn from a stationary joint distribution.

The law of the iterated logarithm tells us how fast $\hat{q}_t$ converges to q, and we want to infer from this the rate at which $p(d_{0t}, a)$ and $p(d_{0t}, b)$ converge to the "equilibrium" first stage signals $p(d_0, a)$ and $p(d_0, b)$. For this we need some additional regularity assumptions. Assume that the payoff function u is C^2 (twice continuously differentiable) in d, and that the second derivative is always negative. This implies that d_{0t}, as a function of $\hat{q}$, is C^1. Secondly, assume that the signal function p is C^1 in d, so that $p(d_{0t}, a)$ and $p(d_{0t}, b)$, as functions of $\hat{q}$, are C^1. By the law of the iterated logarithm, there is a constant $K > 0$ such that

$$\limsup_{t\to\infty} \frac{|\hat{q}_t - q|}{K\sqrt{(\log\log t)/t}} < 1$$

with probability one. Since $p(\cdot, a)$ and $p(\cdot, b)$ are C^1 in $\hat{q}_t$, there is some $\lambda > 0$ such that, for almost every state sequence $\{s_t\}_{t=1}^{\infty}$,

$$|p_t - p(d_0, s_t)| < \lambda K \sqrt{\frac{\log\log t}{t}}$$

for large t. For each t, let $\epsilon_t = [(\log\log t)/t]^{1/3}$. Note that ϵ_t does not involve the constants λ and K which are unknown to the decisionmaker. We can now define the estimated conditional probability of a given p_t. For a sequence of observed states, $\{s_\tau\}_{\tau=1}^{t-1}$, and signals, $\{p_\tau\}_{\tau=1}^{t-1}$, and a current signal p_t, let

$$\hat{q}_t(a \mid p_t) = \frac{\#\{\tau < t : \quad |p_\tau - p_t| < \epsilon_\tau \quad and \quad s_\tau = a\}}{\#\{\tau < t : \quad |p_\tau - p_t| < \epsilon_\tau\}}.$$

That is, $\hat{q}_t(a \mid p_t)$ is the frequency of a conditional on the contemporaneous signal being within ϵ_τ of p_t. (If the denominator is zero, define the estimate arbitrarily.) With probability one, for large τ and $t > \tau$,

$$|p_\tau - p(d_0, s_\tau)| < \frac{\epsilon_\tau}{2}$$

and

$$|p_t - p(d_0, s_t)| < \frac{\epsilon_t}{2} < \frac{\epsilon_\tau}{2},$$

so $|p_\tau - p_t| < \epsilon_\tau$ if $p(d_0, s_\tau) = p(d_0, s_t)$ and only if $|p(d_0, s_\tau) - p(d_0, s_t)| < \epsilon_\tau$. Since $\epsilon_\tau \to 0$, the last inequality will be satisfied for large τ, t only if $p(d_0, s_\tau) = p(d_0, s_t)$. Therefore the estimate $\hat{q}_t(a \mid p_t)$ behaves asymptotically like the true conditional frequency of $s_t = a$ given $p(d_0, s_t)$, and thus converges to the true conditional probability. Hence $d_{1t} \to d_1$ with probability one. In summary, the estimates $\hat{q}_t$ and $\hat{q}_t(a \mid p_t)$ converge, so the decisions d_{0t} and d_{1t} converge to their respective equilibrium values d_0 and d_1 with probability one.

The possibility of "learning from scratch", as demonstrated in the above result, depends critically on the recursive nature of the dynamic model. The estimated conditional probability $\hat{q}_t(a \mid p_t)$ is not affected by the previous estimate $\hat{q}_{t-1}(a \mid p_{t-1})$, so the estimation problem is not in the nature of a fixed-point approximation problem.

6. Nonrecursive dynamics

Unfortunately, many interesting real time trading models cannot be formulated recursively. For example, suppose that traders are buying and selling shares of a firm. The ultimate goal may be to maximize end-state utility, or utility of an affordable consumption stream. In any event, in a several period model, the possibility of capital gains arises. Now the intertemporal link is more complicated than in the simple model just discussed. Intertemporal effects accrue not just from learning from signals, but also from the effect of current decisions on the set of actions feasible in the future. This additional connection can give rise to the same kinds of discontinuities upon which the analysis of static REE's faltered. For examples in market models see Border and Jordan [1980] and Jordan [1982].

To see how this can happen in our one decisionmaker model, add to the original model the additional constraint that

$$d_1 + d_2 \leq 1,$$

and consider the specification

$$\begin{aligned} u(d,a) &= -d^2, \\ u(d,b) &= -(d-r)^2, \\ p(d,a) &= d, \\ p(d,b) &= 1-2d. \end{aligned}$$

This is the same specification used to illustrate recursive dynamics, but with an additional intertemporal constraint. The decisionmaker maximizes the expected sum of utilities in the two stages. In this model we can construct counterexamples to the existence of equilibrium.

Denote by $v(d,a)$ (resp. $v(d,b)$) the maximal utility obtainable in the second period in state a (resp. b) if the first period action is d. Suppose first that the state is revealed in the first period. Then

$$\begin{aligned} v(d,a) &= 0, \\ v(d,b) &= \begin{cases} 0 & \text{if } 1-d \geq r; \\ -(1-d-r)^2 & \text{if } 1-d < r. \end{cases} \end{aligned}$$

If $v(d,b) = 0$, then the intertemporal connection has no effect on the second period. In this case, as before, $d_1 = (1-q)r$. Substituting this into $v(d,b)$, we see that if the true state is revealed by first period signals, $v(d,b) = 0$ if and only if $1/(2-q) \geq r$.

To construct our counterexample to the existence of equilibrium, suppose that $1/(2-q) < r$. Then the first period problem for the decisionmaker is to choose d to maximize

$$-qd^2 - (1-q)(d-r)^2 - (1-q)(1-d-r)^2.$$

The solution has $d_1 = (1-q)/(2-q)$. The signals possible as a result of the first period action are

$$\begin{aligned} p_{a1} &= (1-q)/(2-q), \\ p_{b1} &= 1 - 2(1-q)/(2-q). \end{aligned}$$

Suppose that $q = 1/2$ (requiring $r > 2/3$). Then $p_{a1} = p_{b1}$ and so the state cannot be known in period 2. If the state is to be unknown in period 2, the maximization problem becomes one of maximizing

$$-q(d_1^2 + d_2^2) - (1-q)[(d_1-r)^2 + (d_2-r)^2]$$

subject to

$$d_1 + d_2 \leq 1.$$

The unconstrained optimum is

$$d_1 = d_2 = (1-q)r.$$

This is feasible, since in this case

$$d_1 + d_2 = 2(1-q)r = r < 1,$$

because $q = 1/2$.

If these are the decisions, then

$$\begin{aligned} p_{a1} &= (1-q)r, \\ p_{b1} &= 1 - 2(1-q)r. \end{aligned}$$

But these signals must reveal the state since, by our assumptions, $(1-q)r > 1/3$, while $(1-q)r = 1/3$ would be required for $p_{a1} = p_{b1}$. Equilibrium thus fails to exist, because of the same kind of discontinuity in information structures that arose in the example of non-existence of the static REE.

The analysis of this example suggests the possibility for a generic equilibrium existence result, although none has so far been demonstrated. Obviously this solution lacks some of the appealing features of the equilibria that exist when the model is recursive, but it shares the property that information irrelevant to its holder will not be revealed.

REFERENCES

Anderson, R. M. and H. Sonnenschein, "On the existence of rational expectations equilibrium," **J. Econ. Theory** 26 (1982), 261-278.

Blume, L. and D. Easley, "Learning to be rational," **J. Econ. Theory** 26 (1982), 340-351.

Blume, L. and D. Easley (1983), "Rational expectations equilibrium: an alternative approach," **J. Econ. Theory**, forthcoming.

Border, K. and J. Jordan, "Expectations equilibrium with expectations conditioned on past data," **J. Econ. Theory** 22 (1980), 395-406.

Bray, M., "Learning, estimation, and the stability of rational expectations equilibrium," **J. Econ Theory** 26 (1982), 318-340.

Jordan, J., "A dynamic model of expectations equilibrium," **J. Econ. Theory** 28 (1982), 235-254.

Jordan, J., "Learning rational expectations: the finite state case," U. of Minn. discussion paper no. 82-167, (1982a).

Jordan, J. and R. Radner, "Rational expectations in microeconomic models: an overview," **J. Econ. Theory** 26 (1982), 201-223.

Kobayashi, T., "A convergence theorem on rational expectations equilibrium with price information," working paper no. 79, Economic Series, IMSSS, Stanford U. (1977).

Radner, R., "Equilibre des marchés à terme et au comptant en cas d'incertitude," **Cahiers Econ. C.N.R.S. Paris** 4 (1967), 35-52.

Radner, R., "Rational expectations equilibrium: generic existence and the information revealed by prices," **Econometrica** 47 (1979), 655-678.

Radner, R., "Equilibrium under uncertainty," in **Handbook of Mathematical Economics** (K. Arrow and M. Intriligator, eds.), vol. 2, chap. 20, North Holland, Amsterdam, 1982.

Reiter, S., "On expectations equilibrium," mimeographed notes, Northwestern University (1976).

Vol. 157: Optimization and Operations Research. Proceedings 1977. Edited by R. Henn, B. Korte, and W. Oettli. VI, 270 pages. 1978.

Vol. 158: L. J. Cherene, Set Valued Dynamical Systems and Economic Flow. VIII, 83 pages. 1978.

Vol. 159: Some Aspects of the Foundations of General Equilibrium Theory: The Posthumous Papers of Peter J. Kalman. Edited by J. Green. VI, 167 pages. 1978.

Vol. 160: Integer Programming and Related Areas. A Classified Bibliography. Edited by D. Hausmann. XIV, 314 pages. 1978.

Vol. 161: M. J. Beckmann, Rank in Organizations. VIII, 164 pages. 1978.

Vol. 162: Recent Developments in Variable Structure Systems, Economics and Biology. Proceedings 1977. Edited by R. R. Mohler and A. Ruberti. VI, 326 pages. 1978.

Vol. 163: G. Fandel, Optimale Entscheidungen in Organisationen. VI, 143 Seiten. 1979.

Vol. 164: C. L. Hwang and A. S. M. Masud, Multiple Objective Decision Making – Methods and Applications. A State-of-the-Art Survey. XII, 351 pages. 1979.

Vol. 165: A. Maravall, Identification in Dynamic Shock-Error Models. VIII, 158 pages. 1979.

Vol. 166: R. Cuninghame-Green, Minimax Algebra. XI, 258 pages. 1979.

Vol. 167: M. Faber, Introduction to Modern Austrian Capital Theory. X, 196 pages. 1979.

Vol. 168: Convex Analysis and Mathematical Economics. Proceedings 1978. Edited by J. Kriens. V, 136 pages. 1979.

Vol. 169: A. Rapoport et al., Coalition Formation by Sophisticated Players. VII, 170 pages. 1979.

Vol. 170: A. E. Roth, Axiomatic Models of Bargaining. V, 121 pages. 1979.

Vol. 171: G. F. Newell, Approximate Behavior of Tandem Queues. XI, 410 pages. 1979.

Vol. 172: K. Neumann and U. Steinhardt, GERT Networks and the Time-Oriented Evaluation of Projects. 268 pages. 1979.

Vol. 173: S. Erlander, Optimal Spatial Interaction and the Gravity Model. VII, 107 pages. 1980.

Vol. 174: Extremal Methods and Systems Analysis. Edited by A. V. Fiacco and K. O. Kortanek. XI, 545 pages. 1980.

Vol. 175: S. K. Srinivasan and R. Subramanian, Probabilistic Analysis of Redundant Systems. VII, 356 pages. 1980.

Vol. 176: R. Färe, Laws of Diminishing Returns. VIII, 97 pages. 1980.

Vol. 177: Multiple Criteria Decision Making-Theory and Application. Proceedings, 1979. Edited by G. Fandel and T. Gal. XVI, 570 pages. 1980.

Vol. 178: M. N. Bhattacharyya, Comparison of Box-Jenkins and Bonn Monetary Model Prediction Performance. VII, 146 pages. 1980.

Vol. 179: Recent Results in Stochastic Programming. Proceedings, 1979. Edited by P. Kall and A. Prékopa. IX, 237 pages. 1980.

Vol. 180: J. F. Brotchie, J. W. Dickey and R. Sharpe, TOPAZ – General Planning Technique and its Applications at the Regional, Urban, and Facility Planning Levels. VII, 356 pages. 1980.

Vol. 181: H. D. Sherali and C. M. Shetty, Optimization with Disjunctive Constraints. VIII, 156 pages. 1980.

Vol. 182: J. Wolters, Stochastic Dynamic Properties of Linear Econometric Models. VIII, 154 pages. 1980.

Vol. 183: K. Schittkowski, Nonlinear Programming Codes. VIII, 242 pages. 1980.

Vol. 184: R. E. Burkard and U. Derigs, Assignment and Matching Problems: Solution Methods with FORTRAN-Programs. VIII, 148 pages. 1980.

Vol. 185: C. C. von Weizsäcker, Barriers to Entry. VI, 220 pages. 1980.

Vol. 186: Ch.-L. Hwang and K. Yoon, Multiple Attribute Decision Making – Methods and Applications. A State-of-the-Art-Survey. XI, 259 pages. 1981.

Vol. 187: W. Hock, K. Schittkowski, Test Examples for Nonlinear Programming Codes. V. 178 pages. 1981.

Vol. 188: D. Bös, Economic Theory of Public Enterprise. VII, 142 pages. 1981.

Vol. 189: A. P. Lüthi, Messung wirtschaftlicher Ungleichheit. IX, 287 pages. 1981.

Vol. 190: J. N. Morse, Organizations: Multiple Agents with Multiple Criteria. Proceedings, 1980. VI, 509 pages. 1981.

Vol. 191: H. R. Sneessens, Theory and Estimation of Macroeconomic Rationing Models. VII, 138 pages. 1981.

Vol. 192: H. J. Bierens: Robust Methods and Asymptotic Theory in Nonlinear Econometrics. IX, 198 pages. 1981.

Vol. 193: J.K. Sengupta, Optimal Decisions under Uncertainty. VII, 156 pages. 1981.

Vol. 194: R. W. Shephard, Cost and Production Functions. XI, 104 pages. 1981.

Vol. 195: H. W. Ursprung, Die elementare Katastrophentheorie. Eine Darstellung aus der Sicht der Ökonomie. VII, 332 pages. 1982.

Vol. 196: M. Nermuth, Information Structures in Economics. VIII, 236 pages. 1982.

Vol. 197: Integer Programming and Related Areas. A Classified Bibliography. 1978 – 1981. Edited by R. von Randow. XIV, 338 pages. 1982.

Vol. 198: P. Zweifel, Ein ökonomisches Modell des Arztverhaltens. XIX, 392 Seiten. 1982.

Vol. 199: Evaluating Mathematical Programming Techniques. Proceedings, 1981. Edited by J.M. Mulvey. XI, 379 pages. 1982.

Vol. 200: The Resource Sector in an Open Economy. Edited by H. Siebert. IX, 161 pages. 1984.

Vol. 201: P. M. C. de Boer, Price Effects in Input-Output-Relations: A Theoretical and Empirical Study for the Netherlands 1949–1967. X, 140 pages. 1982.

Vol. 202: U. Witt, J. Perske, SMS – A Program Package for Simulation and Gaming of Stochastic Market Processes and Learning Behavior. VII, 266 pages. 1982.

Vol. 203: Compilation of Input-Output Tables. Proceedings, 1981. Edited by J. V. Skolka. VII, 307 pages. 1982.

Vol. 204: K.C. Mosler, Entscheidungsregeln bei Risiko: Multivariate stochastische Dominanz. VII, 172 Seiten. 1982.

Vol. 205: R. Ramanathan, Introduction to the Theory of Economic Growth. IX, 347 pages. 1982.

Vol. 206: M.H. Karwan, V. Lotfi, J. Telgen, and S. Zionts, Redundancy in Mathematical Programming. VII, 286 pages. 1983.

Vol. 207: Y. Fujimori, Modern Analysis of Value Theory. X, 165 pages. 1982.

Vol. 208: Econometric Decision Models. Proceedings, 1981. Edited by J. Gruber. VI, 364 pages. 1983.

Vol. 209: Essays and Surveys on Multiple Criteria Decision Making. Proceedings, 1982. Edited by P. Hansen. VII, 441 pages. 1983.

Vol. 210: Technology, Organization and Economic Structure. Edited by R. Sato and M.J. Beckmann. VIII, 195 pages. 1983.

Vol. 211: P. van den Heuvel, The Stability of a Macroeconomic System with Quantity Constraints. VII, 169 pages. 1983.

Vol. 212: R. Sato and T. Nôno, Invariance Principles and the Structure of Technology. V, 94 pages. 1983.

Vol. 213: Aspiration Levels in Bargaining and Economic Decision Making. Proceedings, 1982. Edited by R. Tietz. VIII, 406 pages. 1983.

Vol. 214: M. Faber, H. Niemes und G. Stephan, Entropie, Umweltschutz und Rohstoffverbrauch. IX, 181 Seiten. 1983.

Vol. 215: Semi-Infinite Programming and Applications. Proceedings, 1981. Edited by A. V. Fiacco and K. O. Kortanek. XI, 322 pages. 1983.

Vol. 216: H. H. Müller, Fiscal Policies in a General Equilibrium Model with Persistent Unemployment. VI, 92 pages. 1983.

Vol. 217: Ch. Grootaert, The Relation Between Final Demand and Income Distribution. XIV, 105 pages. 1983.

Vol. 218: P. van Loon, A Dynamic Theory of the Firm: Production, Finance and Investment. VII, 191 pages. 1983.

Vol. 219: E. van Damme, Refinements of the Nash Equilibrium Concept. VI, 151 pages. 1983.

Vol. 220: M. Aoki, Notes on Economic Time Series Analysis: System Theoretic Perspectives. IX, 249 pages. 1983.

Vol. 221: S. Nakamura, An Inter-Industry Translog Model of Prices and Technical Change for the West German Economy. XIV, 290 pages. 1984.

Vol. 222: P. Meier, Energy Systems Analysis for Developing Countries. VI, 344 pages. 1984.

Vol. 223: W. Trockel, Market Demand. VIII, 205 pages. 1984.

Vol. 224: M. Kiy, Ein disaggregiertes Prognosesystem für die Bundesrepublik Deutschland. XVIII, 276 Seiten. 1984.

Vol. 225: T. R. von Ungern-Sternberg, Zur Analyse von Märkten mit unvollständiger Nachfragerinformation. IX, 125 Seiten. 1984

Vol. 226: Selected Topics in Operations Research and Mathematical Economics. Proceedings, 1983. Edited by G. Hammer and D. Pallaschke. IX, 478 pages. 1984.

Vol. 227: Risk and Capital. Proceedings, 1983. Edited by G. Bamberg and K. Spremann. VII, 306 pages. 1984.

Vol. 228: Nonlinear Models of Fluctuating Growth. Proceedings, 1983. Edited by R. M. Goodwin, M. Krüger and A. Vercelli. XVII, 277 pages. 1984.

Vol. 229: Interactive Decision Analysis. Proceedings, 1983. Edited by M. Grauer and A. P. Wierzbicki. VIII, 269 pages. 1984.

Vol. 230: Macro-Economic Planning with Conflicting Goals. Proceedings, 1982. Edited by M. Despontin, P. Nijkamp and J. Spronk. VI, 297 pages. 1984.

Vol. 231: G. F. Newell, The M/M/∞ Service System with Ranked Servers in Heavy Traffic. XI, 126 pages. 1984.

Vol. 232: L. Bauwens, Bayesian Full Information Analysis of Simultaneous Equation Models Using Integration by Monte Carlo. VI, 114 pages. 1984.

Vol. 233: G. Wagenhals, The World Copper Market. XI, 190 pages. 1984.

Vol. 234: B. C. Eaves, A Course in Triangulations for Solving Equations with Deformations. III, 302 pages. 1984.

Vol. 235: Stochastic Models in Reliability Theory. Proceedings, 1984. Edited by S. Osaki and Y. Hatoyama. VII, 212 pages. 1984.

Vol. 236: G. Gandolfo, P. C. Padoan, A Disequilibrium Model of Real and Financial Accumulation in an Open Economy. VI, 172 pages. 1984.

Vol. 237: Misspecification Analysis. Proceedings, 1983. Edited by T. K. Dijkstra. V, 129 pages. 1984.

Vol. 238: W. Domschke, A. Drexl, Location and Layout Planning. IV, 134 pages. 1985.

Vol. 239: Microeconomic Models of Housing Markets. Edited by K. Stahl. VII, 197 pages. 1985.

Vol. 240: Contributions to Operations Research. Proceedings, 1984. Edited by K. Neumann and D. Pallaschke. V, 190 pages. 1985.

Vol. 241: U. Wittmann, Das Konzept rationaler Preiserwartungen. XI, 310 Seiten. 1985.

Vol. 242: Decision Making with Multiple Objectives. Proceedings, 1984. Edited by Y. Y. Haimes and V. Chankong. XI, 571 pages. 1985.

Vol. 243: Integer Programming and Related Areas. A Classified Bibliography 1981–1984. Edited by R. von Randow. XX, 386 pages. 1985.

Vol. 244: Advances in Equilibrium Theory. Proceedings, 1984. Edited by C. D. Aliprantis, O. Burkinshaw and N. J. Rothman. II, 235 pages. 1985.

Vol. 245: J. E. M. Wilhelm, Arbitrage Theory. VII, 114 pages. 1985.

Vol. 246: P. W. Otter, Dynamic Feature Space Modelling, Filtering and Self-Tuning Control of Stochastic Systems. XIV, 177 pages. 1985.

Vol. 247: Optimization and Discrete Choice in Urban Systems. Proceedings, 1983. Edited by B. G. Hutchinson, P. Nijkamp and M. Batty. VI, 371 pages. 1985.

Vol. 248: Plural Rationality and Interactive Decision Processes. Proceedings, 1984. Edited by M. Grauer, M. Thompson and A. P. Wierzbicki. VI, 354 pages. 1985.

Vol. 249: Spatial Price Equilibrium: Advances in Theory, Computation and Application. Proceedings, 1984. Edited by P. T. Harker. VII, 277 pages. 1985.

Vol. 250: M. Roubens, Ph. Vincke, Preference Modelling. VIII, 94 pages. 1985.

Vol. 251: Input-Output Modeling. Proceedings, 1984. Edited by A. Smyshlyaev. VI, 261 pages. 1985.

Vol. 252: A. Birolini, On the Use of Stochastic Processes in Modeling Reliability Problems. VI, 105 pages. 1985.

Vol. 253: C. Withagen, Economic Theory and International Trade in Natural Exhaustible Resources. VI, 172 pages. 1985.

Vol. 254: S. Müller, Arbitrage Pricing of Contingent Claims. VIII, 151 pages. 1985.

Vol. 255: Nondifferentiable Optimization: Motivations and Applications. Proceedings, 1984. Edited by V. F. Demyanov and D. Pallaschke. VI, 350 pages. 1985.

Vol. 256: Convexity and Duality in Optimization. Proceedings, 1984. Edited by J. Ponstein. V, 142 pages. 1985.

Vol. 257: Dynamics of Macrosystems. Proceedings, 1984. Edited by J.-P. Aubin, D. Saari and K. Sigmund. VI, 280 pages. 1985.

Vol. 258: H. Funke, Eine allgemeine Theorie der Polypol- und Oligopolpreisbildung. III, 237 pages. 1985.

Vol. 259: Infinite Programming. Proceedings, 1984. Edited by E. J. Anderson and A. B. Philpott. XIV, 244 pages. 1985.

Vol. 260: H.-J. Kruse, Degeneracy Graphs and the Neighbourhood Problem. VIII, 128 pages. 1986.

Vol. 261: Th. R. Gulledge, Jr., N. K. Womer, The Economics of Made-to-Order Production. VI, 134 pages. 1986.

Vol. 262: H. U. Buhl, A Neo-Classical Theory of Distribution and Wealth. V, 146 pages. 1986.

Vol. 263: M. Schäfer, Resource Extraction and Market Structure. XI, 154 pages. 1986.

Vol. 264: Models of Economic Dynamics. Proceedings, 1983. Edited by H. F. Sonnenschein. VII, 212 pages. 1986.